# Dressed for Eternity

**Dressed for Eternity**

by Marilynn Dawson

All Scripture quoted from the King James Version (Public Domain) unless otherwise stated.

Copyright © 2013 by Marilynn Dawson

All rights reserved. No part of this book may be used or reproduced in any manner whatsoever without written permission, except in the case of brief quotations embodied in critical articles or reviews.

This work is licensed under the Creative Commons Attribution-NoDerivs 3.0 Unported License. To view a copy of this license, visit http://creativecommons.org/licenses/by-nd/3.0/ or send a letter to Creative Commons, 444 Castro Street, Suite 900, Mountain View, California, 94041, USA.
Copyrighted October 6, 2013

ISBN 978-1-928160-34-2

## DEDICATION

This book is dedicated to my two grown children, Ashley and Isaiah Dawson, as they seek to enter the adult world in a manner that announces them as members of the Bride of Christ.

## SHOUT OUT

Shout-out to my two faithful proofers/editors, Shannon and Michele. You guys have been with me since "the beginning" and I value your friendship, sisterhood, and pickiness!

## THANK YOU

I'd also like to thank Rik Hall, Nat Davis, and the friends we have over in the Indie Christian Authors Group on Facebook, for all your encouragement and support.

# Table of Contents

Introduction .................................................................................................. 1

## Section One

**The Twelve Foundations Stones of Aaron's Breastplate and the New Jerusalem** .................................................................................... 11
Sardis - The first Stone in Aaron's Breastplate............................... 15
Pitdah, or Topaz - The Second Stone in Aaron's Breastplate............ 19
The Chrysoprase or Emerald - The Third Stone in Aaron's Breastplate..... 23
Anthrax(Garnet) or Jacynth - The Fourth Stone in Aaron's Breastplate..... 29
Sapphire, sometimes referred to as Chalcedony or Aqua-marine - The Fifth Stone in Aaron's Breastplate................................................. 33
Jasper - The Sixth Stone in Aaron's Breastplate............................ 37
Ligure - The Seventh Stone in Aaron's Breastplate....................... 41
Agate or Emerald - The Eighth Stone in Aaron's Breastplate........ 45
Amethyst - The Ninth Stone in Aaron's Breastplate...................... 49
Chrysolite, Chrysoberyl in modern times - The Tenth Stone of Aaron's Breastplate................................................................................. 53
Beryl (or is it Onyx or Diamond?)- The Eleventh Stone of Aaron's Breastplate................................................................................. 57
Onyx - The Twelfth Stone of Aaron's Breastplate ........................ 61
**The New Jerusalem**................................................................... 65
Pearl - The Gates of the New Jerusalem........................................ 67
Gold - The Streets of the New Jerusalem...................................... 73

## Section Two

**Ancient Jewish bridal attire and Food Fit for the Bride of Christ**....... 77
'Broidered Work - Ancient Jewish Bridal Attire............................. 83
Badger Skin - Ancient Jewish Bridal Attire................................... 87
Linen - Ancient Jewish Bridal Attire............................................. 91
Silk - Ancient Jewish Bridal Attire................................................ 95
Ornaments - Ancient Jewish Bridal Attire..................................... 99
Silver Bracelets - Ancient Jewish Bridal Attire............................. 105
Chains - Ancient Jewish Bridal Attire........................................... 109

# Section Two Continued...

Forehead Jewels or Nose Jewels - Ancient Jewish Bridal Attire............115
Earrings - Ancient Jewish Bridal Attire..................................119
Crown - Ancient Jewish Bridal Attire.....................................125
**Food Fit for the Bride of Christ**.....................................131
Fine Flour - Food fit for the Bride of Christ............................133
Honey - Food Fit for the Bride of Christ.................................137
Olive Oil - Food Fit for the Bride of Christ.............................141

# Section Three

**The Great Clothing Exchange**..........................................145
Robe of Righteousness....................................................147
Beauty for Ashes.........................................................159
Oil of Joy...............................................................171
Garments of Praise.......................................................181

# Section Four

**"Without Spot or Wrinkle"**............................................193
Sanctification...........................................................195
**Spots and Wrinkles**...................................................205
Spots....................................................................209
Wrinkles.................................................................212
Learning how to do spiritual laundry.....................................221
Parable of the 10 Virgins................................................231

# Section Five

**Modesty**..............................................................235
Cultural Expressions of Modesty..........................................237
What is Modesty?.........................................................241
Does all this talk of Modesty mean it's wrong to look nice?..............261

# Conclusion

Recap..................................................................................................267

# Appendices

**APPENDIX A**........................................................................................I
**APPENDIX B**......................................................................................IX
**MORE FROM THIS AUTHOR**.......................................................XIX

## Introduction to "Dressed for Eternity"

While I was writing "Becoming the Bride of Christ: A Personal Journey" between 2010 and 2012, strange questions began to re-enter my mind as I learned what it meant to live everyday life as the Bride of Christ. These questions first came forward when God had introduced Himself as my unseen Husband in March of 2007. I was filled with bewilderment at that time, not fully understanding the journey I was about to embark on. I wasn't ready to answer it, but the initial question that came to me later that summer of '07, was: What if God wants me studying the spiritual meanings behind the finery He speaks of putting on His Bride in Scripture, then learn to "put on" the definitions of those descriptions as the accessorizing that pleases and impresses Him? This was a confusing question back then, as God had just finished driving home to me that He delighted to make me as I am via Psalm 139. The thought wouldn't leave me that there must be some measure of aesthetic appreciation in our Lord to choose for us the shapes He delights to give us. So the question became, what kind of aesthetic appearance pleases God? What ways of accessorizing and visual improvements impress Him? True beauty is not on the outside, it comes from within. He teaches this rather emphatically in Scripture.

I left the subject alone and carried on with the journey as it was at that time, eventually publishing a written record for others to engage in as well. (See the "More from this author" page at the back of this book)

Recently, the question has come back to mind, but with a much more focused angle to it.

## "How does God Adorn His Bride in the Scriptures?"

At first glance, this question seems entirely scandalous, particularly to the protestant evangelical or charismatic Christian. It is of no consequence to those who adhered to the Greco-Roman deity worship back in ancient times. It is also of no consequence to those who adhere to the concept of worshipping the Mother of Jesus as Mary, Queen of Heaven.

## Introduction

However, to those of neither persuasion, this is a jarring question for sure! God does not have a wife! Or does He?

We see in the Old Testament Scriptures, references to God betrothing Himself to Israel and later divorcing Himself from that betrothal.

> Isaiah 50:1 *Thus saith the LORD, Where is the bill of your mother's divorcement, whom I have put away?* or which of my creditors is it to whom I have sold you? Behold, for your iniquities have ye sold yourselves, and for your transgressions is your mother put away.

> Isaiah 54:5-6 For thy Maker is thine husband; the LORD of hosts is his name; and thy Redeemer the Holy One of Israel; The God of the whole earth shall he be called. ⁶For the LORD hath called thee as a woman forsaken and grieved in spirit, and a wife of youth, when thou wast refused, saith thy God.

> Jeremiah 3:6-14 The LORD said also unto me in the days of Josiah the king, Hast thou seen that which backsliding Israel hath done? she is gone up upon every high mountain and under every green tree, and there hath played the harlot. ⁷And I said after she had done all these things, Turn thou unto me. But she returned not. And her treacherous sister Judah saw it. ⁸*And I saw, when for all the causes whereby backsliding Israel committed adultery I had put her away, and given her a bill of divorce;* yet her treacherous sister Judah feared not, but went and played the harlot also. ⁹And it came to pass through the lightness of her whoredom, that she defiled the land, and committed adultery with stones and with stocks. ¹⁰And yet for all this her treacherous sister Judah hath not turned unto me with her whole heart, but feignedly, saith the LORD. ¹¹And the LORD said unto me, The backsliding Israel hath justified herself more than treacherous Judah. ¹²Go and proclaim these words toward the north, and say, Return, thou backsliding Israel, saith the LORD; and I will not cause mine anger to fall upon you: for I am merciful, saith the LORD, and I will not keep anger for ever. ¹³Only acknowledge thine iniquity, that thou hast transgressed against the LORD thy God, and hast scattered thy ways to the strangers under every green tree, and ye have not obeyed my voice, saith the LORD.

> *[14]Turn, O backsliding children, saith the LORD; for I am married unto you: and I will take you one of a city, and two of a family, and I will bring you to Zion:* (Authors note: we see this come to pass when Christ comes to save His people from their sins, grafting all, both gentile and Jew, into the vine. See Romans 11 and Galatians 3:7-9, 26-29)

This concept of betrothal, divorce, and marriage to the people of Israel carries on in Hosea:

> Hosea 2:2 *Plead with your mother, plead: for she is not my wife, neither am I her husband:* let her therefore put away her whoredoms out of her sight, and her adulteries from between her breasts;

> Hosea 2:19-20 And I will betroth thee unto me for ever; yea, I will betroth thee unto me in righteousness, and in judgment, and in lovingkindness, and in mercies. [20]I will even betroth thee unto me in faithfulness: and thou shalt know the LORD.

In the New Testament, we see Christ referenced in relation to the Church in a passage on marriage in Ephesians.

> Ephesians 5:21-27 Submitting yourselves one to another in the fear of God. [22]Wives, submit yourselves unto your own husbands, as unto the Lord. [23]For the husband is the head of the wife, even as Christ is the head of the church: and he is the saviour of the body. [24]Therefore as the church is subject unto Christ, so let the wives be to their own husbands in every thing. [25]Husbands, love your wives, even as Christ also loved the church, and gave himself for it; [26]That he might sanctify and cleanse it with the washing of water by the word, [27]That he might present it to himself a glorious church, not having spot, or wrinkle, or any such thing; but that it should be holy and without blemish.

## Introduction

We see John the Baptist speaking of joy in his role as the Friend of the Bridegroom.

> John 3:29  He that hath the bride is the bridegroom: but the friend of the bridegroom, which standeth and heareth him, rejoiceth greatly because of the bridegroom's voice: this my joy therefore is fulfilled.

Christ Himself makes mention of His role as the Bridegroom:

> Mark 2:18-20  And the disciples of John and of the Pharisees used to fast: and they come and say unto him, Why do the disciples of John and of the Pharisees fast, but thy disciples fast not? *19And Jesus said unto them, Can the children of the bridechamber fast, while the bridegroom is with them? as long as they have the bridegroom with them, they cannot fast. 20But the days will come, when the bridegroom shall be taken away from them, and then shall they fast in those days.*

The Apostle Paul mentions the Bride again in his letter to the church at Corinth:

> 2 Corinthians 11:1-3  Would to God ye could bear with me a little in my folly: and indeed bear with me. *2For I am jealous over you with godly jealousy: for I have espoused you to one husband, that I may present you as a chaste virgin to Christ.* 3But I fear, lest by any means, as the serpent beguiled Eve through his subtilty, so your minds should be corrupted from the simplicity that is in Christ.

We see the Bride mentioned again in the closing verses of the book of Revelation.

> Revelation 21:2  And I John saw the holy city, new Jerusalem, coming down from God out of heaven, prepared as a bride adorned for her husband.

> Revelation 22:17  And the Spirit and the bride say, Come. And let him that heareth say, Come. And let him that is athirst come. And whosoever will, let him take the water of life freely.

What becomes clear in these verses, is that God intended for Israel to be His future Bride, but due to Israel's continued rejection of God and His teachings, He chose to prepare the Bride of Christ and we see God the Son wanting to present His Bride to God the Father without spot or wrinkle.

From time to time in the Scriptures, there are references to how God adorns His Bride. Some of these are in the Old Testament and some are in the New Testament. There are references to jewels, to gold and silver, to fine linens, belts, cords, etc. The Scriptures tell us that upon acceptance of Jesus Christ as Lord of our lives, He grants to us His Robe of Righteousness. Interspersed among these passages, and sometimes immediately following them, are references to how this raiment has been spoiled and what is necessary to clean it up again, to be made presentable to the Father by Christ the Son.

## Customs Then and Now

Understanding the various pieces of attire given to the Bride of Christ requires at least an introductory understanding of Jewish wedding practises back in the times when Scripture was written.

As can be appreciated, wedding customs have changed quite a bit over time. What is now done all at once in a ceremony under a temporary shelter, used to take anywhere from one to several years to complete. Without a basic understanding of the ancient ceremony in a nutshell, the pieces discussed and their correlation to the Bride of Christ could get very easily lost or even worse, create confusion. As God is not the author of confusion, let us briefly look at this ceremony:

Focus on Jerusalem (focusonjerusalem.com) has created a very handy short-form notation of the ancient Jewish wedding ceremony and its contrast to the Bride of Christ.

First we have the Shiddukhin. This is the first step, where the marriage is arranged between the father of the groom, and the father of the bride.

## Introduction

Depending on what point in history you consider, the bride may or may not have any consent at this stage. Various sources suggest that this step is sometimes done by the suitor himself.

Next we have the Mohar, also known as The Bride Price. This was required by law and was paid by the father of the groom. Otherwise known as the dowry, it reflected the perceived value of the bride.

Although not required, sometimes the groom would give Mattan or Love Gifts as an expression of his love for her.

The bride's father would add to her dowry by giving her Shiluhim, to equip her for her new life. This was actually part of her family inheritance. As you will see when we come to the discussion on head decorations, many girls would be given this gift by their fathers to show prospective suitors the worth and wealth of the family to which she belonged. This gave way to referring to this headpiece as "the family jewels" and if a single coin got lost, it was a very frantic affair.

The Ketubah was the actual Marriage Contract stating the Mohar, the Rights of the bride, and the promises of the groom. This is very like the legal documents we sign today at modern wedding ceremonies, the major difference being that this was signed at the time the suitor came asking for the daughter's hand.

Once the Ketubah was signed, the father of the bride would call her in, and the suitor would present her with the Kiddushin, or "cup of acceptance". If she accepted the cup, the betrothal was sealed. If she did not accept it, then according to the terms of the Mohar, the betrothal would be annulled.

## Preparation Time:

This step would initiate a period of preparation for both the bride and the groom. The groom would return to his father's house to build a room, known in ancient times as the Chuppah or Huppah.

Based on ancient historical records, by the time Christ used this terminology at the Last Supper, this had been the third iteration of the usage of the term "Chuppah" in the wedding ceremony.

The bride had preparations of her own to do which will be covered at various places in this book.

The final step in the ceremony was the Nissuin. This was when the father of the groom would say that all was ready and the son could go get his bride and bring her home. At the time of the Last Supper, this took the form very much like that of an abduction. However, this would probably be the most joyous abduction anyone would ever experience, as this was the culmination of the wedding. The bride and her attendants had been ready for some time, possibly up to a year or more, waiting for this unannounced day to arrive. The groom would come with his attendants, one blowing the shofar and the groom calling out to his bride. There would be quite the parade back to his father's house followed by a coronation of the King and Queen (as bride and groom were called on their wedding day), a marriage feast, and the consummation of which John the Baptist was so pleased to be named a friend to witness.

It is a point of interest for the author, that research on this shortened list of events has been elaborated on in different ways over time as well as by various Jewish writers. So while there are differences depending on when you look in history, this was the generally-understood ancient Jewish wedding ceremony in a nutshell.

## The Bride's Preparations

I wish to spend a few minutes now discussing the preparations of the bride. These are important for the Church to take note of, because it is due to these steps being forgotten by Israel that God found Himself issuing a writ of divorce from His betrothal to her.

The most important of her preparations was, and for the modern observing Jewish bride, still is, the Mikveh, which is a ceremonial purification bath, preferably in moving water (as opposed to still), when available.

## Introduction

The concept of doing Mikveh as a ceremonial washing to purify one's self from past sins has been done throughout Jewish history, not merely for bridal prep, but for other important situations as well. This is why when John the Baptist came baptizing for sins, the people had questions.

> John 3:23-30  And John also was baptizing in Aenon near to Salim, because there was much water there: and they came, and were baptized. [24]For John was not yet cast into prison.  [25]Then there arose a question between some of John's disciples and the Jews about purifying.  [26]And they came unto John, and said unto him, Rabbi, he that was with thee beyond Jordan, to whom thou barest witness, behold, the same baptizeth, and all men come to him.  [27]John answered and said, A man can receive nothing, except it be given him from heaven.  [28]Ye yourselves bear me witness, that I said, I am not the Christ, but that I am sent before him. [29]He that hath the bride is the bridegroom: but the friend of the bridegroom, which standeth and heareth him, rejoiceth greatly because of the bridegroom's voice: this my joy therefore is fulfilled.  [30]He must increase, but I must decrease.

As we go through this book, we will see just how important this concept of Mikveh is for the Bride of Christ.

The ancient Jewish bride was to be sewing her bridal outfit and displaying her undivided devotion to her groom. She was to complete her preparations with anticipation that her groom could come at any time.

Ancient Yemeni Jewish brides had a very complicated, very flashy bridal outfit to prepare and assemble. It would appear that this is the oldest known ancient Jewish bridal attire available upon which to conduct our study. However, similarities between it and a few passages of Scripture suggest that if this was not the outfit worn by Israeli Jewish brides, that what the writers saw was very close.

## Dressed for Eternity

To this day, Yemenite Jewish brides continue to wear the ancient headdress and outfit. At least one other author has given the headdress the term "Bride Price". You will see just how appropriate that term is when we reach that section of our discussion.

Various authors have written entire books on the ancient Jewish bridal practises, so I will not delve deeper at this stage. But with the introduction given here, let us begin our first discussion, by looking at how the Bride of Christ is described in the book of Revelation. Let us take a moment and read the entire quoted passage:

Revelation 21:2  And I John saw the holy city, new Jerusalem, coming down from God out of heaven, prepared as a bride adorned for her husband.

Revelation 21:9-27  And there came unto me one of the seven angels which had the seven vials full of the seven last plagues, and talked with me, saying, Come hither, I will shew thee the bride, the Lamb's wife. [10]And he carried me away in the spirit to a great and high mountain, and shewed me that great city, the holy Jerusalem, descending out of heaven from God, [11]Having the glory of God: and her light was like unto a stone most precious, even like a jasper stone, clear as crystal; [12]And had a wall great and high, and had twelve gates, and at the gates twelve angels, and names written thereon, which are the names of the twelve tribes of the children of Israel: [13]On the east three gates; on the north three gates; on the south three gates; and on the west three gates. [14]And the wall of the city had twelve foundations, and in them the names of the twelve apostles of the Lamb. [15]And he that talked with me had a golden reed to measure the city, and the gates thereof, and the wall thereof. [16]And the city lieth foursquare, and the length is as large as the breadth: and he measured the city with the reed, twelve thousand furlongs. The length and the breadth and the height of it are equal. [17]And he measured the wall thereof, an hundred and forty and four cubits, according to the measure of a man, that is, of the angel. [18]And the building of the wall of it was of jasper: and the city was pure gold, like unto clear glass. [19]And the foundations of the wall of the city were garnished with all manner of precious stones.

# Introduction

> The first foundation was jasper; the second, sapphire; the third, a chalcedony; the fourth, an emerald; [20]The fifth, sardonyx; the sixth, sardius; the seventh, chrysolite; the eighth, beryl; the ninth, a topaz; the tenth, a chrysoprasus; the eleventh, a jacinth; the twelfth, an amethyst. [21]And the twelve gates were twelve pearls; every several gate was of one pearl: and the street of the city was pure gold, as it were transparent glass. [22]And I saw no temple therein: for the Lord God Almighty and the Lamb are the temple of it. [23]And the city had no need of the sun, neither of the moon, to shine in it: for the glory of God did lighten it, and the Lamb is the light thereof. [24]And the nations of them which are saved shall walk in the light of it: and the kings of the earth do bring their glory and honour into it. [25]And the gates of it shall not be shut at all by day: for there shall be no night there. [26]And they shall bring the glory and honour of the nations into it. [27]And there shall in no wise enter into it any thing that defileth, neither whatsoever worketh abomination, or maketh a lie: but they which are written in the Lamb's book of life.

We will focus on the Twelve Foundation Stones of the New Jerusalem in the first section of this book.

**Dressed for Eternity**

## The Twelve Foundation Stones of the New Jerusalem

Examining the various pieces of raiment and adornment found in the Scriptures, begins with the puzzling and, as it turns out, rather confusing correlation between the precious stones found in Aaron's Breastplate in Exodus 28 and the precious stones that make up the foundations of the New Jerusalem, described in Revelation 21.

Exodus 28:15-21 And thou shalt make the breastplate of judgment with cunning work; after the work of the ephod thou shalt make it; of gold, of blue, and of purple, and of scarlet, and of fine twined linen, shalt thou make it. [16]Foursquare it shall be being doubled; a span shall be the length thereof, and a span shall be the breadth thereof. [17]And thou shalt set in it settings of stones, even four rows of stones: the first row shall be a sardius, a Topaz, and a carbuncle: this shall be the first row. [18]And the second row shall be an Emerald, a sapphire, and a Diamond. [19]And the third row a ligure, an Agate, and an amethyst. [20]And the fourth row a Beryl, and an onyx, and a jasper: they shall be set in gold in their inclosings. [21]And the stones shall be with the names of the children of Israel, twelve, according to their names, like the engravings of a signet; every one with his name shall they be according to the twelve tribes.

Revelation 21:2 And I John saw the holy city, new Jerusalem, coming down from God out of heaven, prepared as a bride adorned for her husband.

Revelation 21:9-12, 14, 19-21 And there came unto me one of the seven angels which had the seven vials full of the seven last plagues, and talked with me, saying, Come hither, I will shew thee the bride, the Lamb's wife. [10]And he carried me away in the spirit to a great and high mountain, and shewed me that great city, the holy Jerusalem, descending out of heaven from God, [11]Having the glory of God: and her light was like unto a stone

## The 12 Stones of Aaron's Breastplate

most precious, even like a jasper stone, clear as crystal; [12]And had a wall great and high, and had twelve gates, and at the gates twelve angels, and names written thereon, which are the names of the twelve tribes of the children of Israel: [14]And the wall of the city had twelve foundations, and in them the names of the twelve apostles of the Lamb. [19]And the foundations of the wall of the city were garnished with all manner of precious stones. The first foundation was jasper; the second, sapphire; the third, a chalcedony; the fourth, an Emerald; [20]The fifth, sardonyx; the sixth, sardius; the seventh, chrysolite; the eighth, Beryl; the ninth, a Topaz; the tenth, a chrysoprasus; the eleventh, a jacinth; the twelfth, an amethyst. [21]And the twelve gates were twelve pearls; every several gate was of one pearl: and the street of the city was pure gold, as it were transparent glass.

There are 12 stones in Aaron's Breastplate, and 12 foundation stones of the New Jerusalem. Each of the 12 stones on the breastplate bore the name of a tribe of Israel according to birth order. Members of the Early Church chose to assign the names of the 12 Apostles to the 12 foundation stones of the New Jerusalem although as we see in Revelation, John did not. It was with some naivety that this author would even consider that there would be any problem between these correlations.

Due to various bits and pieces of historical, genealogical, archaeological, ancient church, and astronomical records, uncovering the most commonly accepted assignments as best understood by various researchers and scholars proved time consuming. Thanks to a well-quoted Early Church source, it only took five points of research to confirm the commonly accepted assignments of the 12 Apostles to the 12 foundation stones. However it would take more than nine points of research from both Jewish and Christian sources before a common thread would finally be found as to which tribe was assigned to which stone on Aaron's breastplate! The assignments along with their Scriptural, historical and archaeological reasons ranged so wildly from one scholar to another that I was beginning to think I'd never find a consensus!

However, before the Tribes and Apostles could be assigned, a consensus was needed regarding how each stone looked and what they themselves were called. The names of the stones change from the breastplate to the foundation of the

New Jerusalem, but the equation between the two has long been accepted down through history. So it was a matter of matching up from various points of research, the names with the colours and the Hebrew and Greek with the common modern terms. Suffice to say that after two days of extensive research, enough of a basis was arrived at to facilitate this study.

Two sources ended up on top of the pack when all was said and done, and they will be made available in the research appendix at the back of this book.

In coming pages, we will embark together on a study of each stone in Aaron's breastplate. We will cover such topics as:
1. What its properties are,
2. Why it was generally assigned to which tribe
3. Who the apostle is that it was assigned to, and
4. What, if any, correlation there is to why that stone was used to adorn the New Jerusalem, the future home of the Bride of Christ.

Our journey will take us through geology, history, and Scripture. Are you ready?

## Sardis - The first Stone in Aaron's Breastplate

The first Stone in Aaron's Breastplate, and generally considered by some to be the sixth stone of New Jerusalem's 12 Foundations, is Sardius, also known as Carnelian - a variant of Chalcedony. Depending on whom you read, this is referred to by even more names: Sardion, Sardonyx, Sardis, Sardius, Carnelian, and even Chalcedony itself, of whom the Sardius mentioned in Exodus is the red-brown variety, not the orangish variety. The Hebrew word for this stone according to Strong's Hebrew and Greek Dictionary as provided by e-Sword, is:

אדם

'ôdem

*o'-dem* From "a-dam"; *redness*, that is, the *Ruby, garnet*, or some other red gem: - sardius.

אדם

'âdam

aw-dam'

To *show blood* (in the face), that is, *flush* or turn rosy: - be (dyed, made) red (ruddy).

Apparently discovered first in Sardius of Lydia, the Egyptians were the likely manner in which the Hebrews obtained it when they fled Egypt.

## Make-up and Characteristics

Now let's examine the make-up and characteristics of this stone. First, as mentioned above, we know that it is reddish in nature. Some have referred to this stone as Ruby due to its colour, although that would not be accurate considering both the Greek and Hebrew references to this stone refer to either Sardius, Carnelian, or Chalcedony. The Ruby is a variant of the mineral Corundum, not Chalcedony.

## The 12 Stones of Aaron's Breastplate

See the appendix for clarification offered via further resources.

It is interesting to note, that while the names are interchangeable, Sard is actually harder and darker than Carnelian. Considering most researched sources mention Sard or Sardius as opposed to Carnelian, we will go with the fact that this stone is dark red in colour, marked with iron oxide impurities and of a hard, tough nature.

According to various sources, this stone was referred to in ancient times as one that purifies. It is described by some sources as "the blood red" stone. Red of course has been attributed to the concept of passion down through the centuries. When you combine that with the generally understood meaning of Rueben's name: "Behold, a son", the potential meaning for this stone becomes much deeper.

## Rueben and Philip - Associations with the Stone

This stone is most commonly ascribed to Rueben of the 12 Tribes of Israel although some attribute it to Judah. Of the 12 Apostles, Philip is generally assigned to this stone, although some scholars place Bartholomew with it instead. We must remember that these associations of the Apostles are not "set in stone", nor actually listed in such association in Scripture! The 12 Tribes' stone assignments are even more widely varied, some based on modern assumptions of birth order, some on ancient historical assumptions of birth order, and still others based on Camp order rather than birth order. For the purposes of this study, we will go with Rueben and Philip, as those are referenced most often after enough digging among the scholars is accomplished to achieve any kind of consensus.

Rueben's name means "Behold, a son". Rueben was the eldest among his brothers in Jacob's household, and the one who spared Joseph's life by suggesting they dig a pit to place him in, hoping later he'd be able to retrieve him. He is known for his sorrow at the shared lie told by the brothers to their father when Joseph did not return.

## Dressed for Eternity

We don't gain much insight from the meaning of Philip's name as to why he has typically been associated with this stone. However, he asks Christ a question that gets a similar response to Rueben's name. Philip asks Christ to "Show us the Father" in John 14:8. Christ's response is "he that hath seen me hath seen the Father" in verse 9.

Indeed, as Rueben's name proclaims, "Behold, a Son!"

**What does this mean for the Bride of Christ?**

> Matthew 1:21 And she shall bring forth a son, and thou shalt call his name JESUS: for he shall save his people from their sins.

We see in the meaning of Rueben's name a prophetic call out to the Son of Man who would later come, the One of which we write as Jesus Christ, or as John observes, our Heavenly Bridegroom. We observe then, that this stone has us looking straight into the Sonship of Christ and the cleansing Blood shed for the remission of sins.

It is thus imperative, for the man or woman of God who claims to be a member of the Church, the Bride of Christ, to ensure that he or she has passed under the Blood of Christ and received forgiveness for their sin. Failure to repent of one's sin and accept the cleansing flow of the Blood of Christ results in disqualification from their place in the Bride of Christ.

Secondly, when considering the tattered nature of Christ's Robe of Righteousness on the body of the Bride, we must acknowledge that since passing through that Crimson Flood, we have from time to time wilfully engaged in sin again! The only way to remove sin's stain from our robes, is to repent and seek forgiveness. But here is where another natures of Sardis comes into play. Being human, our sinful nature is hard, and can be very tough to deal with. We can't cleanse ourselves of our sin. We can't get rid of it on our own. Only Christ is strong enough to overcome our sin and cleanse us from all unrighteousness.

## The 12 Stones of Aaron's Breastplate

1 John 1:8-9  If we say that we have no sin, we deceive ourselves, and the truth is not in us. ⁹If we confess our sins, he is faithful and just to forgive us our sins, and to cleanse us from all unrighteousness.

# Dressed for Eternity

## Pitdah, or Topaz - The Second Stone in Aaron's Breastplate

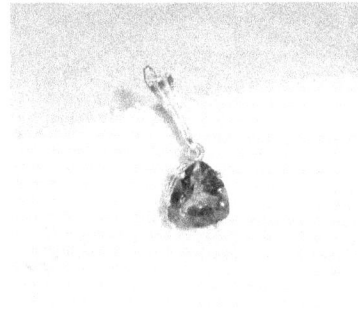

Pitdah, or Topaz as most scholars have come to refer to it, sits as the second stone in Aaron's Breastplate and the 9th stone of the 12 Foundations of the New Jerusalem. While some grades of the stone we now call Topaz can have a yellowish, brown or greenish hue, gemologists are more likely to say that the ancient stone referred to as Topaz was closer to that of Peridot, although mined from the generally understood location of an island in the Red Sea.

## Make-up and Characteristics

Commonly understood characteristics include the fact that the wide-ranging available colours of Topaz and the varying degrees of yellow-green in Peridot, are generally derived from impurities in the stone itself. The exception is modern-day Topaz that through heating and/or application of colour, has been known to take on blueish hues as well. In fact, when most people think of Topaz today, they think of the artificial blue colour. The generalized shape of this stone in the wild is that of a rhombic prism. Both the Peridot and the Topaz are characterized by a white streak going through the stone.

History leads us to believe that it was widely available in its more semi-precious varieties around the ancient Middle East. We are told that once again, it was a stone readily available from the Egyptians, Phoenicians etc. So characteristic number one, it was common. In its higher grade forms, it was highly prized by the Hebrews of that day, as evidenced by Job's words:

> Job 28:19 "The Topaz of Ethiopia shall not equal it, neither shall it be valued with pure gold."

The Topaz is said to have similar hardness to that of a Ruby, while its lustre is similar to that of a Diamond.

## The 12 Stones of Aaron's Breastplate

Ancient descriptions of this stone suggest it was layered, with the bottom layer having a reddish hue while the upper layer held the yellowish or greenish hue, clearly not the same stone as most describe today.

## Simeon and Matthew - Associations with the Stone

Simeon's name means: "To hearken" or "one who hears" or "hear". The similarity between Simeon and this stone appears to be in the last characteristic noted above. Jewish historical lore suggests that the two-toned nature of this stone carried with it the implication of morality. Due to the fact Simeon is noted in the Scriptures as having gone to rescue his sister, one can see where this suggestion might rise. Other meanings of his name include: "to proclaim", "to announce", "to write", and "to cut". This last definition might allude to the ancient description of this stone as well.

It is said that the standard under which the Tribe of Simeon camped had the symbol of a city on a green background. This is in keeping with the suggested stone having a greenish hue to it. It is noteworthy to mention however, that different sources place this banner's background under different colours and therefore ascribe different stones to this tribe in the breastplate.

> Luke 5:27-32  And after these things he went forth, and saw a publican, named Levi, sitting at the receipt of custom: and he said unto him, Follow me.  [28]And he left all, rose up, and followed him.  [29]And Levi made him a great feast in his own house: and there was a great company of publicans and of others that sat down with them.  [30]But their scribes and Pharisees murmured against his disciples, saying, Why do ye eat and drink with publicans and sinners?  [31]And Jesus answering said unto them, They that are whole need not a physician; but they that are sick.  [32]I came not to call the righteous, but sinners to repentance.

Matthew's name in simple English means: "Gift of God". His Hebrew name, Levi, meant "Join to", which is of note considering when Jesus called him, Matthew left his tax-collecting post and joined himself to the cause of Christ.

Due to the kind of work Matthew did before he was called by Christ, deductions about his personality, skills and abilities have emerged by various writers. It can't escape notice that Publicans, tax-collectors who worked for Rome, were incredibly disliked in the Roman Empire! Even worse, any Jew found working for the Romans, especially in this capacity, was hated even more! So it is consequently observed that Matthew needed to have a tough skin, a keen understanding of traded goods, and the ability to account for everything meticulously! We see then how Matthew's personal qualities match up with this stone's quality of hardness, and yet with the wealthy lustre of the Diamond. Matthew was by no means poor! The banquet thrown for Christ in Luke 5:29 would have been no small affair and according to Luke, was well attended by what the Jews of the day would have considered, "the baser sort". So while the everyday Jew hated him, clearly he was well-known and appreciated by those of his demographic.

**What does this mean for the Bride of Christ?**

Christ is looking for a Bride with combat boots on. The moral purity offered in this stone along with its hardness and lustre speak to this loudly! The Bride of Christ is meant to be beautiful, gentle, pure, proclaiming the goodness of Christ while shaking off the fiery darts of the enemy, which are the attacks that come within and without the Church. She does this with the Shield of Faith:

> Ephesians 6:16 Above all, taking the shield of faith, wherewith ye shall be able to quench all the fiery darts of the wicked.

An immoral attitude does not become the Bride of Christ. Engagement in immorality defiles the Christian, contributing to the spots and wrinkles Christ wants to cleanse and remove before presenting her to the Father. This defilement may be spiritual as described to Ezekiel of Jerusalem's behaviour straying from God, or it may be physical as in the concept of adultery or fornication outside the marriage bed. It should be the desire of every born-again Christian to lead lives of purity before the world and before God, not putting any other gods before Him, and holding true to virginity or to one's spouse as the situation demands.

## The 12 Stones of Aaron's Breastplate

A toughened attitude toward God also contributes to those spots and wrinkles in the Robe of Righteousness. There is no room for a set jaw before the Heavenly Bridegroom. The only toughness God desires, is that which is provided by the Shield of Faith as it stops all attacks from the enemy! The Bride must not be consumed by what the world thinks, but must be strong and unbreakable against "fear of man" and do what she has been called to do regardless of what those around her think.

Her tenderness toward God and toward the hurting is of ultimate beauty in the eyes of God. Scripture says:

> 1 Peter 3:3-4  Whose adorning let it not be that outward adorning of plaiting the hair, and of wearing of gold, or of putting on of apparel; ⁴But let it be the hidden man of the heart, in that which is not corruptible, even the ornament of a meek and quiet spirit, which is in the sight of God of great price.

> Proverbs 8:11  For wisdom is better than rubies; and all the things that may be desired are not to be compared to it.

## The Chrysoprase or Emerald - The Third Stone in Aaron's Breastplate

The third stone in Aaron's Breastplate, and considered to be the fourth stone of the foundations of New Jerusalem, is the Chrysoprase or Emerald. Some scholars have suggested this stone is the Carbuncle. However, it appears the word Carbuncle refers more to the style of cut than to the gem itself. Most sources say this third stone
of Aaron's Breastplate was of a greenish hue, although occasional sources suggest the burnt red of the fourth stone instead. Our discussion then, will centre on the Chrysoprase or Emerald.

## Make-up and Characteristics

Similarities between these stones exist primarily in colour and hardness, and perhaps in shape if they had been cut in the Carbuncle manner, which is to say, a rounded, roughly squarish/rectangle cut. Both the Chrysoprase and Emerald range from pale green to darker greens depending on the level of Chromium (Emerald) or Nickel (Chrysoprase) found in each. An interesting note about Chrysoprase occurs in a book written in 1904:

> "On exposing a natural chrysoprase to light or heat its colour becomes paler, though this may be restored by placing the stone in a damp medium. It is surprising that the colour of the natural gem should be susceptible to the action of light and heat, whilst the artificial product is quite unaffected." (Precious Stones, by Max Bauer; trans. L. J. Spencer, 1904.)

## The 12 Stones of Aaron's Breastplate

Both stones are said to have a hardness between 6 and 7, or even 7.5 for the Emerald, placing them in the middle of the Mohs Scale of Hardness. See the link provided for this scale in the appendix. This rating places them in the middle of the scale, suggesting they are much softer than harder gems such as the Diamond, which is the hardest of all.

While this author did not find locales where the Chrysoprase may have originated, the Emerald was well-known to be mined in Upper Egypt for many centuries, with some mines being reopened for a time in the 1800's. Once again we see where the Hebrews obtained their jewels that God would pronounce use for in Temple Worship and Ceremony.

The yellowish-green and light-affected nature of the Chrysoprase as noted by Max Bauer above, confers with other writings by Rabbinical sources that believed when this stone was in artificial light, it took on the colour of flaming red with yellow flashes through it, earning it the name "Lightning Stone" as the Hebrew word for this third stone indicates: "Baraketh". By day it was said that this stone took on an amber (greenish-yellow) hue. It is felt then, that this is what Paul was referring to when he called Christ the Morning Star. See another discussion of this stone in the links provided in the appendix.

## Levi and Thaddaeus - Associations with the Stone

The Tribe most commonly associated with this stone is Levi. Levi's name means "attached" or "joined to". As we know from the Scriptures, Levi was the tribe chosen to serve in the Temple as priests to perform the work of the Temple and minister God's Word to the nation of Israel. It is commonly accepted that the colour green stands for Life in both Christian, Jewish, and many secular circles. Any time we see the green grass grow, the green tree sprout its leaves, and the green stems of the flowers coming up out of the earth, we know Spring has sprung and we hold celebrations of life, typically around Easter time or the time of the Spring Equinox. So it is said that this stone was a type of the Life to come, and a type of the eternal judgement so immediately upon our heads. When out of the Light of God, this stone's darker, fiery and flashing features come forth, but when in the Light of God, the softer greenish-yellow comes forth.

The Levite tribe was "joined to the altar" so to speak, with the High Priest in both role and appearance, taking on a type of who Christ is and what He came to do for mankind. In Christ, we have life and life eternal. Away from Christ, we live in darkness and face terrible and eternal judgement.

The apostle generally associated with this stone is Thaddaeus. Thaddaeus is generally associated with "Judas, not Iscariot" in the Gospels, and according to sources, the use of the surname Thaddaeus was preferable to the name Judas due to Iscariot's betrayal of Christ. The various names ascribed to Thaddaeus give a string of interesting meanings:

- Thaddaeus: "Gift of God" in Greek, or "Breast" in Hebrew
- Lebbaeus: "Heart or Courageous"
- Judas, a Greek derivative of the Hebrew Judah: "Praise Yahweh"
- Judas Thaddaeus would then mean: Praise Yahweh for the Gift of God.

The source used for this information remarks that Iscariot means "the men of the city" in Hebrew, causing the author to comment that "Judas, not Iscariot" would read "Praise Yahweh, but not from the men of the city".

In light of our desired discussion, this is very interesting. We may not know much about this particular Apostle from either Scripture or historical records, but his name alone, in combination with the Tribe Levi being associated with the properties of this stone in Aaron's Breastplate, offers insight. As noted already, the Tribe of Levi was set apart to serve in the Temple. They were not given land when the Hebrews entered Canaan either. They truly were not "men of the city". They were men of the Temple. Their service pointed to the eventual gift of God as prophesied by the Prophets. The "Gift of God" of course, is the gift of Salvation offered through Jesus Christ, granting us eternal life with Him in Heaven, avoiding the terrible judgements brought on our own heads through refusal to accept this gift.

So in Thaddaeus's name, we see both the meaning of the stone's colours, and the service of Levi all wrapped up into one name!

# The 12 Stones of Aaron's Breastplate

## What does that mean for the Bride of Christ?

The Bride of Christ is to live in the Light. By living in the Light, we offer hope to the world around us, shining forth the life-giving Light of God upon a darkened world. Failure to live in the Light means living in death and in danger of eternal judgement. Scripture state:

> John 3:17-21 For God sent not his Son into the world to condemn the world; but that the world through him might be saved. $^{18}$He that believeth on him is not condemned: but he that believeth not is condemned already, because he hath not believed in the name of the only begotten Son of God. $^{19}$And this is the condemnation, that light is come into the world, and men loved darkness rather than light, because their deeds were evil. $^{20}$For every one that doeth evil hateth the light, neither cometh to the light, lest his deeds should be reproved. $^{21}$But he that doeth truth cometh to the light, that his deeds may be made manifest, that they are wrought in God.

> 1 John 1:5-9 This then is the message which we have heard of him, and declare unto you, that God is light, and in him is no darkness at all. $^{6}$If we say that we have fellowship with him, and walk in darkness, we lie, and do not the truth: $^{7}$But if we walk in the light, as he is in the light, we have fellowship one with another, and the blood of Jesus Christ his Son cleanseth us from all sin. $^{8}$If we say that we have no sin, we deceive ourselves, and the truth is not in us. $^{9}$If we confess our sins, he is faithful and just to forgive us our sins, and to cleanse us from all unrighteousness.

The Bride of Christ received the Great Commission, and is not to hide her light under a bowl, but is to be set out on a hill for all to see.

Some verses to ponder:

> John 3:14-21 And as Moses lifted up the serpent in the wilderness, even so must the Son of man be lifted up: $^{15}$That whosoever believeth in him should not perish, but have eternal life. $^{16}$For God so loved the world,

that he gave his only begotten Son, that whosoever believeth in him should not perish, but have everlasting life. ¹⁷For God sent not his Son into the world to condemn the world; but that the world through him might be saved. ¹⁸He that believeth on him is not condemned: but he that believeth not is condemned already, because he hath not believed in the name of the only begotten Son of God. ¹⁹And this is the condemnation, that light is come into the world, and men loved darkness rather than light, because their deeds were evil. ²⁰For every one that doeth evil hateth the light, neither cometh to the light, lest his deeds should be reproved. ²¹But he that doeth truth cometh to the light, that his deeds may be made manifest, that they are wrought in God.

Matthew 5:14-16 Ye are the light of the world. A city that is set on an hill cannot be hid. ¹⁵Neither do men light a candle, and put it under a bushel, but on a candlestick; and it giveth light unto all that are in the house. ¹⁶Let your light so shine before men, that they may see your good works, and glorify your Father which is in heaven.

## Anthrax (Garnet) or Jacynth - The Fourth Stone in Aaron's Breastplate

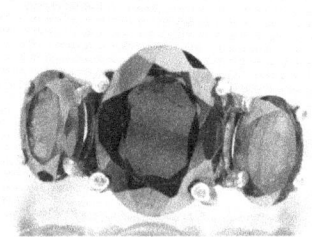

Depending on the sources you read, and in what time period of history they were written, you will find yourself looking at the fourth stone of the first row of Aaron's Breastplate and wondering what on earth they are talking about! An excellent case in point is provided in a discussion over at Christianhospitality.org of this particular stone. By the time you get to the end of this stone's historical breakdown, you end up with a very similar description to two stones in particular, the Anthrax (Garnet) and the Jacynth. Even how the Hebrew word is spelled is up for debate, depending on one's understanding of the ancient Hebrew versus modern Hebrew (Yiddish) presentations. Matters aren't helped by the modern-day dictionary discussion of the Anthrax (Garnet), which appears to be as wide-ranging as the Topaz, minus the ability to appear in any colour resembling blue. However, there are enough similarities between the modern and ancient descriptions of these two stones to settle on them for the purposes of our discussion.

### Make-up and Characteristics

In observing that Anthrax (Garnet) and Jacynth are both known to have varying hues, it is interesting to note that while the Jacynth's orange-red colouring is its most prominent hue, the hue of the Anthrax (Garnet) that is most commonly referred to is that of burning embers, reddish coal, or a red appearing over a dark/dark green background. These stones are similar in that regard, but the Anthrax (Garnet) is darker. In hardness, they are both rated around a 7 on the Mohs scale (see the Mohs scale link in the appendix), causing one gem researcher to note that due to this rating, jewellers should take care in setting these stones as they are known to be brittle. It should be mentioned that the Jacynth was known to be mined in the African region.

# The 12 Stones of Aaron's Breastplate

## Judah and Simon - Associations with the Stone

Psalm 22:3 But thou art holy, O thou that inhabitest the praises of Israel.

Judah is the tribe of Israel most commonly ascribed to this stone. His name means "Praise" or "Praise of Jehovah". It would appear, based on various imagery available down through the ages, that dark red has been considered one of the colours of royalty along with the likes of deep purple, royal blue, and rich Emerald green. So it is said, that such a colour is fitting for this tribe, as it would be from the Tribe of Judah that Israel's eternal King would come. Indeed it is from this tribe that King David was born, and then from his line would come Mary, virgin mother of Jesus Christ. Scripture tells us that God inhabits the praises of His people! The connotation is not lost on the author. Out of praise Christ came.

Early Church writings and various scholars ascribe Simon to this particular stone. His name literally means "rock or stone" in the Greek. Some speculate that perhaps the name was a derivative of Shimeon, which as we learned already, means "hearken" or "one who hears". So we either have a rock with ears or we have one who hears The Rock, referring to Christ Himself. Most conjecture about this apostle's personality comes from the added description given to him any time his name is mentioned in the gospels, from Matthew and Mark calling him Simon the Canaanite, to Dr. Luke calling him Simon the Zealot. Apparently the name "Canaanite" refers less to the ancient land of Canaan upon which Israel was settled, and more to do with the Greek word used with a similar definition to Luke's choice of wording. Being a doctor, Luke was the disciple to write his book with much detail, so it appears this particular Simon among the disciples, had been part of the radical group in Israel known as The Zealots at the time Christ called him.

## What does this mean for the Bride of Christ?

Burning embers suggest hot coals. They can also suggest a fire that risks burning out. How is the Bride of Christ to keep the fires burning, but through the praises of her people lifted high to the Throne of God!

Ephesians 5:18-21 And be not drunk with wine, wherein is excess; but be filled with the Spirit; [19]Speaking to yourselves in psalms and hymns and spiritual songs, singing and making melody in your heart to the Lord; [20]Giving thanks always for all things unto God and the Father in the name of our Lord Jesus Christ; [21]Submitting yourselves one to another in the fear of God.

Colossians 3:15-17 And let the peace of God rule in your hearts, to the which also ye are called in one body; and be ye thankful. [16]Let the word of Christ dwell in you richly in all wisdom; teaching and admonishing one another in psalms and hymns and spiritual songs, singing with grace in your hearts to the Lord. [17]And whatsoever ye do in word or deed, do all in the name of the Lord Jesus, giving thanks to God and the Father by him.

Psalm 22:3 But thou art holy, O thou that inhabitest the praises of Israel.

Truly it is in her praises that God shows up. Worship ensues as spirit meets Spirit and as God communes with the heart of man, and the heavenly Bridegroom is pleased. Anyone who has been around a campfire will know that if you take a piece of wood out of the fire and set it off to one side, the flames on that piece will eventually die down and go out. However, if that piece of wood is added back into the fire, its embers flare up again and join the others as hot as before.

For many in the Church, the fervent fire of their faith has burned low. The coals flicker and are at risk of dying out altogether because eyes have been shifted off the object of their worship and onto the differences and divisions among them instead. Christ would desire that we turn our hearts back to Himself, join arms with our fellow believers once more and allow ourselves to once again be fanned by the eternal flame of the Holy Spirit to bring intense pleasure to our God and King.

## The 12 Stones of Aaron's Breastplate

Hebrews 10:22-25 Let us draw near with a true heart in full assurance of faith, having our hearts sprinkled from an evil conscience, and our bodies washed with pure water. [23]Let us hold fast the profession of our faith without wavering; (for he is faithful that promised;) [24]And let us consider one another to provoke unto love and to good works: [25]Not forsaking the assembling of ourselves together, as the manner of some is; but exhorting one another: and so much the more, as ye see the day approaching.

## Sapphire, sometimes referred to as Chalcedony or Aqua-marine - The Fifth Stone in Aaron's Breastplate

Sapphire, the fifth stone in Aaron's Breastplate, and the 2nd foundation stone of New Jerusalem, has a bit of an identity crisis as far as what this stone really refers to in the time of Ancient Hebrew. It has been confused by some authors due to its Greek word, as that which referred to Lapis Lazuli, a semi-precious blue stone. It is said that we get the name for this stone from the Hebrew word: Sapir. Still, some sources call this stone Chalcedony and others call it Aqua-Marine. It's interesting to note that all three stones have similar qualities.

### Make-up and Characteristics

Sapphire is most known for its deep blue colour, although it comes in lighter shades or even different colours altogether. On the Mohs hardness scale, it is right behind the Diamond, at a rating of 9. This has meant that this stone, similar to the Diamond, has found its way into various commercial uses requiring a very hard stone to complete a job. Similar to Aqua-marine, some variants of Sapphire, particularly that mined in Tanzania, Africa, can change colour.

Chalcedony has been known to come in a wide range of colours that include a grayish-blue. It's softer than the other two at roughly 6 - 7 on the Mohs scale. It too, was readily available at the time the Hebrews left Egypt.

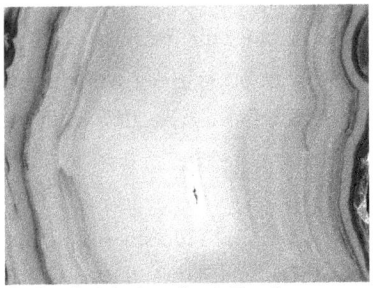
© Darknightsky - Stock Free Images

Aqua-marine comes in varying shades of colour as well, but is most prized for its blueish tint. It is generally of the lighter colour blue/green, but can be a deep blue on occasion.

## The 12 Stones of Aaron's Breastplate

As mentioned, it can be prone to colour changes. See the link in the appendix to learn why this might be. Suffice to say for this discussion, that exposure to light and heat makes it susceptible to changes in brightness and colour. As a member of the Beryl family, it has a hardness rating of 7.5 to 8 roughly.

While any of these stones could have been the stone mentioned for the fifth place on Aaron's Breastplate, the one most commonly attributed is the Sapphire. If that was indeed the case, then we now have two stones on Aaron's Breastplate that were known to change colour when exposed to light and heat.

## Issachar and Paul - Associations with the Stone

The name Issachar means "reward", "rewarded", or "hired worker" depending on the source you go with. It is very possible the name has all those meanings together. Some say that members of this tribe became well-respected members of David's Mighty Men and that due to their ability to discern the times, they were listened to by others. In combination with blue often standing for the thought of heaven, the heavens, or the sky, it is easy to see how in light of the blue nature of this stone, the hired worker will be rewarded.

Paul, also known by his Hebrew name, Saul, has been added to this list by most sources due to a shuffling of the 12 Apostles thanks to some saying Judas Iscariot lost his place among the original 12. This is as widely held a consensus as those who would replace Judas with Mattias according to references in the book of Acts. However, due to the Early Church largely assuming this stone's association with Paul, he is who we will go with for the purposes of this study. Not everyone agrees with him being added to the original 12 and have called him "the False Apostle" while others simply refer to him as the Apostle to the Gentiles.

Paul's original Hebrew name, Saul means "asked for, prayed for, or borrowed". His Greek name, Paul means "small". Indeed as one looks up into the heavens on a starry night, one can feel very small! But when paired with Issachar's meaning, we have a reward for the small one who asked and prayed for something.

## What does this mean for the Bride of Christ?

If the blue nature of this stone by any gem mentioned above is referenced to the concept of heaven, and if we believe that in relation to heaven, we are small; then it behooves us to take seriously the statement God makes in James:

> James 4:2-3 Ye lust, and have not: ye kill, and desire to have, and cannot obtain: ye fight and war, yet ye have not, because ye ask not. ³Ye ask, and receive not, because ye ask amiss, that ye may consume it upon your lusts.

We should also take seriously the words in Hebrews:

> Hebrews 11:6 But without faith it is impossible to please him: for he that cometh to God must believe that he is, and that he is a rewarder of them that diligently seek him.

Scripture also says in James:

> James 1:17 Every good gift and every perfect gift is from above, and cometh down from the Father of lights, with whom is no variableness, neither shadow of turning.

God doesn't change. The angels told the disciples that in the same manner in which they saw Him go, which was up into the heavens, Christ would return.

> Acts 1:9-11 And when he had spoken these things, while they beheld, he was taken up; and a cloud received him out of their sight. ¹⁰And while they looked stedfastly toward heaven as he went up, behold, two men stood by them in white apparel; ¹¹Which also said, Ye men of Galilee, why stand ye gazing up into heaven? this same Jesus, which is taken up from you into heaven, shall so come in like manner as ye have seen him go into heaven.

The Bride of Christ looks to the heavens, eagerly awaiting the Bridegroom's trumpet announcing His return for the Church to gather her up into the clouds

### The 12 Stones of Aaron's Breastplate

with Him to go to the Marriage Supper of the Lamb ahead of His Second Coming. It should be noted here that Christ's return for the Church, and The Second Coming when He sets foot on the Mount of Olives where every eye shall see Him, are two different events in the end-time passages of Scripture. However, delving into a full discussion of that is beyond the scope of this section. What is important to note, is that Christ's promise is to those who long for His appearing. (see Appendix B for a discussion on rapture and tribulation concepts)

> 2 Timothy 4:8  Henceforth there is laid up for me a crown of righteousness, which the Lord, the righteous judge, shall give me at that day: and not to me only, but unto all them also that love his appearing.

We are to be eagerly awaiting the day that our Heavenly Bridegroom is coming, and preparing ourselves for that day. The parable of the 10 virgins applies here, but not to the unsaved and saved as some have taught. It instead applies to the current state of the Church in general. There will be those who are not ready when the Trumpet blows. They will not rise to meet Christ in the air, but will instead be left on this earth to endure the Tribulation period, becoming numbered among those of the Tribulation saints.

It behooves us then, to be sure we are in full submission to the Holy Spirit's efforts in our lives. We know He is actively working in us when we exhibit the Fruit of the Spirit.

> Galatians 5:22-25  But the fruit of the Spirit is love, joy, peace, longsuffering, gentleness, goodness, faith,  [23]Meekness, temperance: against such there is no law.  [24]And they that are Christ's have crucified the flesh with the affections and lusts.  [25]If we live in the Spirit, let us also walk in the Spirit.

## Jasper - The Sixth Stone in Aaron's Breastplate

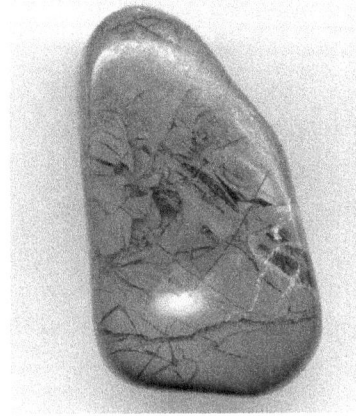

Jasper, as its commonly called, or Fire Opal as some have referred to it, is the sixth stone in Aaron's Breastplate, the 8th stone in the foundations of New Jerusalem. Keep in mind these are the most commonly agreed upon placements among an incredibly diverse scholarly, theological, historical and archaeological spectrum of gemology, and history in both Jewish and Christian research and definitions. As in other discussion so far where more than one stone is suggested, it's interesting to look at their various similarities as to why they were chosen.

## Make-up and Characteristics

Jasper is called such, largely due to its Hebrew and Greek wording. The Greek translation of the Hebrew word comes out as Isapis, commonly interpreted as Jasper into English. Once again we see the availability of this stone in the time of the Hebrews fleeing Egypt, as there is a yellow-red Jasper gem known as "Egyptian Jasper". This stone is said to be both opaque, and strongly yellow and red in colour. It's considered one of the more sensitive or softer stones at 6.5-7 on the Mohs hardness scale.

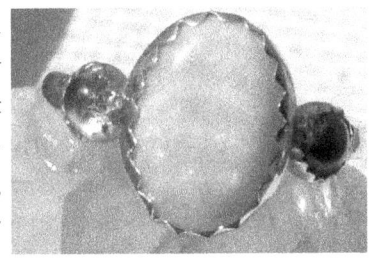

Fire Opal is also considered an orange-red stone, and as a result, one of the more flashy and eye-catching stones in the Opal family. It is said to be found in Ethiopia and ranges a 6-7.5 on the Mohs hardness scale. Apparently, due to the fact the Fire Opal has a high water content, it is a difficult stone to prepare, age, or treat in any way. Some stones will go cloudy if the water content has in some way left the stone. This stone is also known to dry out and crack too.

## The 12 Stones of Aaron's Breastplate

So we see availability to the Egyptians who showered the Hebrews with precious things as they fled. We see very similar colourations in the two stones, and we see similar softness.

## Zebulun and Peter - Associations with the Stone

Various meanings of Zebulun's name are "exaltation", "habitation", "to exalt" "home" and "honour". Zebulun's lot in the Promised Land was to settle on the coast. It is said that Zebulun's sea ports were a welcome sight to sailors.

Peter's name of course, means "Rock" as his full name was actually Simon-Peter. Peter is known in the Gospels for having a fiery personality, a "speak first, think later" attitude, and fierce loyalty! He was present when the Holy Spirit fell on the 120 in the Upper Room, and became instrumental in the Early Church.

## What does this mean for the Bride of Christ?

> Matthew 16:18 And I say also unto thee, That thou art Peter, and upon this rock I will build my church; and the gates of hell shall not prevail against it.

> Romans 9:30-33 What shall we say then? That the Gentiles, which followed not after righteousness, have attained to righteousness, even the righteousness which is of faith. [31]But Israel, which followed after the law of righteousness, hath not attained to the law of righteousness. [32]Wherefore? Because they sought it not by faith, but as it were by the works of the law. For they stumbled at that stumblingstone; [33]As it is written, Behold, I lay in Sion a stumblingstone and rock of offence: and whosoever believeth on him shall not be ashamed.

Christ our Rock is our habitation. Indeed we are to honour and exalt His place in our lives. One of the symbols of the Holy Spirit is fire, which is often drawn artistically using red, orange, and yellow colours, all of which are represented by the stones discussed here. Our hearts are to be Christ's home, and He says in the Scriptures:

John 14:15  If ye love me, keep my commandments.

John 15:9-13  As the Father hath loved me, so have I loved you: continue ye in my love. [10]If ye keep my commandments, ye shall abide in my love; even as I have kept my Father's commandments, and abide in his love. [11]These things have I spoken unto you, that my joy might remain in you, and that your joy might be full. [12]This is my commandment, That ye love one another, as I have loved you. [13]Greater love hath no man than this, that a man lay down his life for his friends.

John 14:16-18  And I will pray the Father, and he shall give you another Comforter, that he may abide with you for ever; [17]Even the Spirit of truth; whom the world cannot receive, because it seeth him not, neither knoweth him: but ye know him; for he dwelleth with you, and shall be in you. [18]I will not leave you comfortless: I will come to you.

Acts 2:1-4  And when the day of Pentecost was fully come, they were all with one accord in one place. [2]And suddenly there came a sound from heaven as of a rushing mighty wind, and it filled all the house where they were sitting. [3]And there appeared unto them cloven tongues like as of fire, and it sat upon each of them. [4]And they were all filled with the Holy Ghost, and began to speak with other tongues, as the Spirit gave them utterance.

It is the Holy Spirit who has been sent to come alongside us and prepare us for that wedding day in the sky! He is the One who opens our eyes and illuminates our hearts to the teachings of Christ and all we are to do to prepare ourselves for that day.

Our lives are to be marked by the Fire of the Holy Spirit, built on the Rock, which is Christ Himself.

# Ligure - The Seventh Stone in Aaron's Breastplate

The seventh stone in Aaron's Breastplate, often called the Ligure, and sometimes referred to as the Sapphire or Lapis Lazuli, is an interesting stone. If known by the name Ligure, as given in the Scriptural account of the stones necessary for Aaron's Breastplate, we meet with historical ambiguity and even scepticism. One source redeems it by giving a bit of history where the stone was typically found in the lower part of France. In addition, the name in Hebrew comes from a similar word meaning Lynx, as in, the large cat. Ligure is apparently formed from amber of a tree also referred to as a lynx, giving way to some of the mythological references to this stone that have created so much scepticism.

While several sources all agree that this was the seventh stone, at the same time, an equal number of sources claim it was the blue of the Sapphire or Lapis Lazuli rather than the yellowish green of the Ligure.

## Make-up and Characteristics

Ligure, as noted above, is generally a yellowish-green in nature, and apparently giving the appearance of millet, or small grains. It is gathered by some to have supposed to have been a form of Agate. Being made out of amber, it is also considered quite a hard stone.

Sapphire is most known for its deep blue colour, although it comes in lighter shades or even different colours altogether. On the Mohs hardness scale, it is right behind the Diamond, at a rating of 9. This has meant that this stone, similar to the Diamond, has found its way into various commercial uses requiring a very hard stone to complete a job. This stone has been available from various locations in Africa.

# The 12 Stones of Aaron's Breastplate

Lapis Lazuli is not a precious stone per se, but is known as semi-precious. It is often found in colours ranging from blue mid-tones to dark blue, and is thought to have been the stone that John saw as one of the 12 foundation stones in the New Jerusalem. Lapis Lazuli has been around since ancient times, and according to Wikipedia, was sourced from Afghanistan by ancient Egypt as their supplier of the stone. It is a softer stone at only 5 - 5.5 on the Mohs hardness scale.

## Dan and Andrew - Associations with the Stone

The meaning of Dan, is "judge", "to judge", "to be vindicated". A somewhat more descriptive meaning is given by his Mother, Rachael when she says, "Hashem has judged me and heard my voice". One of his descendants, Samson, would also be judged and sent to the Philistines. Other definitions say Dan as a tribe was to judge among his own tribe and people as an equal.

Andrew's name in Greek means "manly, manliness, or strong man". Scripture doesn't give us a Hebrew version of his name. From what can be gathered of his role among the Disciples and later the Early Church, it is safe to surmise that he was an unassuming character who was quick to judge the nature of Jesus as the Christ, and introduce others to Him.

## What does this mean for the Bride of Christ?

The understanding of this seventh place in Aaron's Breastplate would suggest that the Bride of Christ can be a confusing and sometimes contentious body of Believers. We're soft at some moments, tough as nails at others. But whether we shine the Light of Christ, insist on living the Life of Faith, or point heavenward (yellow, green, blue), we are all living out the Great Commission one way or another, even if we don't agree on how that's done or what that looks like.

**Dressed for Eternity**

But regardless of our take on living the Christian faith in the world, we are to correctly judge that Jesus Christ is Lord, that one day He will judge the world and those who turned their backs, and to bring others to that saving knowledge as well.

> Philippians 2:9-11  Wherefore God also hath highly exalted him, and given him a name which is above every name: [10]That at the name of Jesus every knee should bow, of things in heaven, and things in earth, and things under the earth; [11]And that every tongue should confess that Jesus Christ is Lord, to the glory of God the Father.

# Dressed for Eternity

## Agate or Emerald - The Eighth Stone in Aaron's Breastplate

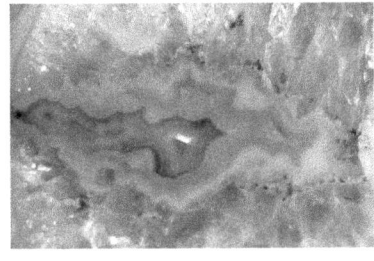

This eighth stone in Aaron's Breastplate is largely considered to be the Agate, although some say the Emerald as well. Interestingly, definitions of the Agate vary widely while most sources agree that the colour of the stone being referred to is a deep green colour. The Hebrew word for this stone is "Shebo" and in the Greek, "Achates", from which it is surmised to have come to the word Agate. There is disagreement on what this stone actually looks like, but for the purposes of this study, we'll look at why it's been compared to the Emerald.

## Make-up and Characteristics

The Agate is an interesting precious stone. The layered nature in which it is formed lends itself to a wide variety of appearances and colour combinations. One of the outer formative layers is generally described as dark greenish. A quote from Wikipedia puts it this way:

> "The first deposit on the wall of a cavity, forming the "skin" of the Agate, is generally a dark greenish mineral substance, like celadonite, delessite or "green earth", which are rich in iron probably derived from the decomposition of the augite in the enclosing volcanic rock. This green silicate may give rise by alteration to a brown iron oxide (limonite), producing a rusty appearance on the outside of the Agate-nodule."

This appears very similar to a quote taken from the 1911 Britannica which states:

> "The first deposit on the wall of a cavity, forming the "skin" of the Agate, is generally a dark greenish mineral substance, like celadonite, delessite or "green earth," which are hydrous silicates rich in iron, derived probably from the decomposition of the augite in the mother-rock.

## The 12 Stones of Aaron's Breastplate

This green silicate may give rise by alteration to a brown oxide of iron (limonite), producing a rusty appearance on the outside of the Agate-nodule."

This stone has a waxy lustre and ranks around 6.5 - 7 on the Mohs hardness scale.

The striped nature of the stone, in combination with the dark green hue that most scholars agree on, make the outer layer's colouration a candidate for this stone on Aaron's Breastplate.

The Emerald stone, as is commonly understood, is green. The darker the hue, the richer the appearance of the stone. Not only is this stone found in Egypt and actually mined there, but is found in other places as well around the Mediterranean and beyond. Once again, we have a stone the Egyptians easily had in their possession, to give to the Hebrews as they fled the land. This stone, while on a level of hardness at 6.5-8 on the Mohs scale, is still considered fragile and not very tough, generally due to how the stone is formed. This would be in keeping with the colour's reference to life, and that while life is enduring, it is also fragile.

Unfortunately, this particular gem stone gets imitated via synthetic means as often as the Sapphire.

## Gad and John - Associations with the Stone

Gad's name means "a troop", "to overcome", "good fortune" or "fortunate". It is noted among scholars of the Tribes of Israel, that Gad would be the first to take land in the Land of Canaan. We know from Exodus that this land was rich and fertile. Gad overcame the inhabitants, obtaining the good fortune of their portion of the new Land of Israel.

Some scholars have referred to the green gem as Beryl. When the Emerald is looked up, that is what is found, a member of the Beryl mineral family. It is surmised that in ancient times, the Beryl was used for "good fortune", one of the meanings of Gad's name.

John's name in the Greek comes from the Hebrew name "Yohanan" meaning "Yahweh is/has been gracious". We aren't really told which John is referred to in the Early Church's assignment of the stones to the 12 Apostles. It is hinted that this may have been John, the brother of James, sons of Zebedee. This is the John that some scholars say gave us the Gospel of John, 1st and 2nd John, and Revelation in the New Testament. These two brothers were nicknamed "Sons of Thunder" by those who knew them in the time of Christ, more than likely because of their high-tempered ways of doing things. Their Mother didn't help much either, when she demanded they each have a place on Christ's throne when he ascended into Heaven. Boisterous seemed to be the manner of the day for these two according to Biblical and historical lore. But one thing was certain, John was part of Christ's inner circle, and was known as the Beloved Disciple or The One that Jesus Loved. (note: some say this description was for another John who may have been a relative as well as a disciple)

## What does this mean for the Bride of Christ?

For members of the Bride of Christ such as myself, this is an encouraging term of endearment. Not all of us are crafted at the finer points of interpersonal communication. Some of us are seen as proverbial "bulls in a china shop" when it comes to expressing strong opinions. But yet, we see in the Scriptures that Christ endeared Himself to such a disciple. Like the stones mentioned here, life for many Christians is banded and striped with the colours of life, sin, death and rebirth. But like the Emerald and its Beryl mineral family, we can say with Gad that we have the good fortune of embracing eternal life at the death and resurrection of its giver, Jesus Christ, our Lord. We may crumble under intense pressure, but the heavenly Bridegroom does not. Earthly life is fragile, but in Christ, the promise of Eternal Life is unbreakable!

## The 12 Stones of Aaron's Breastplate

2 Corinthians 4:7-9 (NIV) But we have this treasure in jars of clay to show that this all-surpassing power is from God and not from us. [8]We are hard pressed on every side, but not crushed; perplexed, but not in despair; [9]persecuted, but not abandoned; struck down, but not destroyed.

# Dressed for Eternity

## Amethyst - The Ninth Stone in Aaron's Breastplate

Amethyst is one of the few stones in Aaron's Breastplate that is not contested by any other stone. Amethyst is the 12th stone in the foundations of the New Jerusalem. So many of the stones have been so widely contested that it's nice to settle on just one for a change.

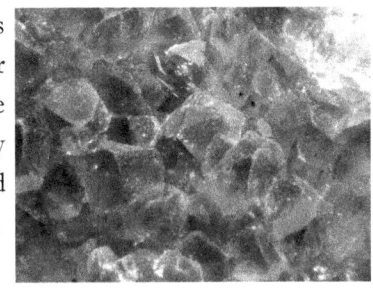

## Make-up and Characteristics

Amethyst is a member of the quartz family and shows up in the wild in the form of quartz crystal geodes. Amethyst can still be found in Africa and was widely used by Egyptians in their jewelry. On the Mohs hardness scale, it ranks a 7, which gemologists says is good for jewelry creation. This gem has long been associated with royalty, and the Greek name from which it comes, means "not drunk" which some scholars take to mean it was used as an amulet, while other scholars say it refers to the deep rich wine-like purple in many of the gem's naturally found iterations.

## Naphtali and Mattias - Associations with the Stone

Naphtali's name means "wrestler". It is interesting to note that Naphtali, along with Asher and Dan, brought up the rear whenever Israel was on the move in the desert. Remember we learned that Dan was to be a leader among his brethren and the Tribe of Dan commands this last quarter of the nation. Reviewing Jacob's blessings over his sons reveals that Naphtali was referred to as having "beautiful words", or as other scholars say, having eloquent speech. Eloquence is indeed one of the things commonly attributed to royalty.

## The 12 Stones of Aaron's Breastplate

This stone would not be complete without some controversy attached to it. This time, that controversy isn't in the stone itself, but in the concept of the 12th disciple instead. While some have said it was Paul, and indeed there is enough consensus as to agree with some in the Early Church who granted Paul a name on the 12 foundations of the New Jerusalem, others feel it is instead Matthias, who was voted into position in the book of Acts.

Matthias, in the book of Acts, replaced Judas, who, as we know from the Scriptures, had committed suicide after betraying Jesus for 30 pieces of silver. Not much is known about Matthias, other than that he was present not merely during John the Baptist's preaching, but apparently followed Christ's teachings as well. His name in Hebrew means "Gift of God".

In this discussion we have a few things of note.

- The royal colour purple present in the stone called Amethyst.
- Eloquent speech said of one whose name means "wrestle" or "wrestler"
- Contention between man's election or God's appointment.
- The Hebrew version of Matthias meaning "Gift of God".

## What does this mean for the Bride of Christ?

The Bride of Christ is destined for royalty one day. One day, Scripture says we will rule and reign with Him when He returns for the 1,000 year reign on the earth.

> 2 Timothy 2:10-13 Therefore I endure all things for the elect's sakes, that they may also obtain the salvation which is in Christ Jesus with eternal glory. [11]It is a faithful saying: For if we be dead with him, we shall also live with him: [12]If we suffer, we shall also reign with him: if we deny him, he also will deny us: [13]If we believe not, yet he abideth faithful: he cannot deny himself.

Revelation 20:6   Blessed and holy is he that hath part in the first resurrection: on such the second death hath no power, but they shall be priests of God and of Christ, and shall reign with him a thousand years.

In order for this destiny to be fulfilled, there is some wrestling that has to take place in the life of the Christian. We cannot be complacent about how we live our lives every day. We must be constantly aware that there is an enemy out there who wants nothing more than to strip our royal heritage from us and drive us into hell.

Secondly, we must be mindful of our speech.  Scripture offers many admonitions on this issue, the books of Proverbs and James being foremost in this author's mind. Scripture says that it isn't the words of the worldly wise that will win souls, but the foolishness of preaching that will rescue souls from the grasp of the enemy camp.

> 1 Corinthians 3:18-19   Let no man deceive himself. If any man among you seemeth to be wise in this world, let him become a fool, that he may be wise.  [19]For the wisdom of this world is foolishness with God. For it is written, He taketh the wise in their own craftiness.

> 1 Corinthians 1:17-19   For Christ sent me not to baptize, but to preach the gospel: not with wisdom of words, lest the cross of Christ should be made of none effect.  [18]For the preaching of the cross is to them that perish foolishness; but unto us which are saved it is the power of God. 19  For it is written, I will destroy the wisdom of the wise, and will bring to nothing the understanding of the prudent.

Thirdly, we must be mindful of seeking God's wisdom in all that we set about to do. As the Scriptures say, it shouldn't be "tomorrow we will do this or that" but "Lord-willing, and with His blessing, we shall do this or that" and seek God in the major and minor decisions of life.

**The 12 Stones of Aaron's Breastplate**

> James 4:13-15  Go to now, ye that say, To day or to morrow we will go into such a city, and continue there a year, and buy and sell, and get gain: [14]Whereas ye know not what shall be on the morrow. For what is your life? It is even a vapour, that appeareth for a little time, and then vanisheth away. [15]For that ye ought to say, If the Lord will, we shall live, and do this, or that.

God wants to be included in everyday life! Even the simple things, if God's allowed to have a say, can turn out quite different than originally planned.

Lastly, we must remember that our salvation is God's gift to us through Jesus Christ our Lord. We will never realize the royalty set out for us if we do not accept Him as Lord and Saviour of our lives and seek to live out that gift in everyday life.

> Ephesians 2:8-9  For by grace are ye saved through faith; and that not of yourselves: it is the gift of God:  [9]Not of works, lest any man should boast.

## Chrysolite, Chrysoberyl in modern times - The Tenth Stone of Aaron's Breastplate

Chrysolite and Chrysoberyl are the same stone, only having changed names in more modern times. The original name was used up to the Victorian age. This is the tenth stone in Aaron's Breastplate, and the seventh foundation stone in the New Jerusalem. Occasionally, scholars will refer to this gem simply as Beryl, which is a different stone altogether. There are however, Beryls that can be a yellowish-green in colour, similar to the Chrysoberyl.

## Make-up and Characteristics

The Chrysoberyl is classified as the third hardest stone on the Mohs Scale, at 8.5. It is typically a yellowish-green in colour with the stones used for gems being more yellow than green. Beryl can come in yellowish-green, but is more known for its sea-green colourations. Beryl has been mined in various places around Africa. Chrysoberyl has been found in Madagascar and Zimbabwe in Africa as well. So the stones the Egyptians gave to the Hebrews could easily have been either one, though most sources seem to settle on the Chrysolite, now named Chrysoberyl.

## Asher and Bartholomew - Associations with the Stone

Asher's name means "blessed", "happy", "prosper", "straight", "honest", and "go, lead or guide". When Jacob blessed Asher, he said, "his bread shall be fat, and he shall yield royal dainties." Jewish sources say his name means "good fortune", and that his tribe would indeed be fortunate among Israel, as some of the best produce would come out of that portion of the land.

# The 12 Stones of Aaron's Breastplate

Bartholomew's name in Hebrew means "son of a plowman", but like so many in today's society, it seems as if he became known by his last name instead of his first name. We learn of his first name in the book of John where he is called Nathanael. The meaning of Nathanael, which is a derivative of the Hebrew name, means "given/gift of God" or "God has given".

Nathanael begins his time among Christ's disciples in a very pessimistic observation, "no good thing can come from Nazareth" (see John 1:46), when Philip wants to introduce him to Christ. But Jesus sees him as a realist, and a learner, a true Israelite needing a sign, so he grants him one by observing that He'd previously seen him "under the tree". This is all the proof Nathanael needed, and he became one of the 12. He and Philip become inseparable partners in ministry.

## What does this mean for the Bride of Christ?

Colours have meanings in Scripture, and if we were to take the meanings of yellow and green and put them together, we'd have "glorious life". When compared to the meaning of Asher's name, we see an amazing similarity! Indeed, God said in His Word:

> John 10:10 The thief cometh not, but for to steal, and to kill, and to destroy: I am come that they might have life, and that they might have it more abundantly.

This isn't merely speaking of life on this earth, but life spent sharing in His glory for all eternity!

It is said that the Chrysoberyl, though plentiful and beautiful, often doesn't make it into jewelry. The stone is somehow unassuming, like some scholars' descriptions of Bartholomew; and possibly due to its plentifulness, somehow looked down on as in the city of Nazareth where our Lord grew up. Even so, God can take what the world casts aside, and use it for His glory, bringing light and life to those it touches.

In the same way, God wants to use us, His Children, to reach out to those around us with the Light of the Gospel of Eternal Life. It doesn't matter how gifted a person may think they are. It doesn't matter how social they are, or how quiet they are. God created each of us with a purpose to be used for His glory and desires, if we will let Him. All we have to do is answer His call, get up from under our tree, and walk into the blessings and joy God has for us.

# Dressed for Eternity

## Beryl (or is it Onyx or Diamond?)- The Eleventh Stone of Aaron's Breastplate

The Eleventh stone in Aaron's Breastplate has three stones competing for the position. What is generally understood by most scholars, is that this 5th foundation stone of the New Jerusalem is of a whitish or clear tone. This is important to point out early, as the same research done for this stone may easily show up in the 12th stone, due to incredible similarities that lead to the different appearances. The stones in contention are the Beryl, the Onyx, and the Diamond.

### Make-up and Characteristics

Beryl is most often suggested for this stone because of the Hebrew and Greek names' definitions. According to sources cited in Wikipedia, Beryl can range from aqua-marine to reddish to clear to green. Amazingly enough, at various times and places, all of these colours have been cited by various scholars as *the* colour of this particular stone! But while there is much discrepancy, one thing seems, pardon the pun, clear! When the stones of Aaron's Breastplate are referred to only by colour, it is likely that the Eleventh stone will be called "White", more than any of the other colours.

The Diamond needs no introduction. The strongest stone on the Mohs scale at 9, this stone not only graces many an expensive necklace, watch and bracelet, but it works hard in commercial enterprises too on the edge of cutting tools, computerized equipment, etc.

Onyx is another wide-ranging stone in its appearance. The most popular colour being black, and therefore modified to appear that way throughout the ages, its unadulterated colours tend more to banded red and white,

## The 12 Stones of Aaron's Breastplate

or white with other colours. Apparently this banding has been put to good use in ancient times, with the white layer being exposed and then carved away from the darker layer underneath to act as a kind of precious-stone relief.

All three of these stones have been readily available from ancient times to the present in Africa. So it would be of no surprise to the author if they were also included among the many gems showered on the Hebrews as they fled Egypt.

### Joseph and Thomas - Associations with the Stone

One of the tidbits of information in my research that proved to be of resounding agreement, was the assigning of this stone to either Joseph, or one of his sons. The larger agreement was that this stone belonged to Joseph. Joseph was Rachel's oldest son to Jacob, and the son sold into slavery who would be raised up out of prison to spare Egypt during 7 years of famine.

Joseph's name means "May God add", and his son's names mean "fruitful" and "son of my forgetfulness". Indeed as these meanings imply, God caused Joseph to "forget" his hardships, to bring fruitfulness to Egypt, and to add blessings to his Father's family.

Thomas's name means "Twin" in both the Hebrew and Greek renditions. Scripture does not tell us about his twin however. Thomas is most known for his questioning after Christ rose from the dead. However it is also important to note that he was loyal, faithful, and devoted to Christ in the Gospel accounts as well. His greatest act of courage was after Christ raised Lazarus from the tomb and the disciples got word that murderous intent was waiting in Jerusalem. Thomas suggested they all go to die with Him (see John 11:16).

### What does this mean for the Bride of Christ?

In the Diamond, we have transparency and strength. In the Beryl we have transparency through colour. In the Onyx we have white offset by colour. Strength and transparency are two things offered and expected of the Bride of Christ. In our weakness, God imparts His strength to get us through.

> 2 Corinthians 12:9  And he said unto me, My grace is sufficient for thee: for my strength is made perfect in weakness. Most gladly therefore will I rather glory in my infirmities, that the power of Christ may rest upon me.

When we stand before Christ, we stand bare of anything that would protect and hide us from His all-seeing, all-knowing eyes. We must be willing to give our lives for the One Who gave His life for us.

> 1 John 3:16  Hereby perceive we the love of God, because he laid down his life for us: and we ought to lay down our lives for the brethren.

As we allow ourselves to be vulnerable in His hand, God does indeed add to our lives a measure of fruitfulness only found in surrender and submission to the Holy Spirit. We are to turn our backs on our former ways, to "forget them" so to speak, and to turn 100% toward Christ, our Heavenly Bridegroom. We are asked to be loyal, to be faithful, and to endure to the end, receiving a crown of life in the process.

> James 1:12  Blessed is the man that endureth temptation: for when he is tried, he shall receive the crown of life, which the Lord hath promised to them that love him.

> Revelation 2:10  Fear none of those things which thou shalt suffer: behold, the devil shall cast some of you into prison, that ye may be tried; and ye shall have tribulation ten days: be thou faithful unto death, and I will give thee a crown of life.

**Dressed for Eternity**

## Onyx - The Twelfth Stone of Aaron's Breastplate

The final stone in Aaron's Breastplate and the first foundation stone in the New Jerusalem, is generally thought to be the Onyx, or as some scholars have more specifically called it, the Sardonyx. Some scholars have suggested the rose quartz, Pink Tourmaline, or Jasper as well. The majority however, have focused on the Onyx/Sardonyx stone. What is interesting in discussions of this stone, is the description of the colour. Most feel that due to the Hebrew and Greek names, as well as how these stones were often described by ancient writers, it was known to have a nail or bone-like colouring, suggesting to many that it was of a pinkish, or red/white - pinkish colouration. We'll look at these stones with that understanding.

## Make-up and Characteristics

As in previous discussions of the Jasper and Onyx stones, these occur in nature in a wide array of colours and colour combinations. It is of interest to note however, that both these stones do have pink or pale skin-coloured varieties. In the Onyx, the Sardonyx variant with its red and white striping can easily appear pinkish or skin-toned at a quick glance. Both stones are in the same place on the Mohs hardness scale at 6 - 7 roughly. Both also get their pinkish tone from whitish and reddish portions of the stone, whether banding on the Onyx, or irregularities of the Jasper. Both stones were easy to come by for the Egyptian people prior to the Hebrews fleeing Pharaoh.

# The 12 Stones of Aaron's Breastplate

## Benjamin and James - Associations with the Stone

Benjamin's name means "son of my right hand". This is a very prophetic meaning, as Benjamin became a staunch supporter of Judah, King David's tribe. Jacob's blessing over Benjamin indicated his would become a warlike tribe, and in choosing to stand with Judah, that did become the case as Israel split in half and central Israel became hotly contested from time to time.

The name James is apparently the English word for Jacob, and as such, bears the same meaning, "supplanter". Like his brother John, he is looked on in the various Gospel accounts as faithful, loyal, zealous, and in Luke 9:52-54, would have called down fire on Christ's detractors if Jesus Himself had not rebuked him first. Just like his brother, he'd misunderstood what Christ meant about His Kingdom and stood eagerly by his Mother as she requested that her two sons sit at His side when Christ entered His throne in Heaven. Yes, he most definitely was one of the "Sons of Thunder".

## What does this mean for the Bride of Christ?

Red stands for the Blood of Christ that washes away the deathly stain of sin from the human heart.

> 1 John 1:7 But if we walk in the light, as he is in the light, we have fellowship one with another, and the blood of Jesus Christ his Son cleanseth us from all sin.

White stands for the purity Christ displayed and that we can only afford through His sacrifice for our sins.

> Psalm 51:7 Purge me with hyssop, and I shall be clean: wash me, and I shall be whiter than snow.

The fleshly colour generally ascribed to the 12th stone points to Christ's body which was beaten, bruised, and whipped, about which it is written in Isaiah 53:

> Isaiah 53:5 But he was wounded for our transgressions, he was bruised for our iniquities: the chastisement of our peace was upon him; and with his stripes we are healed.

Jesus stands at the right hand of the Father interceding for His Bride according to the book of Hebrews, and one day the thunderous trumpet will sound and the Bride of Christ will rise to meet Him in the air.

> Hebrews 7:25 Wherefore he is able also to save them to the uttermost that come unto God by him, seeing he ever liveth to make intercession for them.

> 1 Thessalonians 4:16-17 For the Lord himself shall descend from heaven with a shout, with the voice of the archangel, and with the trump of God: and the dead in Christ shall rise first: $^{17}$Then we which are alive and remain shall be caught up together with them in the clouds, to meet the Lord in the air: and so shall we ever be with the Lord.

This stone reminds us of the sacrifice Jesus made for us on the Cross, of our fleshly nature, and that it is only by His shed Blood that we can be cleansed of all unrighteousness and made clean and white before Him.

# Dressed for Eternity

## The New Jerusalem

> Revelation 21:2  And I John saw the holy city, new Jerusalem, coming down from God out of heaven, prepared as a bride adorned for her husband.

> Revelation 21:9-12, 14, 19-21  And there came unto me one of the seven angels which had the seven vials full of the seven last plagues, and talked with me, saying, Come hither, I will shew thee the bride, the Lamb's wife. [10]And he carried me away in the spirit to a great and high mountain, and shewed me that great city, the holy Jerusalem, descending out of heaven from God, [11]Having the glory of God: and her light was like unto a stone most precious, even like a jasper stone, clear as crystal; [12]And had a wall great and high, and had twelve gates, and at the gates twelve angels, and names written thereon, which are the names of the twelve tribes of the children of Israel: [14]And the wall of the city had twelve foundations, and in them the names of the twelve apostles of the Lamb. [19]And the foundations of the wall of the city were garnished with all manner of precious stones. The first foundation was jasper; the second, sapphire; the third, a chalcedony; the fourth, an emerald; [20]The fifth, sardonyx; the sixth, sardius; the seventh, chrysolite; the eighth, beryl; the ninth, a topaz; the tenth, a chrysoprasus; the eleventh, a jacinth; the twelfth, an amethyst. [21]And the twelve gates were twelve pearls; every several gate was of one pearl: and the street of the city was pure gold, as it were transparent glass.

As seen above, we have only covered the 12 Foundation Stones of the New Jerusalem so far. This was due to their pairings with the 12 Stones of Aaron's Breastplate. However, there are two other items in this passage that will complete our look at the New Jerusalem's adornment as a bride coming out of Heaven.

No one has ever seen pearls so large they could comprise an entire gate. Nor have we seen gold so pure that it's like transparent glass. But let us take a moment or two now to look at these final two pieces of jewelled adornment in this section of our discussion.

# Dressed for Eternity

## Pearl - The Gates of the New Jerusalem

The New Jerusalem, described by John as coming down from the heavens adorned as a Bride for her husband, does not just feature 12 gemstone foundations, but 12 gates made of pearl as well.

Revelation 21:12-13, 21  And had a wall great and high, and had twelve gates, and at the gates twelve angels, and names written thereon, which are the names of the twelve tribes of the children of Israel:  On the east three gates; on the north three gates; on the south three gates; and on the west three gates.  And the twelve gates were twelve pearls; every several gate was of one pearl: and the street of the city was pure gold, as it were transparent glass.

## The Pearly Gates

Various sources I came across in my research tried to assign tribal names to the foundation stone colours on their maps. But as we see in the verses about the New Jerusalem above, it wasn't the stone foundations that bore the names of the Tribes of Israel, but the gates instead. This is why in my studies, I looked at the 12 foundation stones from the perspective of the 12 stones on Aaron's Breastplate.

It is interesting that the 12 Tribes receive such prominent placement on these gates. Before we merge our Tribal studies together, let's look at the make-up and characteristics of the pearl.

# The New Jerusalem

## Make-up and Characteristics

As is commonly known by those who live in coastal waters, there are two types of pearls that fetch a decent price on the markets.

- The wild or natural pearls, which may or may not be round in shape, and
- The cultured pearls that are carefully monitored by humans to be sure they form correctly from the specially formulated seeded irritant placed in the clam or oyster.

Before the advent of cultured pearls, divers used to harvest oysters and clams by the hundreds in order to find just a few pearls. This is why in history and in Scripture, anything of incredibly rare occurrence and value, is likened to that of a precious pearl.

A wild or cultured pearl is created when a microscopic irritant ends up, or is placed, in the mantle folds of the clam or oyster. The crustacean addresses this irritant by coating it repeatedly in the same mother-of-pearl substance that coats the interior of its own shell. After sufficient time passes, a pearl is formed. The iridescent nature of the shimmering surface is caused by light passing through and bouncing off the repeated layers of the pearl. Fake synthetic pearls try to imitate this, but often unsuccessfully to the trained eye. The calcium carbonate nature of the pearl renders it susceptible to dissolving in vinegars and other acetic acids.

According to Marge Dawson, author of "Pearls of Creation: A-Z of Pearls 2nd Edition", there is a very simple test that can tell you if you are buying real or fake pearls.

Take a white cloth with you and place the pearls on the cloth away from direct light to examine how the colours of the nacre show through.

Take two pearls and gently rub them against each other. Real pearls will feel slightly rough, as if rubbing two pieces of fine-grain sandpaper together.

# Dressed for Eternity

Fake pearls will slide over each other smoothly with no roughness detected at all.

When trying to come up with a way to describe the colours of pearl, difficulty set in. Mother-of-Pearl itself can range from pure white, to having any number of shades of almost all other colours. Although my own eyes have not seen brown or black, apparently there is the rare occasion when one will find a black pearl. The shimmering metallic-like colours that shift and move in the light are caused by light being reflected among the various layers that make up the pearl body.

## The Tribes and the Pearls

This produces a very interesting analogy as we consider the various colours of the precious stones and the various colours associated to each of the 12 Tribes. It is only speculation then, but it may very well be that each massive pearl making up each of the 12 gates of the New Jerusalem, may reflect the colour that God assigned to each tribe of Israel. It will be interesting to see just which colours God thought each tribe embodied and how the meanings of those colours match with the meanings of their names.

It is purely conjecture as well, but quite plausible, that due to the wide range of naturally-occurring colours in the wild, natural pearls, that God might assign each Tribe to the pearl that matches the colour He gave them. It would be fun, to map a chart of naturally occurring pearl colours, to the colours found in the 12 stones, and see where that leads us. Would these colours be placed according to camp placement around the Tabernacle? Some scholars feel this will happen, but as usual, there is lack of consensus as to how that would look due to linear rather than columnar positioning. But it will be an interesting addition to this study once appropriate information is found.

## What does this mean for the Bride of Christ?

> Proverbs 27:9   Ointment and perfume rejoice the heart: so doth the sweetness of a man's friend by hearty counsel.

## The New Jerusalem

> Proverbs 27:17 Iron sharpeneth iron; so a man sharpeneth the countenance of his friend.

Just as you can tell real pearls from fake by their smoothness or roughness, Scripture says that the hearty council of a man sharpens the countenance of his friend.

> Matthew 7:13 Enter ye in at the strait gate: for wide is the gate, and broad is the way, that leadeth to destruction, and many there be which go in thereat:

The easy road is smooth, paved with promises, but in the end is merely an imitation of the real thing and ultimately leads to hell. The road to heaven is narrow, rough, and paved in the shed blood of Jesus Christ our Lord, without whom we would never see heaven's shores. When life seems too easy, the Bride of Christ should ask herself if she's truly living a life set apart unto her Heavenly Bridegroom.

Each pearl has a dominant colour, with other colours playing over the surface in the shimmering context already noted. while the dominant colour is given by the clam or oyster's coating. The shimmer is caused by the reflection of light. For the Bride of Christ, this is of immense importance as we consider that we are to be reflections of Christ in our everyday lives. When people look at us, they should be able to see the Light of Christ reflected in how we talk and act, in the places we go and things we buy, in the entertainment we choose and the friends we make. Each member of the Bride of Christ has been given a dominant colour, or personality. But the colours that play across the surface of our lives should be those of the varying facets of our Lord and Maker, Jesus Christ.

Some verses to think about:

> Psalm 36:7-10 How excellent is thy lovingkindness, O God! therefore the children of men put their trust under the shadow of thy wings. [8]They shall be abundantly satisfied with the fatness of thy house; and thou shalt make them drink of the river of thy pleasures. [9]For with thee is the

fountain of life: in thy light shall we see light. ¹⁰O continue thy lovingkindness unto them that know thee; and thy righteousness to the upright in heart.

Proverbs 4:18  But the path of the just is as the shining light, that shineth more and more unto the perfect day.

Proverbs 6:23  For the commandment is a lamp; and the law is light; and reproofs of instruction are the way of life:

Isaiah 9:2  The people that walked in darkness have seen a great light: they that dwell in the land of the shadow of death, upon them hath the light shined.

Isaiah 42:5-9  Thus saith God the LORD, he that created the heavens, and stretched them out; he that spread forth the earth, and that which cometh out of it; he that giveth breath unto the people upon it, and spirit to them that walk therein:  ⁶I the LORD have called thee in righteousness, and will hold thine hand, and will keep thee, and give thee for a covenant of the people, for a light of the Gentiles;  ⁷To open the blind eyes, to bring out the prisoners from the prison, and them that sit in darkness out of the prison house.  ⁸I am the LORD: that is my name: and my glory will I not give to another, neither my praise to graven images.  ⁹Behold, the former things are come to pass, and new things do I declare: before they spring forth I tell you of them.

Isaiah 58:6-8  Is not this the fast that I have chosen? to loose the bands of wickedness, to undo the heavy burdens, and to let the oppressed go free, and that ye break every yoke?  ⁷Is it not to deal thy bread to the hungry, and that thou bring the poor that are cast out to thy house? when thou seest the naked, that thou cover him; and that thou hide not thyself from thine own flesh?  ⁸Then shall thy light break forth as the morning, and thine health shall spring forth speedily: and thy righteousness shall go before thee; the glory of the LORD shall be thy rereward.

Matthew 5:14-16  Ye are the light of the world. A city that is set on an hill

## The New Jerusalem

cannot be hid. [15]Neither do men light a candle, and put it under a bushel, but on a candlestick; and it giveth light unto all that are in the house. [16]Let your light so shine before men, that they may see your good works, and glorify your Father which is in heaven.

John 12:35-36   Then Jesus said unto them, Yet a little while is the light with you. Walk while ye have the light, lest darkness come upon you: for he that walketh in darkness knoweth not whither he goeth. [36]While ye have light, believe in the light, that ye may be the children of light. These things spake Jesus, and departed, and did hide himself from them.

Acts 13:46-48   Then Paul and Barnabas waxed bold, and said, It was necessary that the word of God should first have been spoken to you: but seeing ye put it from you, and judge yourselves unworthy of everlasting life, lo, we turn to the Gentiles. [47]For so hath the Lord commanded us, saying, I have set thee to be a light of the Gentiles, that thou shouldest be for salvation unto the ends of the earth. [48]And when the Gentiles heard this, they were glad, and glorified the word of the Lord: and as many as were ordained to eternal life believed.

Romans 13:10-14   Love worketh no ill to his neighbour: therefore love is the fulfilling of the law. [11]And that, knowing the time, that now it is high time to awake out of sleep: for now is our salvation nearer than when we believed. [12]The night is far spent, the day is at hand: let us therefore cast off the works of darkness, and let us put on the armour of light. [13]Let us walk honestly, as in the day; not in rioting and drunkenness, not in chambering and wantonness, not in strife and envying. [14]But put ye on the Lord Jesus Christ, and make not provision for the flesh, to fulfil the lusts thereof.

1 John 1:7   But if we walk in the light, as he is in the light, we have fellowship one with another, and the blood of Jesus Christ his Son cleanseth us from all sin.

When the Light of God shines over us, do we shine as those who are mentioned in these verses?

# Dressed for Eternity

## Gold - The Streets of the New Jerusalem

What can be said about gold that hasn't already been said? Gold has been the epitome of wealth, the essence of all things bright, clear, shiny, rich, and royal. Gold has been the standard by which countries and empires have measured their wealth and traded their goods. It has graced many palaces, crowns, jewelry, and even used in the plating of many implements in the ancient Hebrew Tabernacle. King Solomon overlaid much of the woodwork in his temple with gold, and it was a world wonder until it was destroyed by the Romans in 70 A.D.

Today we will discuss the properties of gold, and what it means to the Bride of Christ. We have left Aaron's Breastplate and now focus on the last remaining description of the New Jerusalem before going on to other passages in the Bible where God adorns His Bride.

## Make-up and Characteristics

Gold is an interesting metal. It is one of the few metals that can maintain its beauty and lustre without concern over exposure to the elements. By itself, gold is a very soft metal and quite malleable. For a metal worker to get it to hold its shape, gold must be mixed with another metal to form a gold alloy. The percentage of gold in the alloy is what lends to the concept of ranking pieces of jewelry according to karats. 24 karat gold is considered the higheest alloy concentration available while still maintaining strength to hold form and desired appearance.

Gold's ability to resist corrosion by most chemicals, conduct electricity, and its malleability have led it into more than just wealth and accessories. Gold also finds itself working hard for a living in various commercial settings such as dentistry, where gold is often used in tooth crowns and caps.

## The New Jerusalem

Typically, gold is a yellowish colour, but when combined with various alloys, can take on the appearance of white or rose, and even other colours less common. Gold has been mined all over the world from ancient times to the present.

## Analogy in Scripture

Gold's refining process is so ancient that it was easily used as a reference point when God spoke through the prophets. He gives the analogy of the Refiner sitting at his fire, boiling the impurities to the surface and skimming them off until he sees his reflection. This analogy describes how God will refine His people, until they reflect His face to the world around them.

> Zechariah 13:9  And I will bring the third part through the fire, and will refine them as silver is refined, and will try them as gold is tried: they shall call on my name, and I will hear them: I will say, It is my people: and they shall say, The LORD is my God.

> Malachi 3:2-3  But who may abide the day of his coming? and who shall stand when he appeareth? for he is like a refiner's fire, and like fullers' soap: [3]And he shall sit as a refiner and purifier of silver: and he shall purify the sons of Levi, and purge them as gold and silver, that they may offer unto the LORD an offering in righteousness.

We see God adorning His Bride with gold in Ezekiel and Song of Solomon. They are described as chains of gold around their neck.

> Song of Solomon 1:10  Thy cheeks are comely with rows of jewels, thy neck with chains of gold.

> Ezekiel 16:13  Thus wast thou decked with gold and silver; and thy raiment was of fine linen, and silk, and broidered work; thou didst eat fine flour, and honey, and oil: and thou wast exceeding beautiful, and thou didst prosper into a kingdom.

## Dressed for Eternity

In Ezekiel, gold and silver are the metals described for the earrings, bracelet, necklace, forehead ornament and crown. As we are only discussing the metal right now, we won't go into those other presentations for today. But these are mentioned to point out that in the New Jerusalem, the gold considered so precious by the world's standards, will be used as pavement instead.

> Revelation 21:21  And the twelve gates were twelve pearls; every several gate was of one pearl: and the street of the city was pure gold, as it were transparent glass.

God Himself appreciates the appearance of gold or He wouldn't use it, but the lowly position in which it is placed in eternity should help us put this precious metal into perspective.

### What does this mean for the Bride of Christ?

In John's description of the streets paved with gold, he mentions that they are of the purest gold, and transparent at that. No gold known to man has ever been transparent, but as best the human mind could fathom when seeing this magnificent city come down out of heaven, such was the description chosen by John.

This would suggest that the Bride of Christ has gone through the purifying flames of trial and testing. The dross of sin has been removed from her soiled garments of righteousness, and she stands pure before God, transparent before Him, confident that she can bare everything to Him in complete transparency, and He is pleased. His glory is reflected in her, as described of the New Jerusalem, and there is no evil in her.

We've heard it said many times throughout the Church age, that trials and temptations come to test us, to see if we've learned the ways of God and are walking in them, bringing to the surface issues that God wants to address in our lives. We are told in Scripture:

## The New Jerusalem

1 Peter 4:12-13  Beloved, think it not strange concerning the fiery trial which is to try you, as though some strange thing happened unto you: [13]But rejoice, inasmuch as ye are partakers of Christ's sufferings; that, when his glory shall be revealed, ye may be glad also with exceeding joy.

Just as pure gold is malleable and easily pliant in the hand of the smithy and the jeweller, so God desires that we would be moldable in His hands just like the concept of wet clay on the potter's wheel (another analogy we won't go into for the purposes of this discussion). God longs to see His glory reflected in our lives. Gold, the colour, represents God's glory in the Christian usage of colour in Scripture. The more we allow difficult times to refine us; the more we reflect His glory, the more pliable we are in His hands, and the more intimate a relationship we can then enjoy with the Creator of the Universe. A couple cannot truly enjoy each other if they are not transparent with each other. Nor can we enjoy an intimate relationship with Jesus Christ if we do not let Him see into every area of our lives. One day the Bride of Christ will stand before Him pure and transparent, radiating His glory.

# Dressed for Eternity

## Introduction to Jewish bridal attire, similarities to the Armour of God, and the Bride of Christ

Understanding the bridal adornment in Ezekiel requires an understanding of everyday attire given in Isaiah. Thankfully, an extensive discussion on this was available over at Ancient Hebrew's website. (see appendix for link) Their discussion is not exhaustive by any means, but provided enough assistance that between the author's descriptions, viewing several passages of Scripture in parallel layout in e-Sword, and via use of the Strong's Hebrew Lexicon, I was able to come up with enough information to get a general overview of the average kinds of clothing and ornamentation typically worn in ancient Israel.

This understanding is important, because if we go with more modern definitions, we can miss what God was trying to say. The armour of God, for example, has been paired with Medieval knights' trappings instead of the armour Paul observed on the Roman guards who stood over him every day while in prison. Understanding that Roman armour protected primarily the front of the soldier, and you get a better idea of what is meant in the passage in Ephesians.

For the comparative discussion desired between the Bride of Christ and the attire God uses to clothe His Bride in Scripture, some notes may be drawn between the occasional ancient attire and that of the Roman guard.

# Dressed for Eternity

## Men and Women's Clothing

*King Jehu of Israel bows before Shalmanezer III of Assyria. Source: zyworld.com*

It was common in ancient times, just as it is now, for everyday folk to wear jewelry if they had it, plain, decorative or special-purpose belts and head coverings, etc. As is still custom in various Middle Eastern regions, the concept of male and female robes were very much in play in the ancient times. Different cuts and styles denoted male and female just as different cuts and styles today in western society denote a male or female pair of jeans. These differences were to be strictly enforced as part of the Levitical law that God gave to the Jewish people in the desert.

> Deuteronomy 22:5 The woman shall not wear that which pertaineth unto a man, neither shall a man put on a woman's garment: for all that do so are abomination unto the LORD thy God.

It is important then, to understand that a man's robe was not to be worn on a woman, and vice versa. Men's robes often went to the knee or to the mid-calf, with only official robes typically going to the ankle. Women's robes always went to the ankle. Their cloaks and mantels were wider and longer as well, and often sported a hood of sorts. Men's head scarves were often wrapped around their head similar to the concept of a turban, and even alluded to as such by the Young's Literal Translation calling the King James Version's "bonnet" a "head tire". I had to look up what was meant by tires; "tires round like the moon" referred to a round pendant on a necklace, while "tire" or "tyre" referred to the wrapping of the headscarf around the head.

## Ancient Jewish Bridal Attire

This was in contrast to the woman's head scarf typically being allowed to fall down the back of her head. Some men wore their head scarves this way, and when they did, both genders used a strip of cloth or rope to tie around their head to keep the headscarf in place. Not all women wore such a headband, but when they did, it was often decorated the way women today decorate scarves with jewelry, necklaces, or plain and decorated cloth wound together.

## Jewelry

Then as now, men and women wore jewelry, although the author of the mentioned article found that men wearing earrings was a bit weird. Perhaps in their culture, they have never seen men do that, though this particular author has. Neck chains were worn by both genders, but only on special occasions, and the bridal neck chains were quite different from others a woman might wear at other times. Rings too were worn by both men and women. Men of noble stature usually wore them as a status symbol, while women of any status wore them for beauty, special occasions, or also to denote status. Just as jewelry can denote wealth today; it was no different back then. The wealthier you were back in ancient Israel, the more you could afford precious (as opposed to semi-precious) stones, and more detailed and more finely crafted jewelry. A Bride's adornment then, was of the highest value a family could afford, and typically provided to her by her betrothed husband in the form of a dowry.

Pictured here is what that dowry looked like then, and now, on a Yemini Jewish Bride. I first found this attire in an ancient artifact photo from the Israel Museum. The more research I did, the more I discovered this practise for young Jewish Yemeni brides continues to this day and has even been the focus of at least one Jewish post-holocaust novel about the headpiece, known to the young heroine's family as "The Bride Price".

## Dressed for Eternity

Such a title clearly describes the nature of the dowry displayed on this headpiece and various descriptions state that it can weigh several kilograms.

Whenever possible, as this study progresses, images will be offered of the various pieces discussed, and it is my hope that such images will come from the time period in which the referenced Scriptures were written. Some of these discussions will include Scriptures where God speaks of various teachings that are compared to pieces of jewelry and why that comparison is made.

# Dressed for Eternity

## 'Broidered Work - Ancient Jewish Bridal Attire

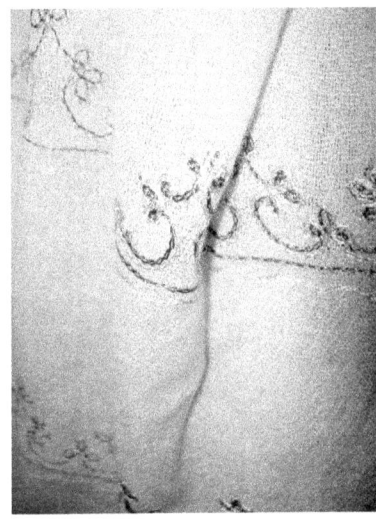

Embroidery... This is a skill that has truly been passed down through the ages of time. Historical writings say that prior to being written about in the Torah, the Hebrew people had picked up the art from the Egyptians, their hosts prior to enslavement by the Pharaohs. Truly it was a beautiful art, as God appointed men to oversee its use in the creation of the Temple implements.

Below is a section out of the 1902 Encyclopedia Britannica 9th Edition (Ninth Edition):

"EMBROIDERY is the art of working with the needle flowers, fruits, human and animal forms upon wool, silk, linen, or other woven texture. That it is of the greatest antiquity we have the testimony of Moses and Homer, and it takes precedence of painting, as the earliest method of representing figures and ornaments was by needle-work traced upon canvas. "

"The Jews are supposed to have derived their skill in needle-work from the Egyptians, with whom the art of embroidery was general; they produced figured cloths by the needle and the loom, and practised the art of introducing gold thread or wire into their work. Amasis, king of Egypt, sent to the Minerva of Lindus a linen corslet with figures interwoven and em-broidered with gold and wool; and, to judge from a passage in Ezekiel, they even embroidered the sails of their galleys which they exported to Tyre : " Fine linen with broidered work from Egypt was that which thou spreadest forth to be thy sail." "

"The book of Exodus describes how the curtains of the tabernacle were embroidered by hand, and the garments of Aaron and his sons wrought

## Ancient Jewish Bridal Attire

in needle-work. Aholiab, the chief embroiderer, is specially appointed to assist in the work of decoration. In celebrating the triumph of Sisera, his mother's made to say that he has a " prey of divers colours of needle-work on both sides," meaning that the stuff was wrought on both sides alike, a style of embroidery exhibiting a degree of patience and skill only done by the nations of the East."

This extensive quote from the Encyclopedia Britannica, tells us that creating embroidery so that the design showed through on both sides of the cloth, was a method of embroidery only found in the Middle East. If we understand that the Temple Curtain was 4 inches thick and from what we can tell, embroidered on both sides, the feat is even more impressive.

## Then and Now

Ezekiel 16:10  I clothed thee also with broidered work, and shod thee with badgers' skin, and I girded thee about with fine linen, and I covered thee with silk.

The book of Ezekiel describes the clothing of the Bride, typified by Jerusalem, as having 'broidered work.  Many discussions of the ancient clothing styles worn in the historical period of the Bible in one way or another refer to colour. However, these same writings also mention that most of the clothing of that day was made from either wool or flax.  Linen does not accept dye very well, so the women would embroider designs onto their clothing for festive occasions.  This craft became entrenched in the Jewish culture where now, common Jewish embroidery designs have been digitized for use in embroidery machines.

One piece of embroidery continues to this day in modern Jewish circles on the prayer shawl.  Pictured here is a velvet bag for a prayer shawl.  This bag is embroidered with a design unique to the owner, and bears the owner's name.

# Dressed for Eternity

Some sources say that families and clans would develop their own unique embroidered designs and you knew which clan they were from by the embroidery on their clothing.

## Relation to the Armour of God

In a very similar fashion, Roman armies would be broken into their ranks by large embroidered standards bearing the image of a plant or animal associated with that particular group of soldiers. These standards would be held high as the army paraded into town in processions toward the Emperor.

## What does this mean for the Bride of Christ?

> Song of Solomon 8:6 Set me as a seal upon thine heart, as a seal upon thine arm: for love is strong as death; jealousy is cruel as the grave: the coals thereof are coals of fire, which hath a most vehement flame.
>
> 2 Corinthians 1:20-22 For all the promises of God in him are yea, and in him Amen, unto the glory of God by us. $^{21}$Now he which stablisheth us with you in Christ, and hath anointed us, is God; $^{22}$Who hath also sealed us, and given the earnest of the Spirit in our hearts.
>
> Ephesians 1:12-14 That we should be to the praise of his glory, who first trusted in Christ. $^{13}$In whom ye also trusted, after that ye heard the word of truth, the gospel of your salvation: in whom also after that ye believed, ye were sealed with that holy Spirit of promise, $^{14}$Which is the earnest of our inheritance until the redemption of the purchased possession, unto the praise of his glory.

The Bride of Christ has also been marked by her Lover, bearing His image stamped on her heart. She wears the Robe of Righteousness, given to her by Christ Himself.

## Ancient Jewish Bridal Attire

> Isaiah 61:10  I will greatly rejoice in the LORD, my soul shall be joyful in my God; for he hath clothed me with the garments of salvation, he hath covered me with the robe of righteousness, as a bridegroom decketh himself with ornaments, and as a Bride adorneth herself with her jewels.

Over the years, illustrations have arisen describing life as a tapestry, and how when we look at the tapestry of our lives, sometimes all we see is the messy underside and wonder how God could love us.  We fail to see that God, the master weaver, sees the design on the top side of the tapestry, and He sees something beautiful.

Tapestries are woven, while embroidery is sewed.  In both cases, great attention to detail is applied, with dark and light threads used to bring out the desired presentation.  It is said that gold was sometimes worked in like thread, and as the Hebrews would have learned this from the Egyptians; it is not a stretch to see royalty dressed in robes embroidered with gold.

# Dressed for Eternity

## Badger Skin - Ancient Jewish Bridal Attire

Ezekiel 16:10 I clothed thee also with broidered work, and shod thee with badgers' skin, and I girded thee about with fine linen, and I covered thee with silk.

We are looking at the second item in this verse now, feet shod with badger's skin. The Hebrew word for badger's skin in the KJV, has been debated by some scholars as to whether it truly means the badger, which did and still does live in the region, or the dugong family of the sea cow, which was quite prevalent back then, but almost extinct now. One scholar argues that because the skin is listed among costly elements God told Moses to gather for the Tabernacle, that the skin would not have been as prevalent as the sea cow and therefore is the badger. For the purposes of this study, we'll look at the badger for that very reason.

## Characteristics and Discussion

The first point of interest is that we are unable to consider this footwear without considering its use first mentioned in Scripture, that of the outer covering of the Tabernacle. While the colour is indeed stated as unassuming and drab, the nature of the skin is what God was after. Badger skin has been well-known down through the ages as being excellent protection against the natural elements of storms, dust, and weather. While this author has never held a badger skin in her hands, it is said that due to the way the hair grows on the animal, water, ice, and snow roll off it like water off a duck's back. So while the more colourful and rich fabrics were underneath, the badger skin protected the Tabernacle from all inclement weather the Hebrews would encounter on their travels.

## Ancient Jewish Bridal Attire

In addition, it was to cover the tables, altar, lamp stands, and Ark of the Covenant during travel. This gave a very unassuming appearance to a very important part of Tabernacle setup; protection from the elements when set up and a protective covering during transportation.

## Use as Footwear

Its use then for the bridal garments described in Ezekiel was not merely as footwear for the Bride, but the best footwear money could buy, despite its less eye-catching appearance. Only the best footwear would be given to God's Bride.

The Roman soldiers of Paul's day wore sandals too, and these sandals had to go the distance in more ways than one. They had to stand up to the rigours of walking, marching, and fighting in battle. But in Paul's dissertation in Ephesians 6, these sandals carry the Gospel of peace.

> Ephesians 6:15 And your feet shod with the preparation of the gospel of peace;

They are tough, can stand up to the elements, won't fall apart under the rigours of travel and battle, and bring the message of peace.

## What does this mean for the Bride of Christ?

A couple thoughts can be drawn from today's observations.

> Romans 12:4-5 For as we have many members in one body, and all members have not the same office: $^5$So we, being many, are one body in Christ, and every one members one of another.

> 1 Corinthians 12:23-25 And those members of the body, which we think to be less honourable, upon these we bestow more abundant honour; and our uncomely parts have more abundant comeliness. $^{24}$For our comely parts have no need: but God hath tempered the body together, having given more abundant honour to that part which lacked:

²⁵That there should be no schism in the body; but that the members should have the same care one for another.

First, is the concept that Paul writes about in other letters to the churches regarding the members of Christ's body, the Church. Paul writes that all of us in God's Kingdom have a job to do; we are meant to work together, but some of us have more eye-catching jobs than others. But Paul writes that to those who are less appealing, God has given more grace. They may not be attractive to those on the outside, but their contribution to the Kingdom of God is completely indispensable! Without them, protection would not be afforded to those who need it. Without them, more attractive but less hardy jobs would be destroyed. They are the ones doing the tough, dirty, and sometimes hard tasks that pave the way for others to come in after them. Often times, they are the ones able to stand up against the enemy in a battle, the prayer warrior behind the scenes, the Bible smuggler, the street worker, the soup kitchen cook. They are not on stage or in the public eye, they are not flashy and most people don't want to do their job. But the Gospel would not go forward as successfully as it has without them. When the crowns are handed out in heaven, their reward will be great!

> Isaiah 53:1-3 Who hath believed our report? and to whom is the arm of the LORD revealed? ²For he shall grow up before him as a tender plant, and as a root out of a dry ground: he hath no form nor comeliness; and when we shall see him, there is no beauty that we should desire him. ³He is despised and rejected of men; a man of sorrows, and acquainted with grief: and we hid as it were our faces from him; he was despised, and we esteemed him not.

Secondly is the fact that like the badger skin, Christ Himself was described in Isaiah as having no form that we should desire Him. We are told He would be a Jew of unassuming appearance, and from the outside, no one would want Him. This is likened to the covering of the Tabernacle, how that when you get to know Christ, the deeper you go in Him, the more beautiful He becomes. He is our protection from the influence of the world if we let Him. As a shoe separates the wearer from the dirt and grime of the ground they walk on, hiding ourselves in Christ separates us from the sin of the world around us.

## Ancient Jewish Bridal Attire

We are encouraged to walk in the Spirit so as not to fulfill the lusts of the flesh.

> Galatians 5:16 This I say then, Walk in the Spirit, and ye shall not fulfil the lust of the flesh.

> Isaiah 52:7 How beautiful upon the mountains are the feet of him that bringeth good tidings, that publisheth peace; that bringeth good tidings of good, that publisheth salvation; that saith unto Zion, Thy God reigneth!

Thirdly is the concept, as mentioned in Ephesians 6:15 above, that as we walk in the Spirit, we bring the Gospel of Peace to those around us. Not only are we separated from the world, but we are called as ambassadors to the world to share the Gospel with those who are yet to join the body of Christ. It isn't easy taking the Gospel to the four corners of the earth, but that's what we have been called to do as the Scriptures say:

> Acts 1:8 But ye shall receive power, after that the Holy Ghost is come upon you: and ye shall be witnesses unto me both in Jerusalem, and in all Judaea, and in Samaria, and unto the uttermost part of the earth.

As the saying so famously goes, "These boots were made for walking". Are your feet shod? Are you separated from the ways of the world? Are you doing your bit to take the Gospel to those around you? Have you been called to a mission field at home or abroad? It may not be flattering. It may hurt, cause blisters, develop callouses and sometimes even stink. But God the Father has given the Bride of Christ footwear that will go the distance.

# Dressed for Eternity

## Linen - Ancient Jewish Bridal Attire

The phrase, "fine linen" is found 34 times in the KJV. By the time Solomon wrote the book of Proverbs, fine linen from Egypt had clearly become a matter of boasting. Even today, run a search for "fine linen" and an ad for "Egyptian linens" comes up on my screen. Indeed, the first recorded linen industry was in Egypt roughly 4,000 years ago. The Phoenician traders were known to trade in Egyptian Linen all over the then-known world, even establishing the craft in ancient Ireland. Roman nobles wrote about the incredible work of Egyptian weavers and marvelled at how fine Egyptian Fine Linen was.

## Make-up and Characteristics

Linen is a fabric that, like cotton, comes from a plant. Unlike cotton, the process to get at the longer fibres of the flax plant takes a lot more work. Also unlike cotton, linen does not accept dyes very well, and resists dirt and staining. White linen is recorded as having been worn in Egypt because of the cooler nature of the cloth. Linen has been known down through the ages not merely for its  coolness in extreme heat, but also for its strength. Linen is apparently strongest when it is wet, contrary to all other natural cloth material. According to sources cited by Wikipedia, it was used to help create shields in medieval days because of its strength. However, this strength is also its weakness.

## Ancient Jewish Bridal Attire

Linen that is repeatedly sharply bent will eventually break. This author has a linen dress from Spain. While this dress is very nice to wear in the summer heat, and while it has resisted most stains, the poor thing is ageing. A chocolate stain never did come out, and a handful of small tomatoe stains appear faintly yellow on the front of the dress. The upper half of the back of the dress is now stained yellow because in spite of its cooler nature, I still sweat! Lastly and most recently, the cloth around the leg slits have begun tearing away from the seams. It is the seams where the cloth has been repeatedly bent and sown into place, and after all these years, it is breaking and tearing away.

## Girded about with fine linen

God says in Ezekiel 16, that He girded Jerusalem with fine linen. The definition of "gird" according to Merriam-Webster is "to bind or encircle as with a belt, to fasten such with a sword, to surround, provide, or equip. Another definition is "to prepare for action or gather up one's resources."

Notice those various definitions. Two definitions should be noted in this discussion. The first is "that of enclosing", better described by Dictionary.com as: "to surround; enclose; hem in."

The second is "to bind as with a belt, to fasten, such as a sword."

> Ephesians 6:14 Stand therefore, having your loins girt about with truth, and having on the breastplate of righteousness;

Paul's list of armour in Ephesians 6 references the Belt of Truth. The belt on the Roman Soldier was the most important piece of his armour! This belt not only held his sword, but was the piece that all other armour was in some way attached or fastened to. This belt held leather straps that hung down to cover the skirt of his tunic, so not only did it fasten the armour and hold the sword, but it served to protect his lower body as well.

In Ephesians 6, Truth is seen as that all-important piece that holds everything together, protecting sensitive parts and serving to hold the means of combat.

# Dressed for Eternity

**What does this mean to the Bride of Christ?**

> Exodus 28:39-43  And thou shalt embroider the coat of fine linen, and thou shalt make the mitre of fine linen, and thou shalt make the girdle of needlework.  [40]And for Aaron's sons thou shalt make coats, and thou shalt make for them girdles, and bonnets shalt thou make for them, for glory and for beauty.  [41]And thou shalt put them upon Aaron thy brother, and his sons with him; and shalt anoint them, and consecrate them, and sanctify them, that they may minister unto me in the priest's office.  [42]And thou shalt make them linen breeches to cover their nakedness; from the loins even unto the thighs they shall reach:  [43]And they shall be upon Aaron, and upon his sons, when they come in unto the tabernacle of the congregation, or when they come near unto the altar to minister in the holy place; that they bear not iniquity, and die: it shall be a statute for ever unto him and his seed after him.

It is no wonder then, that linen was a requirement by God for the priestly garments in Temple service in Exodus, and why it is mentioned for the bridal outfit in Ezekiel.  Coarse linen was and still is capable of being made, but finer linen takes more work and therefore was typically owned by the upper classes or priests.  So for God to clothe Jerusalem in fine linen shows the worth and beauty God saw.

The spiritual significance of fine linen for the Bride of Christ is represented by the fact that it resists dirt and stains so easily.  As the Bride of Christ, we too, should resist the stain of sin on our lives.  Sadly, like my dress, not all of us have resisted so well, and our robes are marked by things we never should have allowed ourselves to come into contact with.  Our Robe of Righteousness is meant to be both stain-resistant and sin-resistant.

> 2 Corinthians 12:9  And he said unto me, My grace is sufficient for thee: for my strength is made perfect in weakness. Most gladly therefore will I rather glory in my infirmities, that the power of Christ may rest upon me.

## Ancient Jewish Bridal Attire

> Psalm 93:1 The LORD reigneth, he is clothed with majesty; the LORD is clothed with strength, wherewith he hath girded himself: the world also is stablished, that it cannot be moved.

Secondly, fine linen represents strength, strength that doesn't come from ourselves, but from the One who gave the Bride of Christ her royal garments. Just like the linen, if we act on our own strength, we will eventually break. In our weakness, as the Scriptures say, God is strong. He knows what He's doing as He clothes His Bride. Scripture says that the Heavenly Bridegroom is clothed with strength. Scripture says that His strength is made perfect in weakness. So it is when we as the Bride of Christ allow ourselves to become weak before Him, that He clothes us with His strength.

# Dressed for Eternity

## Silk - Ancient Jewish Bridal Attire

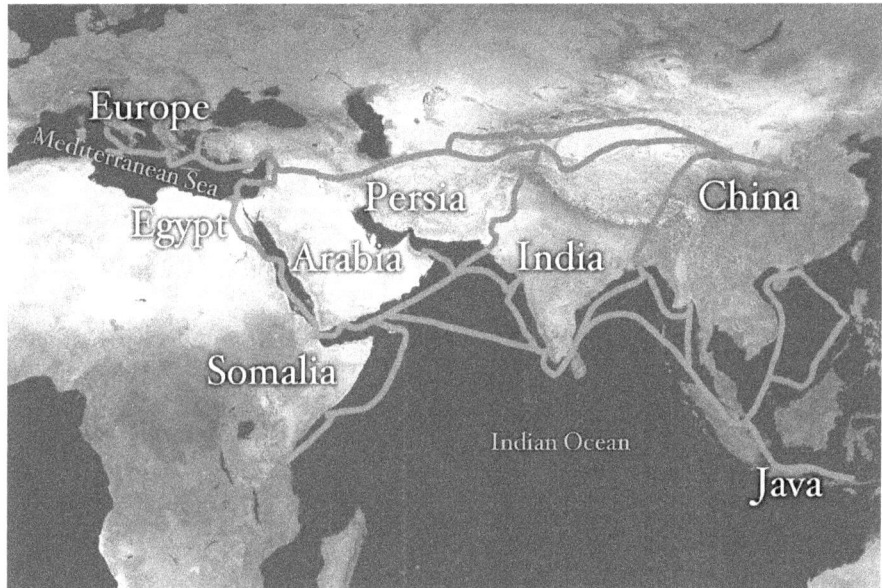

*Land (Red) and Sea (Blue) routes of the Silk Road*

Silk's narrative down through history is an interesting one to say the least. Consideration of God's decoration of silk for Jerusalem once again takes us back to the Tabernacle, and by extension, to Ancient Egypt from where the Hebrews would have obtained such cloth. The question then, is how on earth did Egypt get it? This cloth was not native to that land, nor native to any regions close by.

The answer is found in what can only be described as the beginnings of the Silk Road, long before "official" records were found. The Silk Road is said to have begun with the Han dynasty in China around 206 BC. But when we consider the roughly estimated date of the Exodus, we find ourselves looking at anywhere from 1200 BC to as far back as the 1300's BC. A map pictured here shows the Silk Road as it was understood by those who have tracked its history. Note the sea-routes. This was most likely how the Egyptians obtained it before the later-understood dates of the Silk Road's existence. It is possible they obtained it via caravan trade routes from India as well, as both India and China appear to have discovered silk around the same time.

## Ancient Jewish Bridal Attire

But the fact that the Hebrews had it in their possession prior to the commonly understood discovery and trade of silk, would suggest that such cloth was already being created at least 1000 years before the Syrians and Romans heard of and made record of it. Egyptian mummies have been found with silk in their hair.

## Make-up and Characteristics

Natural silk is derived from special silk worms that create the silk from spinarettes in their heads while creating their cocoon. In ancient times, these cocoons would be found after the larvae had left, apparently producing shorter strands of silk than cultivated cocoons now. Animal rights activists actually prefer this older method of gathering cocoons, as more larvae live than the numbers the farmer chooses to maintain his stock.

Once the cocoons have been soaked in boiling water, the strands are separated from each other. Two or three strands from different cocoons will be wound together to make a workable thread. A cocoon where the larvae did not hatch will produce a single mile-long strand.

Silk, unlike linen, will lose up to 20% of its strength when wet. It shrinks a fair bit when first washed as well. If it is stretched, it generally does not spring back into shape. It is a delicate cloth as a result. It is also prone to being eaten by other bugs. But with all those negatives, it does have some positives. Silk is cool to wear in the summer and helps to trap heat in the winter. Similar to linen, it has been put to a wide range of uses over the centuries including undergarments, pyjamas, handkerchiefs, all the way up to kimonos in China and other garments worn by royalty. Silk has been seen as a status symbol, announcing to the world that the wearer is of the nobility or royalty. Due to how each strand of silk is formed, the shimmering nature of its appearance, no matter the dye given to it, will produce the appearance of other colours as it is turned in the light.

## Dressed for Eternity

**What does this mean for the Bride of Christ?**

God included silk in the setup of the Tabernacle in the wilderness, and includes it in His list of adorning garments for His Bride. It is this author's conjecture that more than any of the other garments covered to this point, silk truly shows the royal, regal nature of this Bride. She is not just any Bride preparing to marry any young man. She has been claimed by royalty, and being given the garments of royalty to wear on her wedding day. The shimmering colours as they appear in the light as she moves display the varying attributes of her noble nature given to her by her Bridegroom.

But she must be careful. Allowing her silk to become consistently soiled will invite the ravages of sin to eat away at it. Trying to prepare for her wedding day while playing in the world will stretch her, to the point where she will not return to what she once was. Scripture says:

> Romans 5:19-21 For as by one man's disobedience many were made sinners, so by the obedience of one shall many be made righteous. [20]Moreover the law entered, that the offence might abound. But where sin abounded, grace did much more abound: [21]That as sin hath reigned unto death, even so might grace reign through righteousness unto eternal life by Jesus Christ our Lord.

> Romans 6:1-7 What shall we say then? Shall we continue in sin, that grace may abound? [2]God forbid. How shall we, that are dead to sin, live any longer therein? [3]Know ye not, that so many of us as were baptized into Jesus Christ were baptized into his death? [4]Therefore we are buried with him by baptism into death: that like as Christ was raised up from the dead by the glory of the Father, even so we also should walk in newness of life. [5]For if we have been planted together in the likeness of his death, we shall be also in the likeness of his resurrection: [6]Knowing this, that our old man is crucified with him, that the body of sin might be destroyed, that henceforth we should not serve sin. [7]For he that is dead is freed from sin.

## Ancient Jewish Bridal Attire

Romans 6:12-16  Let not sin therefore reign in your mortal body, that ye should obey it in the lusts thereof. [13]Neither yield ye your members as instruments of unrighteousness unto sin: but yield yourselves unto God, as those that are alive from the dead, and your members as instruments of righteousness unto God. [14]For sin shall not have dominion over you: for ye are not under the law, but under grace. [15]What then? shall we sin, because we are not under the law, but under grace? God forbid. [16]Know ye not, that to whom ye yield yourselves servants to obey, his servants ye are to whom ye obey; whether of sin unto death, or of obedience unto righteousness?

It is her duty, as the future Bride to the Heavenly Bridegroom, to keep her garments clean from the ravages of sin, to resist the temptation to stretch herself across both sides of grace and sin, and to keep her garments bright and ready for her wedding day.

## Ornaments - Ancient Jewish Bridal Attire

Ezekiel 16:11  I decked thee also with ornaments, and I put bracelets upon thy hands, and a chain on thy neck.

Ezekiel moves from the apparel to the ornamentation in verse 11 of chapter 16. Using the Strong's Concordance and Hebrew Interlinear revealed something very interesting. The word for "ornaments" in the KJV comes from a Hebrew word that in general refers to "trappings, finery, etc", but in this tense, actually refers to something called a headstall! Referring back to the research done for the introductory article for this section, we discover that the ancient peoples of the time period in which these verses were written were indeed known to decorate their camels profusely!

References in Song of Solomon add to the picture. Some scholars believe that by the time Solomon wrote the words to his love song, this particular ornamentation was so well entrenched that he could not help but write about it. He gives three references of interest in this discussion:

Song of Solomon 1:10  Thy cheeks are comely with rows of jewels, thy neck with chains of gold.

Song of Solomon 4:4  Thy neck is like the tower of David builded for an armoury, whereon there hang a thousand bucklers, all shields of mighty men.

**Ancient Jewish Bridal Attire**

As I pondered how to write about the contents of the next couple verses, it hit me, that Ezekiel may very well have used the word "ornaments" and then merely described them in the wording that follows. Sadly, without knowledge of other ancient Jewish bridal outfits, this leaves me looking at the antiquity of the Yemeni outfit and finding myself amazed at how similar its appearance is to what King Solomon wrote about.

**Historical Observations**

Depending on the family, and depending on the dowry, the Yemeni Jewish bridal headdress can contain silver coins or hanging decorations, gold coins or hanging decorations, greenery, flowers, or the two together in varying combinations, etc. Examining this headdress in light of the varying pieces mentioned in Ezekiel reveals them to all be present. The observations of King Solomon about the cheeks, chains and his poetic description of coins all suddenly make sense as well. This makes me wonder if either his Bride was Yemeni in origin, or if the Yemeni headdress was more widespread than what archaeological history leads us to believe.

When Jewish people arrived in Yemen is apparently up for debate. Some say as far back as the early 1400's BC dating, potentially coinciding with the earliest pitched date of the Exodus as a result. Others say the 1200's, which coincides with the later BC dating of the Hebrew exodus from Egypt. Still others put the dates in either the 200's BC, or a mere 40 years before Rome sacked Jerusalem in 70 AD. Legend has it that King Solomon sent Hebrews by boat to the Arabian Peninsula to mine gold and other precious metals. However, if this were the case, then this headdress would have been imported to Yemen, and not the other way around. We are not told in Scripture that certain Jews stayed behind anywhere they travelled, so how they got to Yemen, when they got there, and the apparent popularity of this headdress all have this author fascinatingly puzzled.

# Dressed for Eternity

## The Roman Helmet - Interesting Considerations

What is of interest, however, is the concept of this ornamentation largely covering the Bride's head and neck. Adding to this level of interest, is the nature of this headpiece being said to hold the dowry, or Bride price. A dowry is a price paid to the Father of the Bride, as part of the betrothal ceremony, and as proof that the bridegroom will return for his Bride. She is said to have been "bought with a price". Via this Yemeni headdress, she displays this dowry for all to see on the day of her wedding.

Before we discuss the implications for the Bride of Christ, these two concepts come together nicely in the helmet Paul wrote about in Ephesians. In Ephesians Chapter 6, Paul urges the follower of Christ to put on the helmet of Salvation.

> Ephesians 6:17 And take the helmet of salvation, and the sword of the Spirit, which is the word of God:

By using the Roman helmet, and by adding the term "Salvation", Paul is making two very interesting and yet deep observations.

First is the nature of the Roman helmet. This headpiece was designed to protect the soldier's brain. Some helmets also had nose pieces designed to protect the soldier's nose from impulsion into his face which would otherwise result in possible puncture of his brain and death. In addition, other designs of this helmet feature neck guards aimed at protecting the wearer's back of the neck from blows that may come from above, beside, or in some instances, from behind.

## Ancient Jewish Bridal Attire

> Ephesians 6:10-12 Finally, my brethren, be strong in the Lord, and in the power of his might. ¹¹Put on the whole armour of God, that ye may be able to stand against the wiles of the devil. ¹²For we wrestle not against flesh and blood, but against principalities, against powers, against the rulers of the darkness of this world, against spiritual wickedness in high places.

> 2 Corinthians 10:3-6 For though we walk in the flesh, we do not war after the flesh: ⁴(For the weapons of our warfare are not carnal, but mighty through God to the pulling down of strong holds;) ⁵Casting down imaginations, and every high thing that exalteth itself against the knowledge of God, and bringing into captivity every thought to the obedience of Christ; ⁶And having in a readiness to revenge all disobedience, when your obedience is fulfilled.

Second is the nature of the associated term Paul put with the helmet, that of Salvation. For many years, this term, "The helmet of Salvation" has been used to explain that the enemy always begins his attacks in our mind. If he can get the Bride of Christ thinking bad thoughts, dwelling on temptations, engaging subject matter that she shouldn't, then he can get the follower of Christ to speak and act in ways that draw them away from the faith. Putting on the helmet of Salvation protects the mind of the believer by placing it under the shed Blood of the Lamb. But there is another meaning here when considering this bridal headdress.

> 1 Corinthians 6:19-20 What? know ye not that your body is the temple of the Holy Ghost which is in you, which ye have of God, and ye are not your own? ²⁰For ye are bought with a price: therefore glorify God in your body, and in your spirit, which are God's.

Salvation refers to the act of saving something or someone, an act of purchasing them from slavery to freedom. In this light, we see Paul saying to put on the Bridal headdress! Display to the world that the Bride of Christ has been bought, purchased unto the day of her wedding when the Heavenly Bridegroom will return for Her. Her headdress covers her head and protects her neck, and in some cases, also includes a nose piece that we'll discuss later.

# Dressed for Eternity

The Roman soldiers often added horse hair to their helmets either in locks resembling a ponytail, or in short, stocky few-inch-wide and several inches long strips that make modern-day kids think of broom heads. These additions would be coloured according to the battalion they led. By the very nature of their helmet, they announced their rank and position within the Roman army.

**Introductory Conclusion**

So it is with the Bride of Christ. She too is part of the Army of the Lord. We will discuss in following pages how the neck chains reflect another part of the Roman soldier's outfit as described by the Apostle Paul. But it is interesting to note that those necklaces, particularly those that drape under the Yemeni Jewish Bride's chin, are attached to the headdress.

The Bride of Christ has been bought with a price. She has been given her dowry and is in waiting for her Bridegroom to appear. The question is, will she be found proudly wearing her dowry when He comes?

# Dressed for Eternity

## Silver Bracelets - Ancient Jewish Bridal Attire

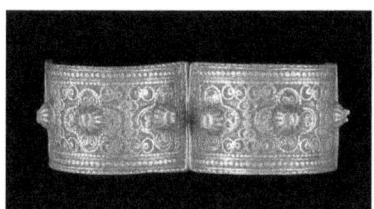

*The bracelet is made of two equal halves, and has three serrated half globules on each side. The decoration combines spirals and circles; a triple bead-molded band frames the decor. Inside of the bracelet is an engraved inscription in Hebrew, Source: Walters Art Museum*

Ezekiel 16:11  I decked thee also with ornaments, and I put bracelets upon thy hands, and a chain on thy neck.

Bracelets are mentioned following the overarcing term "adornments" in Ezekiel 16. While it is hard to find archaeological and historical examples of this. Scripture references the giving of bracelets by suitors several times between Genesis and Ezekiel. Judging from these passages, it was a common practise to include them in a suitor's proposed dowry.

According to Yemenite Jewish history, the bracelets of the bridal attire were made out of silver, and were worn in matching sets. One source I glanced past stated that such bracelets would not only be worn in pairs, but three pairs would be worn between the wrist and the elbow for the wedding day.

Ezekiel, a few verses later, mentions both silver and gold in the adorning of Jerusalem.

> Ezekiel 16:13  Thus wast thou decked with gold and silver; and thy raiment was of fine linen, and silk, and broidered work; thou didst eat fine flour, and honey, and oil: and thou wast exceeding beautiful, and thou didst prosper into a kingdom.

The discussion of gold was already covered in our discussion of golden streets in the New Jerusalem back on page 73. So as our bracelets are the first mention of silver, we will discuss silver next.

# Ancient Jewish Bridal Attire

## Make-up and Characteristics

Similar to gold, silver is a very malleable, ductile metal, but unlike gold, is even more conductive of electricity than copper. The only reason it hasn't been used in place of copper on a wider scale, is cost. Very much like gold, silver is also considered a precious metal and used in both currency and jewelry down through the ages. Silver, while offering a very high polish, tends to tarnish over time as it comes into contact with elements in the atmosphere. This tendency to tarnish has resulted in many silversmiths coming up with protective finishes to prevent such unsightly tarnish. Silver polishes have been sold in stores for many years to keep silverware from colouring and eventually going black.

Refining silver has taken on various forms over the millennia, but only since the industrial age has the method of nitric acid been used as one of the methods. Many modern methods still use smelting furnaces. A PDF whose link is in the appendix, shows one person's attempt to smelt silver in a manner similar to those done during the Middle Ages.

This author's searches for the origins of a silversmith's smelting story as told by a group of women in a Bible study, have failed to unveil the source. However, God does say in Malachi:

> Malachi 3:2-3 But who may abide the day of his coming? and who shall stand when he appeareth? for he is like a refiner's fire, and like fullers' soap: ³And he shall sit as a refiner and purifier of silver: and he shall purify the sons of Levi, and purge them as gold and silver, that they may offer unto the LORD an offering in righteousness.

One of the steps involved in smelting silver is fluxing. This step can take various forms, but the end result is the skimming of the dross from the surface of the silver, until the smithy in ancient times could see his reflection. At that point, the silver was said to be pure.

## What does this mean for the Bride of Christ?

The implications of this refining process for the Bride of Christ are clear. Whether we discuss gold or silver, the refining process is one of very hot temperatures, dross or impurities being skimmed off the top, and the smelter going through the process as many times as necessary to bring forth a metal worthy of the use to which it will be put.

Many times, the Christian life is painted to be all roses and bliss, but in reality, it often has moments of fire and tribulation! This is not always because of those out to attack people of faith, natural disasters striking out of nowhere, or unwanted deaths in the family. They may instead be divine opportunities. If such things seem like haphazard events in the life of the Christian, then they have missed out on the opportunity for God to use those events to refine them, to shape them, to cleanse them, and to form them into the vessels of honour He desires. The Apostle Peter admonishes the church:

> 1 Peter 4:12-13 Beloved, think it not strange concerning the fiery trial which is to try you, as though some strange thing happened unto you: [13]But rejoice, inasmuch as ye are partakers of Christ's sufferings; that, when his glory shall be revealed, ye may be glad also with exceeding joy.

The silver given to the Bride of Christ has gone through just such a refining process. God is pleased with His reflection and with the purity of her nature. She is to wear her purity as part of her dowry, displaying to the world that she is set apart from the sinful impurities and dross of the ways around her.

> Psalm 4:3-5 But know that the LORD hath set apart him that is godly for himself: the LORD will hear when I call unto him. [4]Stand in awe, and sin not: commune with your own heart upon your bed, and be still. Selah. [5]Offer the sacrifices of righteousness, and put your trust in the LORD.

**Dressed for Eternity**

## Chains - Ancient Jewish Bridal Attire

Chains or necklaces are a huge part of the ancient Yemeni Jewish bridal outfit, so much so that you can't see her neck if you tried! They begin directly under her chin, attached to the headdress, and they layer down from there until they cover her entire chest area. Varying imagery of this outfit reveals these chains and necklaces in a multitude of styles, but all of either silver or gold in some fashion. In some images, at least half these chains bear coins on them, while in other images, at least half these chains carry filigree balls or bells on them.

*Traditional lazem necklace from Yemen, beautiful old Bedouin metal piece from North Yemen. This style of jewel was part of the dowry given to the Bride before her marriage. Source: Arabia Felix Jewels*

The concept of wearing a silver or gold chain necklace has been around for at least 4,000 years or more judging from the myriad of archaeological and historical evidence. If a person could afford it, they wore it. If a person could barely afford it, they reserved it for special occasions. But almost everyone had something special they pulled out at festivities to wear around their neck. It is interesting to observe in Scripture, how God likens the obtaining of wisdom and sound teaching to that of a chain:

Proverbs 1:8-9 My son, hear the instruction of thy father, and forsake not the law of thy mother: ⁹For they shall be an ornament of grace unto thy head, and chains about thy neck.

Proverbs 3:3-4 Let not mercy and truth forsake thee: bind them about thy neck; write them upon the table of thine heart: ⁴So shalt thou find favour and good understanding in the sight of God and man.

## Ancient Jewish Bridal Attire

Proverbs 3:21-24  My son, let not them depart from thine eyes: keep sound wisdom and discretion: ²²So shall they be life unto thy soul, and grace to thy neck. ²³Then shalt thou walk in thy way safely, and thy foot shall not stumble. ²⁴When thou liest down, thou shalt not be afraid: yea, thou shalt lie down, and thy sleep shall be sweet.

Proverbs 6:20-23  My son, keep thy father's commandment, and forsake not the law of thy mother: ²¹Bind them continually upon thine heart, and tie them about thy neck. ²²When thou goest, it shall lead thee; when thou sleepest, it shall keep thee; and when thou awakest, it shall talk with thee. ²³For the commandment is a lamp; and the law is light; and reproofs of instruction are the way of life:

This suggests that in ancient times as now, there are people who will not be found without their favourite chain draped around their neck. Both men and women often have a favourite and they'll even wear it in the shower.

## Coins and Shields

Thanks to a reference by Song of Solomon, we have an interesting tie-in here with the Armour of God as discussed by the Apostle Paul in Ephesians. Solomon mentions the two following statements:

Song of Solomon 1:10  Thy cheeks are comely with rows of jewels, thy neck with chains of gold.

Song of Solomon 4:4  Thy neck is like the tower of David builded for an armoury, whereon there hang a thousand bucklers, all shields of mighty men.

**Dressed for Eternity**

These statements have this author wondering if King Solomon was looking at ancient Yemenite Jewish bridal finery in these verses. If you've ever seen a Middle Eastern festive female outfit, or seen a camel or Arabian horse dressed up for a parade, you can't help but have noticed the number of coins attached to the head band, earrings and necklaces. Similarly, the Yemenite Jewish bridal attire in some cases is also bedecked with coins attached to the headpiece and/or necklaces and chains, so much so that it's easy for this author to slip into poetic mode and readily agree with King Solomon that they could appear as scales or shields.

One of the items Paul encourages the believer to put on is the Shield of Faith. The Roman soldier's shield was one of two designs. It was either small and roundish or tall with a rounded rectangular shape meant to protect the entire body hidden behind it. The smaller shield was used by swordsmen to afford the blocking of the opponent's blows, while the larger was used by those who handled the bows and arrows, or the spears. Often times, this larger shield was carried not by the soldier, but by a buckler instead. Hence the various verses in Scripture where God says that He will be our buckler and our shield.

> Psalm 18:30 As for God, his way is perfect: the word of the LORD is tried: he is a buckler to all those that trust in him.

> Psalm 91:3-4 Surely he shall deliver thee from the snare of the fowler, and from the noisome pestilence. ⁴He shall cover thee with his feathers, and under his wings shalt thou trust: his truth shall be thy shield and buckler.

> Proverbs 2:7 He layeth up sound wisdom for the righteous: he is a buckler to them that walk uprightly.

A second item Paul says to put on is the Breastplate of Righteousness. Again, when you look at the ancient Yemeni Jewish bridal attire, you see the chains and necklaces completely covering her chest.

**Ancient Jewish Bridal Attire**

The glory of God and His purity completely covers her heart and lungs. The comparison again to the breastplate the high priest wore in Temple worship must be brought back to mind at this time as well. See the introduction to Aaron's Breastplate on page 11.

**What does this mean for the Bride of Christ?**

The implications for the Bride of Christ are amazing! Gold speaks of God's glory while silver speaks of His purity. God speaks of binding wisdom, discretion, and knowledge like chains about our necks. Decorating the Bride of Christ in this manner then, says several things:

1) First, God is looking for a Bride with brains! Many like to attack Christianity by saying it is a brainless, non-thinking religion. But God to the contrary, asks that the thinking believer take what God has given him/her, and use it to make wise decisions as they go about their daily lives. The Bride of Christ is to be wise, tactful and using discretion in how they interact with others in what they choose to do when with what. The Bride of Christ is to be shrewd, as one place in Scripture puts it, to be wise as serpents and harmless as doves, or as Christ puts it, to be strong yet gentle, to be meek.

Proverbs 2:10-11 When wisdom entereth into thine heart, and knowledge is pleasant unto thy soul; [11]Discretion shall preserve thee, understanding shall keep thee:

Matthew 10:16 Behold, I send you forth as sheep in the midst of wolves: be ye therefore wise as serpents, and harmless as doves.

Matthew 5:5 Blessed are the meek: for they shall inherit the earth.

2) Second, God has decided that the Bride of Christ is worth bedecking in a noble manner. In Jewish wedding customs to this day, the Bride and Groom are called King and Queen for a week surrounding the wedding. They are even to appear in public with escorts during this time. God says the Bride of Christ is worth decorating like that of a

queen, as she will be given to the King of Kings, Jesus Christ Himself. The gold and silver spoken of in Ezekiel attests to this.

3) Third, The Bride of Christ is to look to God for her protection and not seek to provide it herself. This last point is perhaps the most challenging due to modern thought that we have to protect ourselves, that no one else is going to stand up for us. When we take a close look at the Armour of God, we realize that every single piece points to Christ being our Saviour, our protector, our Truth, the object of our faith, the object of the Gospel of peace, and the Word of God, the sword of the Spirit. Here in these chains of gold and silver, we see Him as our shield, even stronger than David's mighty men.

Ephesians 6:16 Above all, taking the shield of faith, wherewith ye shall be able to quench all the fiery darts of the wicked.

Deuteronomy 33:27-29 The eternal God is thy refuge, and underneath are the everlasting arms: and he shall thrust out the enemy from before thee; and shall say, Destroy them. [28]Israel then shall dwell in safety alone: the fountain of Jacob shall be upon a land of corn and wine; also his heavens shall drop down dew. [29]Happy art thou, O Israel: who is like unto thee, O people saved by the LORD, the shield of thy help, and who is the sword of thy excellency! and thine enemies shall be found liars unto thee; and thou shalt tread upon their high places.

Psalm 18:2 The LORD is my rock, and my fortress, and my deliverer; my God, my strength, in whom I will trust; my buckler, and the horn of my salvation, and my high tower.

Psalm 91:1-2 He that dwelleth in the secret place of the most High shall abide under the shadow of the Almighty. [2]I will say of the LORD, He is my refuge and my fortress: my God; in him will I trust.

4) Fourth, The purity of heart found in the glory of God serves as protection over the heart of the believer. The breastplate of Righteousness can only be applied when the wearer is desiring to live a

## Ancient Jewish Bridal Attire

life pure and holy before God the Father. The jewelry that makes up the Yemeni Jewish bridal attire includes gold, silver, and in some cases red choral. Red as we know stands for the shed blood of Jesus Christ, the Bride price paid to ransom the Church from the ravages of sin and wash her clean and white to present to His Father.

Ephesians 6:14 Stand therefore, having your loins girt about with truth, and having on the breastplate of righteousness;

Matthew 26:27-29 And he took the cup, and gave thanks, and gave it to them, saying, Drink ye all of it; $^{28}$For this is my blood of the new testament, which is shed for many for the remission of sins. $^{29}$But I say unto you, I will not drink henceforth of this fruit of the vine, until that day when I drink it new with you in my Father's kingdom.

It behooves the Bride of Christ to use her mind and will in a manner pleasing to God and by extension, pleasing to those around her. It is necessary that she not try to protect herself, but allow God to be her protector instead and to take security in that knowledge and position within His hand.

It bears reminding that the Bride of Christ is royalty. Too often we can forget that as we go about our daily lives, but the Bride of Christ, the church, has been bought into a royal family and will one day rule and reign with Christ at His side.

Lastly, a theme that is developing as this research goes along is that of holiness. The Bride of Christ should be setting herself apart from the world through submission and surrender to the Holy Spirit's work in and through her life. This goes for both men and women in the church body. When we put on the Armour of God, we are putting on the Righteousness of Christ, and the choice to engage in right living will protect our heart from the attacks of the enemy.

# Dressed for Eternity

## Forehead Jewels or Nose Jewels - Ancient Jewish Bridal Attire

"A Jewel on thy Forehead" Ezekiel 16:12 KJV

This phrase in the King James Version has been interpreted by many other translations as a nose jewel reflective of the kind of jewelry typically seen even today in brides from Syria, India, and other places around Middle Eastern countries. The designs of these pieces can range from simply a forehead decoration, to a forehead decoration linked to a nose jewel that has been placed on one side of the Bride's nostril.

Some dictionaries refer to this jewel as a diadem, which is a type of crown or jewelled headband that wraps around the forehead with arms that stretch toward the back of the head. Ezekiel separately mentions a crown, so we'll discuss that decoration more later.

## Discussion of Jewelled Headdresses

In either case, whether a diadem or a draped forehead jewel that may or may not be attached to a nose ring, we do see something similar in the ancient Yemeni Jewish bridal headdress. The images that have been shared so far, being in the public domain, are seen everywhere, but I want us to focus this time on the visible fringe now. This fringe is reminiscent of many copyrighted decorative head pieces this author saw while looking for imagery of this item. Examples from India, Persia, Bedouin women, and even those of the orient, all place jewelled or coin-bedecked chains on the Bride's forehead. Brides from India and Syria may also attach these chains to their nose ring on their special day. This gold or silver decked decoration is not actually part of the towering portion of the headdress, but is instead attached to an embroidered head covering underneath.

## Ancient Jewish Bridal Attire

Coined headdresses have also been seen in documented articles of bridal customs around the Middle East; and it is with this understanding that a deeper appreciation for the parable of the lost coin has been explored.

> Luke 15:8-10 Either what woman having ten pieces of silver, if she lose one piece, doth not light a candle, and sweep the house, and seek diligently till she find it? $^9$And when she hath found it, she calleth her friends and her neighbours together, saying, Rejoice with me; for I have found the piece which I had lost. $^{10}$Likewise, I say unto you, there is joy in the presence of the angels of God over one sinner that repenteth.

Various writings I came across explained the parable of the lost coin in relation to this particular piece of the betrothed Bride's dowry in Jesus' day. The coins attached to the headpiece in ancient times could be changed into currency if the betrothed groom okayed the transaction. In other cases, these forehead jewels were given to the girl when she was of marrying age, to show prospective suitors the wealth of her family. If the family was poor, losing one of these coins would be a big deal. Christ used this as an illustration of how God views the immense value of each lost soul.

## What does this means for the Bride of Christ?

The Bride of Christ wears the pride and joy of all Heaven on her forehead. The Scriptures tell us:

> Ephesians 1:12-14 That we should be to the praise of his glory, who first trusted in Christ. $^{13}$In whom ye also trusted, after that ye heard the word of truth, the gospel of your salvation: in whom also after that ye believed, ye were sealed with that holy Spirit of promise, $^{14}$Which is the earnest of our inheritance until the redemption of the purchased possession, unto the praise of his glory.

Not only is He our helper, our teacher, and our guide, but He is also the seal on our forehead, claiming us as the Bride of Christ.

## Dressed for Eternity

In an alternate way, Scripture speaks of the children of God as being jewels in God's Crown. There is a hymn we used to sing as I was growing up entitled, "Jewels", taken from Malachi 3:17. It is precisely because of verses such as this that this study is taking place.

> Malachi 3:17-18  And they shall be mine, saith the LORD of hosts, in that day when I make up my jewels; and I will spare them, as a man spareth his own son that serveth him.  ¹⁸Then shall ye return, and discern between the righteous and the wicked, between him that serveth God and him that serveth him not.

The coins on the headdress of the Bride of Christ symbolize the dowry given to her by Christ at the Last Supper and later as He stood with His disciples on the hill of ascension. Before rising into the sky He said:

> Acts 1:4-5  And, being assembled together with them, commanded them that they should not depart from Jerusalem, but wait for the promise of the Father, which, saith he, ye have heard of me.  ⁵For John truly baptized with water; but ye shall be baptized with the Holy Ghost not many days hence.

When the 120 were gathered in the Upper Room, it was the Holy Spirit that landed on each head present, as if by a tongue of fire. The receiving of the Holy Spirit in this manner gives the Church power over the enemy, power to preach and to spread the Gospel to all who are lost.

> Acts 1:8  But ye shall receive power, after that the Holy Ghost is come upon you: and ye shall be witnesses unto me both in Jerusalem, and in all Judaea, and in Samaria, and unto the uttermost part of the earth.

God cares deeply for the lost, considering them lost jewels in His own crown, and He sends the Bride of Christ out to find them, not out of fear that her betrothal will be ended by divorce, but out of the urgency of one seeking to find a lost soul before it is damned to hell forever. As each lost soul is found, it is as if another coin has been sewn into the Bride's headdress.

# Dressed for Eternity

## Earrings - Ancient Jewish Bridal Attire

*This is the gold earring found at Tel Megiddo Source: American Friends of Tel Aviv University*

Ezekiel 16:12 And I put a jewel on thy forehead, and earrings in thine ears, and a beautiful crown upon thine head.

Earrings are mentioned 17 times in the Old Testament and in every instance, they are made of gold. Jewelry was one of the ways that men and women stored and displayed their wealth. When God asked the Hebrews to bring offerings of the items necessary to build the very first Tabernacle, both men and women broke off their gold earrings and brought them to Moses.

Exodus 35:22 And they came, both men and women, as many as were willing hearted, and brought bracelets, and earrings, and rings, and tablets, all jewels of gold: and every man that offered offered an offering of gold unto the LORD.

This practise was widespread in Biblical ancient times as we see later in the story of Gideon. He commanded his men to break off the earrings of the defeated invading army, because it was observed the soldiers wore earrings of gold.

Judges 8:23-25 And Gideon said unto them, I will not rule over you, neither shall my son rule over you: the LORD shall rule over you. ²⁴And Gideon said unto them, I would desire a request of you, that ye would give me every man the earrings of his prey. (For they had golden earrings, because they were Ishmaelites.) ²⁵And they answered, We will willingly give them. And they spread a garment, and did cast therein every man the earrings of his prey.

# Ancient Jewish Bridal Attire

## The Egyptian Connection

The Egyptian connection must be remembered, as it was by the hand of the Egyptian people that the Hebrews fled that land with so much wealth. Scripture tells us that they showered gold and silver and precious things upon the Hebrew people as they fled the country before Pharoah.

*Ancient Egyptian gold earring Source: British Museum*

> Exodus 12:33-36  And the Egyptians were urgent upon the people, that they might send them out of the land in haste; for they said, We be all dead men.  ³⁴And the people took their dough before it was leavened, their kneadingtroughs being bound up in their clothes upon their shoulders.  ³⁵And the children of Israel did according to the word of Moses; and they borrowed of the Egyptians jewels of silver, and jewels of gold, and raiment:  ³⁶And the LORD gave the people favour in the sight of the Egyptians, so that they lent unto them such things as they required. And they spoiled the Egyptians.

To that end, a link shared in the appendix mentions a very interesting find in Tel Megiddo that dates to around 1100 BC, well after Israel had conquered Canaan. The archaeological notes about this find suggest the jewelry stash was hidden by the owner, and they never came back for it. There is conjecture about an Egyptian army that came through the area around that time. Considering that the dating of the Hebrew Exodus is somewhere between 1400 and 1200 BC, this stash could very easily have been that of family heirlooms passed down within a Jewish family, rather than having been part of a conquest.

# Dressed for Eternity

The Israel Museum has ancient crescent-shaped gold earrings on display. The British Museum offers images for free under certain terms and conditions, and their image of an ancient Egyptian gold earring is featured on the previous page. These and others like them would no doubt have made up part of the offering of gold given to Moses for the Tabernacle.

As the Jewish culture developed in Yemen, bridal jewelry was largely silver, as shown in the image shared here. However, as times have changed, either gold or silver have been used in bridal attire.

### What does this mean for the Bride of Christ?

Adorning the ears of the Bride of Christ with gold has interesting significance. Scripture urges us:

> James 1:22-25  But be ye doers of the word, and not hearers only, deceiving your own selves. ²³For if any be a hearer of the word, and not a doer, he is like unto a man beholding his natural face in a glass: ²⁴For he beholdeth himself, and goeth his way, and straightway forgetteth what manner of man he was. ²⁵But whoso looketh into the perfect law of liberty, and continueth therein, he being not a forgetful hearer, but a doer of the work, this man shall be blessed in his deed.

Proverbs says:

> Proverbs 25:2  It is the glory of God to conceal a thing: but the honour of kings is to search out a matter.

## Ancient Jewish Bridal Attire

Generally such searching out was the listening to others of whom the matter had been posed. James also shares that the wise person is quick to listen and slow to speak.

> James 1:19 Wherefore, my beloved brethren, let every man be swift to hear, slow to speak, slow to wrath:

As the centuries have gone by, it has become a lament at various points by various people down through the ages that the art of listening in prayer has become faded and almost forgotten. Prayer is meant to be a two-way communication between the child of God, and God Himself. Much liturgy has been created over the years aimed at well-worded, carefully-crafted prayers that remind one more of the Pharisee Christ spoke of in a parable, than the publican beating his chest in abject pleadings for mercy.

> Luke 18:9-14 And he spake this parable unto certain which trusted in themselves that they were righteous, and despised others: [10]Two men went up into the temple to pray; the one a Pharisee, and the other a publican. [11]The Pharisee stood and prayed thus with himself, God, I thank thee, that I am not as other men are, extortioners, unjust, adulterers, or even as this publican. [12]I fast twice in the week, I give tithes of all that I possess. [13]And the publican, standing afar off, would not lift up so much as his eyes unto heaven, but smote upon his breast, saying, God be merciful to me a sinner. [14]I tell you, this man went down to his house justified rather than the other: for every one that exalteth himself shall be abased; and he that humbleth himself shall be exalted.

In fact, when Christ answers the disciples' question to teach them to pray, He makes a point of saying:

> Matthew 6:7-8 But when ye pray, use not vain repetitions, as the heathen do: for they think that they shall be heard for their much speaking. [8]Be not ye therefore like unto them: for your Father knoweth what things ye have need of, before ye ask him.

# Dressed for Eternity

Then Christ launched into what we have come to title, "The Lord's Prayer", which is a great example of how God longs for His people to come to Him. Studying this prayer has been the subject of various books and teachings today. But the one thing still missing, is waiting on God - the meditative reading of His Word and listening to Him speak as part of the conversation.

The second precious metal used in bridal adornment is silver, as we see in the Yemeni Jewish bridal earrings. Silver, just as with white, typifies purity. Gracing the Bride of Christ with silver earrings would say that she is to hear only what is pure and good and true, that what enters her heart through what she hears, pleases God.

> Philippians 4:8 Finally, brethren, whatsoever things are true, whatsoever things are honest, whatsoever things are just, whatsoever things are pure, whatsoever things are lovely, whatsoever things are of good report; if there be any virtue, and if there be any praise, think on these things.

> Proverbs 4:23-27 Keep thy heart with all diligence; for out of it are the issues of life. ²⁴Put away from thee a froward mouth, and perverse lips put far from thee. ²⁵Let thine eyes look right on, and let thine eyelids look straight before thee. ²⁶Ponder the path of thy feet, and let all thy ways be established. 27 Turn not to the right hand nor to the left: remove thy foot from evil.

This is a concept that many in the church have turned aside from. Music, movies, news, TV shows, and even advertisements are often not kind to the heart that wishes to be pure before God. Christ said that what goes into a man's heart will come out in his speech, and that what comes out in his speech is what defiles him.

> Matthew 15:16-20 And Jesus said, Are ye also yet without understanding? ¹⁷Do not ye yet understand, that whatsoever entereth in at the mouth goeth into the belly, and is cast out into the draught? ¹⁸But those things which proceed out of the mouth come forth from the heart; and they defile the man. ¹⁹For out of the heart proceed evil thoughts, murders, adulteries, fornications, thefts, false witness, blasphemies:

## Ancient Jewish Bridal Attire

[20]These are the things which defile a man: but to eat with unwashen hands defileth not a man.

We must take care as Proverbs suggests, and watch what we see, hear, say, and do.

Proverbs 4:23  Keep thy heart with all diligence; for out of it are the issues of life.

The ear that hears is decorated in gold and silver.

Proverbs 25:12  As an earring of gold, and an ornament of fine gold, so is a wise reprover upon an obedient ear.

**Dressed for Eternity**

**Crown - Ancient Jewish Bridal Attire**

We've discussed many parts of the bridal outfit, but one. This final piece in various forms continues to be used in Jewish weddings simply due to the fact that on their wedding day, the Jewish Bride and groom are known as King and Queen in orthodox Jewish circles. To that end, various Jewish cultures have developed customs around this concept, invariably involving a crown of some form.

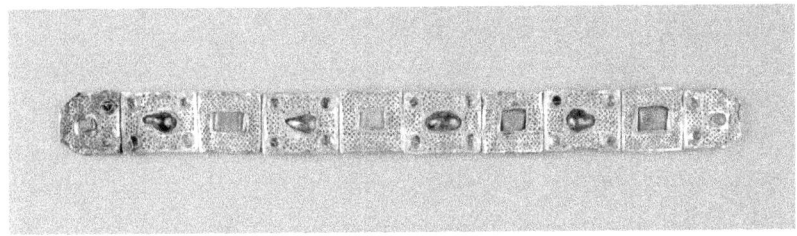

One common iteration of this crown is the diadem. The diadem hasn't changed much from the Roman examples that we have, and in many cases has now been given the name "Tiara" when worn by a lady.

## Ancient Jewish Bridal Attire

In ancient Rome, the diadem was typically made of gold, and either formed into the motif of leaves, or inlaid with precious stones. The illustration of Malachi 3 would suggest that the jewels in God's crown are actually set in a diadem.

The diadem is mentioned 4 times in Scripture and crown 66 times. In most cases, the term crown appears to be more readily interpreted as diadem, but in other cases, one gets the impression its use was most definitely a crown of royalty.

Many references include the word crown or diadem along with terms such as honour, royalty, glory, prize, and life. Whenever God's favour left an Old Testament king, the prophet would remove his crown, or the king was said to have had his crown removed. In various places of Scripture, a crown of glory is mentioned, and in the New Testament, the crown of life is mentioned, and these will be cast before God one day in Heaven.

## Fascination

Crowns have fascinated people down through the ages. Some have been made out of cloth, others out of precious metals such as gold or silver, and most have been decorated in some fashion with precious stones and other artwork. To crown a 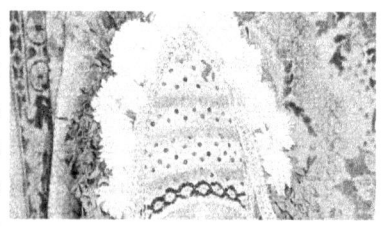 person for a day was to give them a place of honour. Young girls like to dress up as princesses and put a tiara on their heads. As noted above, Jewish brides and grooms wear crowns or tiaras to denote their position that day as king and queen. It is interesting to note while reading various sources on this subject, that some of the kings of ancient lands would make their half-crowns, otherwise known as tiaras or diadems, stand up tall. This was done in Egypt, Assyria, Persia, and other lands as well. We see this in the towering hat worn as part of the Yemeni Jewish bridal headdress. Much like the ancient diadems, we see the Yemeni headdress woven with gold as well.

# Dressed for Eternity

## What does this mean for the Bride of Christ?

> Ezekiel 16:12 And I put a jewel on thy forehead, and earrings in thine ears, and a beautiful crown upon thine head.

The Bride of Christ will wear a crown on her wedding day. According to Ezekiel, it will be a crown of gold, and according to the Apostle James, it will be the crown of life given out to all who endure faithful to the end.

> James 1:12 Blessed is the man that endureth temptation: for when he is tried, he shall receive the crown of life, which the Lord hath promised to them that love him.

> Revelation 2:10 Fear none of those things which thou shalt suffer: behold, the devil shall cast some of you into prison, that ye may be tried; and ye shall have tribulation ten days: be thou faithful unto death, and I will give thee a crown of life.

Being crowned with the glory of God is no small thing, and one the Bride of Christ should not take lightly.

> Psalm 8:5 For thou hast made him a little lower than the angels, and hast crowned him with glory and honour.

> Proverbs 4:7-9 Wisdom is the principal thing; therefore get wisdom: and with all thy getting get understanding. ⁸Exalt her, and she shall promote thee: she shall bring thee to honour, when thou dost embrace her. ⁹She shall give to thine head an ornament of grace: a crown of glory shall she deliver to thee.

God Himself says in Isaiah that He will be to her as a crown and a diadem, meaning it is God who not only crowns His people, but is that very crown Himself. His glory, His presence, will be the covering of the Bride of Christ.

## Ancient Jewish Bridal Attire

> Isaiah 28:5 In that day shall the LORD of hosts be for a crown of glory, and for a diadem of beauty, unto the residue of his people,

To this end, the Bride of Christ should seek to persevere under the pressures of this world and not give up.

> James 1:12 Blessed is the man that endureth temptation: for when he is tried, he shall receive the crown of life, which the Lord hath promised to them that love him.

Those who do not know Christ will throw all manner of dissuasions, discouragements, derailments, and more into the path of the Christ-follower, but we are to remain faithful and not turn to the right hand or to the left.

> Proverbs 4:23-27 Keep thy heart with all diligence; for out of it are the issues of life. ²⁴Put away from thee a froward mouth, and perverse lips put far from thee. ²⁵Let thine eyes look right on, and let thine eyelids look straight before thee. ²⁶Ponder the path of thy feet, and let all thy ways be established. ²⁷Turn not to the right hand nor to the left: remove thy foot from evil.

There will come a day when we will receive this crown of life and we will stand before the Throne so amazed and so grateful that we will throw it down at His feet. This act will not be one of scorn or disfavour, but one of incredible gratitude for all God has brought us through and all He had been to us and done for us.

> 1 Thessalonians 2:19 For what is our hope, or joy, or crown of rejoicing? Are not even ye in the presence of our Lord Jesus Christ at his coming?

> 2 Timothy 4:8 Henceforth there is laid up for me a crown of righteousness, which the Lord, the righteous judge, shall give me at that day: and not to me only, but unto all them also that love his appearing.

> Rev 3:11 Behold, I come quickly: hold that fast which thou hast, that no man take thy crown.

### Dressed for Eternity

We have reached the end of our discussion on ancient Jewish bridal attire, and it is interesting to see the threads that have woven their way along. The glory of God and the purity of heart present in the gold and silver have been present almost this entire journey. We cannot present the glory of God to the world if we are not pure of heart before Him. This means regularly examining ourselves before the Lord, and asking the Holy Spirit to reveal anything to us that needs cleansing, dealing with, etc, and then humbling ourselves to His hand and heart as He washes us clean by the Blood of the Lamb.

> Psalm 139:23-24  Search me, O God, and know my heart: try me, and know my thoughts: [24]And see if there be any wicked way in me, and lead me in the way everlasting.

> 1 Corinthians 11:27-32  Wherefore whosoever shall eat this bread, and drink this cup of the Lord, unworthily, shall be guilty of the body and blood of the Lord. [28]But let a man examine himself, and so let him eat of that bread, and drink of that cup. [29]For he that eateth and drinketh unworthily, eateth and drinketh damnation to himself, not discerning the Lord's body. [30]For this cause many are weak and sickly among you, and many sleep. [31]For if we would judge ourselves, we should not be judged. [32]But when we are judged, we are chastened of the Lord, that we should not be condemned with the world.

It behooves us as the Bride of Christ to look after the dowry God has given us, and to wear it boldly before a world that needs rescuing so that they too may receive this same amazing gift.

# Dressed for Eternity

**Food Fit for the Bride of Christ**

> Ezekiel 16:9-13  Then washed I thee with water; yea, I throughly washed away thy blood from thee, and I anointed thee with oil. [10]I clothed thee also with broidered work, and shod thee with badgers' skin, and I girded thee about with fine linen, and I covered thee with silk. [11]I decked thee also with ornaments, and I put bracelets upon thy hands, and a chain on thy neck. [12]And I put a jewel on thy forehead, and earrings in thine ears, and a beautiful crown upon thine head. [13]Thus wast thou decked with gold and silver; and thy raiment was of fine linen, and silk, and broidered work; thou didst eat fine flour, and honey, and oil: and thou wast exceeding beautiful, and thou didst prosper into a kingdom.

As seen above, we have covered all but the last three items in the list. Flour, honey, and oil don't fit well in clothing or jewellery, so we'll cover them separately in this section instead.

Researching these foods listed here was a fascinating trip through history and archaeology! Just like learning about the pre-dating of Egypt's silk imports, the research on honey also proved to be an eye-opener. So without further adieu, let us begin with Fine Flour.

## Fine Flour - Food fit for the Bride of Christ

When we think of flour in ancient times, images of mortars and pestles come to mind. Research into ancient peoples of the times when Ezekiel lived, reveal varying levels of technology that went into flour and bread making. Because it was so labour-intensive back then to create flour, most civilizations only made enough for that day's use, unless they were able to buy it from a baker who employed slaves or servants to make the flour for him. Due to this, most ground flour was coarse, and sometimes referred to in Scripture as "meal".

> 1 Kings 17:12 And she said, As the LORD thy God liveth, I have not a cake, but an handful of meal in a barrel, and a little oil in a cruse: and, behold, I am gathering two sticks, that I may go in and dress it for me and my son, that we may eat it, and die.

Fine flour then, was much more rare to come by, and typically expensive when found. In order to get fine flour, two things had to happen. First, the bran coat of the flour had to be removed, along with the wheat germ. Once that was done, the flour went through a much more rigorous grinding to produce fine white flour. Then as now, fine white flour produced a much nicer leavened loaf of bread. Yeast wasn't always used and to this day certain kinds of ancient Middle Eastern flat breads are now sold around the world. Pita bread is one example, Indian Naan is another. But the ancients did use yeast as well, typically known as leaven at that time.

# Food Fit for the Bride of Christ

## "The Staff of Life"

Whether "dark" or "white" bread, as the Romans used to call it, or "whole-wheat" or "white bread" as we call it now, bread has been termed "The Staff of Life". Throughout the ages, it has been, and continues to be, a staple food in most societies around the world. Even Scripture refers to bread at various times throughout its pages. The only reason people are starting to worry about bread in today's society, is the fact that technological advances now allow us to genetically modify our food. Wheat has been bred and spliced and enhanced over the years so many times that to find original grain is now referred to as either Legacy grain or Ancient grain. Enhancements that cause it to grow faster, resist pests and other dangers, increase the level of gluten higher than what was naturally found, etc., have resulted in people's intestinal systems rejecting it or reacting in an allergic manner to it. The "Staff of Life" has been broken, and there is now a scramble to maintain the needed grains in modern diets.

Such scientific and technological tampering had not happened yet when Scripture was written, and must be kept in mind when discussing Biblical references to the beneficial and sometimes opulent nature of flour and bread.

## What does this means for the Bride of Christ?

The reference to God giving Jerusalem fine flour to eat is yet another reference to the royalty and nobility granted to the Bride of Christ as heir to the Throne and Joint-Heir with Jesus Christ. Truly, as we examine these verses in Ezekiel, we see that God spared no expense to dress, bedeck, and provide nourishment for the chosen Bride of Christ.

But what should make every Christian stop and ponder with gratitude is just Who this fine flour is and from whence it comes.

## Dressed for Eternity

Our first reference to bread from heaven comes when God fed Manna to the Hebrew people as they travelled in the desert.

> Exodus 16:14-15 And when the dew that lay was gone up, behold, upon the face of the wilderness there lay a small round thing, as small as the hoar frost on the ground. [15]And when the children of Israel saw it, they said one to another, It is manna: for they wist not what it was. And Moses said unto them, This is the bread which the LORD hath given you to eat.

The very word for Manna means "What is it?" It was described as tasting like Coriander seed and sweet like honey. Then in the New Testament, we hear Christ telling His disciples:

> John 6:32-35 Then Jesus said unto them, Verily, verily, I say unto you, Moses gave you not that bread from heaven; but my Father giveth you the true bread from heaven. [33]For the bread of God is he which cometh down from heaven, and giveth life unto the world. [34]Then said they unto him, Lord, evermore give us this bread. [35]And Jesus said unto them, I am the bread of life: he that cometh to me shall never hunger; and he that believeth on me shall never thirst.

Later, as Christ engaged the disciples in a ritual they should have understood but completely missed, known as the betrothal ceremony, He once again referred to Himself in this manner:

> Luke 22:19 And he took bread, and gave thanks, and brake it, and gave unto them, saying, This is my body which is given for you: this do in remembrance of me.

They were blinded momentarily as to what this would mean, but in the hours to come, Christ would be betrayed, whipped, beaten, and hung on a cruel cross. This death on the Cross was necessary to pay the death penalty for sin, and through the shedding of His blood, to achieve the remission of sins for all mankind once and for all. The sacrificial system that had been set up at the time of Moses was now complete. Christ, the sacrificial Lamb of God, would be slain for the world. Of course three days later He rose again, conquering

**Food Fit for the Bride of Christ**

both sin and death, and offering eternal life to all who would come to Him seeking forgiveness. Those who would make Him Lord of their lives would become the Bride of Christ. In Matthew it says:

Matthew 4:1-4  Then was Jesus led up of the Spirit into the wilderness to be tempted of the devil. ²And when he had fasted forty days and forty nights, he was afterward an hungred. ³And when the tempter came to him, he said, If thou be the Son of God, command that these stones be made bread. ⁴But he answered and said, It is written, Man shall not live by bread alone, but by every word that proceedeth out of the mouth of God.

John 1:1-5  In the beginning was the Word, and the Word was with God, and the Word was God. ²The same was in the beginning with God. ³All things were made by him; and without him was not any thing made that was made. ⁴In him was life; and the life was the light of men. ⁵And the light shineth in darkness; and the darkness comprehended it not.

We know from John 1:1-5 that the Word is none other than Jesus Christ Himself, and that it was He who sustained the Israelites in the desert and it is He who sustains the life of the Christian now. We feast on His Words every time we open the pages of Scripture in daily personal devotions. Our soul and our spirit are given new energy and new stamina to continue to resist the wiles of the enemy and his continual attacks. There is a saying, "Seven days without prayer makes one weak". This is true because it is in communication with God that His Word is made alive to us in the Scriptures.

God has not given the Bride of Christ the coarse, dark flour of sin that eats away at her teeth and insides until she eternally dies. No, God has given the Bride of Christ fine flour to eat, the very best furnished for her at the very hands of Christ Himself.

## Honey - Food Fit for the Bride of Christ

Honey has been extolled and written about since records have ever been kept, the oldest of which come from ancient Egypt and ancient China. These records are not so much about the gathering of wild honey, but the care and keeping of the honey bees themselves. Wild honey was gathered as well, but it is an interesting discovery to learn that beekeeping is at least 5,000 years old in some places around the globe.

The composition, breakdown, and benefits of honey receive contradictory treatment depending on whom you go to for such information. There are those who say it is no different than sugar and a potential health hazard. There are those who say it is a complete food due to its amino acids, vitamin profile and complexity of its sugar content. However, there are more voices in scientific circles promoting the benefits of honey than those who aren't. It should be pointed out that pasteurization can remove the benefits otherwise available in raw honey. So it may be that the detractors are looking at pasteurized as opposed to unpasteurized honey in their assessments. These same people claim no difference to man-made syrups using similar sugar breakdowns in their composition. Once again, nothing beats what God created nature to manufacture on its own.

It is an interesting observation that then as now, honey in ancient times was both plentiful as it was costly. While it appears to have been available for the average middle-class on up to the wealthy, there is archaeological and historical evidence that not everyone had access to it, and it was called by at least one ancient poet, Homer, as "liquid gold".

# Food Fit for the Bride of Christ

## Honey's Apparent Historical Controversy

This observation then, of honey being gathered both in the wild and through the keeping of bees, would contradict or perhaps call into a question a relatively new assessment that when God called the land of Canaan, "a land flowing with milk and honey", that honey itself was not meant, but date syrup was meant instead. Now, it is highly possible that date syrup was indeed created from the dates that grow there, and it is possible that the people of that day may have given it the same label as real honey itself. But God is not One to confuse or betray His own people, nor lie to anyone that something is other than it is. To use the term "honey" was to use a term the Hebrews were already aware of having come from Egypt, and they'd know what to expect when the spies entered the land for the first time. There is no indication that the honey in Egypt was made by crushing dates, so the Hebrews would understand God's terminology to literally mean "honey", and not date syrup. This author has yet to dig up certifiable evidence of this apparently new claim about this phrase in Scripture. For the purposes of this discussion, we are using the literal definition of honey as it is prepared by and gathered from bees in their honey combs. Elsewhere in Scripture, King Saul's son is accused of eating honey from a honeycomb against his father's wishes, and references to honey and the honeycomb are made elsewhere in Scripture as well.

> 1 Samuel 14:27 But Jonathan heard not when his father charged the people with the oath: wherefore he put forth the end of the rod that was in his hand, and dipped it in an honeycomb, and put his hand to his mouth; and his eyes were enlightened.

## What does this mean for the Bride of Christ?

The sweetness, healing properties, and value of this naturally-created syrup known as honey down through the ages of time, carry a fair depth of meaning for the Bride of Christ. First off is the value; once again we see that God will spare nothing for to meet the needs of the joint-heir to the throne with His Son, Jesus Christ. She is nobility after all, having been grafted into the vine and as far as God is concerned, deserves nothing but the best.

**Dressed for Eternity**

Secondly, the healing properties of honey must be stressed. The Bride of Christ has been through much and has not always come out the other side unscathed. To the contrary, the Bride of Christ, both within and without, has been the subject of much pain, consequences of choices gone wrong, and attacks from inside and outside the church. She is in need of healing, of cleansing, and of restoring.

Lastly is the sweetness and general nutritional benefit of the honey. We are told in the Scriptures:

> Psalm 34:8 O taste and see that the LORD is good: blessed is the man that trusteth in him.

> Psalm 19:7-10 The law of the LORD is perfect, converting the soul: the testimony of the LORD is sure, making wise the simple. [8]The statutes of the LORD are right, rejoicing the heart: the commandment of the LORD is pure, enlightening the eyes. [9]The fear of the LORD is clean, enduring for ever: the judgments of the LORD are true and righteous altogether. [10]More to be desired are they than gold, yea, than much fine gold: sweeter also than honey and the honeycomb.

We are also told that to dwell on God's Word is sweet to the soul, and as we know, man cannot live on bread alone, but by every word that proceeds from the mouth of God.

> Psalm 119:103 How sweet are thy words unto my taste! yea, sweeter than honey to my mouth!

> Matthew 4:4 But he answered and said, It is written, Man shall not live by bread alone, but by every word that proceedeth out of the mouth of God.

# Dressed for Eternity

## Olive Oil - Food Fit for the Bride of Christ

Olive oil has a long, ancient, and rich history down through the millennia of time. Archaeological historians date the connection between olive oil and Israel to at least 1200 BC if not even as far back as 1400 BC for not only Israel, but the ancient Canaanites as well. Olive presses and storage vats have been uncovered all over the land of Israel, and most notably along the sea coast. By the time Ezekiel was prophet in Israel, the production of olive oil had become a national export to surrounding lands and entire villages had been built around the industry. However, the way Ezekiel mentions the oil in chapter 16 coincides with historical observations that such presses were not everywhere in Israel. Nor was the oil necessarily available to all classes of society, either due to lack of an olive press in the home, or lack of ability to buy the oil from other villages. It wouldn't be until after the Romans took over Israel that the plenteous nature of the oil would reach to every home no matter their class.

But in spite of whether or not the common Hebrew could access the oil or not, it was common to the nation of Israel and featured highly during festivals, ceremonies, and at the King's table. It is even listed among the "Species of Seven" as scholars have come to term the seven major crops that have existed in Israel from antiquity to present day.

## Characteristics

The olive tree itself is one that grows well in rocky, desolate, and often arid or drought-like conditions. To this day the Italians, now the ones famous for olive oil around the world, have sayings about this very ability.

**Food Fit for the Bride of Christ**

It is almost impossible to kill an olive tree by natural means as a result, and the oldest known olive tree in Israel is over 2200 years of age. The leaves of the olive branch have graced many garlands and diadems around the Middle East, being the leaf of choice for the Greeks when creating winners' crowns in their yearly celebrations. It was an olive branch that the dove brought back to Noah when God finally gave permission to rest the ark and disembark.

> Genesis 8:11 And the dove came in to him in the evening; and, lo, in her mouth was an olive leaf pluckt off: so Noah knew that the waters were abated from off the earth.

Consequently, the olive branch has come to mean peace and prosperity.

**What does this mean for the Bride of Christ?**

The symbolism here is deep. Offering olive oil to the Bride of Christ as part of her daily food suggests many things.

First, it says she has persevered. No matter what has been thrown at her, she has stood the test of time and flourished even under the harshest circumstances.

> Mark 13:12-13 Now the brother shall betray the brother to death, and the father the son; and children shall rise up against their parents, and shall cause them to be put to death. [13]And ye shall be hated of all men for my name's sake: but he that shall endure unto the end, the same shall be saved.

Governments and other religions down through time have tried to stamp out Christianity and Judaism wherever it's been found. But instead of wiping out those of the Faith in the One True God, the Church has gone underground and flourished. In fact, it was by such persecution that the Early Church spread out from Jerusalem into every corner of the Roman Empire. The church has gone through many changes, many iterations, and found itself struggling not merely with outside attacks but with internal divisions as well. Indeed, the Church has suffered much over the centuries, but it will remain, and Christ will be returning for those who have stood fast through it all.

## Dressed for Eternity

Second, the Bride of Christ is of the highest nobility, a royalty whose Provider owns the cattle on a thousand hills, and for whom nothing is lacking. She is given the best provision money both can and can't buy, by Her Lord and King, Jesus Christ.

Third, the Bride of Christ will live in peace and prosperity in her new life at the right hand of the Heavenly Bridegroom. Her earthly life may have been full of trials and struggles, but her eternal life is one of peace and abundance. This is not necessarily speaking of material abundance as some would have the reader to believe. But judging from the description of the New Jerusalem, it will one day appear to translate into that on the other side of time.

Fourth, just as olive oil has been used down through the centuries in hygiene, health, and medicinal uses, so God says that He will offer a balm in Gilead.

> Jeremiah 8:22 Is there no balm in Gilead; is there no physician there? why then is not the health of the daughter of my people recovered?

> 1 Samuel 16:13 Then Samuel took the horn of oil, and anointed him in the midst of his brethren: and the Spirit of the LORD came upon David from that day forward. So Samuel rose up, and went to Ramah.

Healing only comes from God, and oil is symbolically representative of the Holy Spirit. The Bride of Christ has access to the oil of the Spirit poured out on Pentecost. Christ gives the parable of the 10 virgins:

> Matthew 25:1-9 Then shall the kingdom of heaven be likened unto ten virgins, which took their lamps, and went forth to meet the bridegroom. ²And five of them were wise, and five were foolish. ³They that were foolish took their lamps, and took no oil with them: ⁴But the wise took oil in their vessels with their lamps. ⁵While the bridegroom tarried, they all slumbered and slept. ⁶And at midnight there was a cry made, Behold, the bridegroom cometh; go ye out to meet him. ⁷Then all those virgins arose, and trimmed their lamps. ⁸And the foolish said unto the wise, Give us of your oil; for our lamps are gone out.

## Food Fit for the Bride of Christ

⁹But the wise answered, saying, Not so; lest there be not enough for us and you: but go ye rather to them that sell, and buy for yourselves.

They are shut out from the feast because you cannot buy the Holy Spirit.

The call is going out. The Bridegroom is coming. But only those who have surrendered to the Lordship of the Holy Spirit in their lives and allowed Him to prune them and cleanse sin away from their lives will be able to enter into the Marriage supper of the Lamb.

This glance at oil concludes Ezekiel's list of food that God deems fit for the Bride of Christ - fine flour, honey, and oil. She does not feast on coarse dry meal, but dines on the Word of God brought to life by the Holy Spirit and meditated on to receive the sweet, filling and long-lasting revelation intended to bring nourishment, cleansing and healing to our lives.

# Dressed for Eternity

## The Great Clothing Exchange

> Isaiah 61:10-11  I will greatly rejoice in the LORD, my soul shall be joyful in my God; for he hath clothed me with the garments of salvation, he hath covered me with the robe of righteousness, as a bridegroom decketh himself with ornaments, and as a bride adorneth herself with her jewels. [11]For as the earth bringeth forth her bud, and as the garden causeth the things that are sown in it to spring forth; so the Lord GOD will cause righteousness and praise to spring forth before all the nations.

> Revelation 19:7-8  Let us be glad and rejoice, and give honour to him: for the marriage of the Lamb is come, and his wife hath made herself ready. [8]And to her was granted that she should be arrayed in fine linen, clean and white: for the fine linen is the righteousness of saints.

In the first four sections we travelled through history and archaeology as we delved into the various forms of adornment, what they were, what they were made of, what their properties were and how that applied to the Bride of Christ. A few times, reference was made to something called, "The Robe of Righteousness".

In these next two sections, we will leave the physical properties behind and focus instead on the spiritual clothing mentioned in Isaiah 61. There are two passages in this chapter that we will cover, the first being the passage above where it mentions this very Robe of Righteousness.

## Robe of Righteousness

The Robe of Righteousness is generally synonymous in Scripture with the garments of Salvation, so we will discuss them as one and the same thing here. The reason for this merger is due to the fact that one cannot accept Christ's gift of Salvation without receiving the Robe of Righteousness. God says that He cannot look on sin, but when we come to Him through Christ, God calls us sons and daughters and joint-heirs with Christ. It is only through the shed Blood of Christ that our sins are washed away and we become justified before God.

> Isaiah 59:1-2 Behold, the LORD'S hand is not shortened, that it cannot save; neither his ear heavy, that it cannot hear: *²But your iniquities have separated between you and your God, and your sins have hid his face from you, that he will not hear.*

> Psalm 51:7-10 Purge me with hyssop, and I shall be clean: wash me, and I shall be whiter than snow. ⁸Make me to hear joy and gladness; that the bones which thou hast broken may rejoice. *⁹Hide thy face from my sins, and blot out all mine iniquities.* ¹⁰Create in me a clean heart, O God; and renew a right spirit within me.

This impartation of righteousness begins way back in Genesis with Abraham when God took him outside the tent to look at the stars:

> Genesis 15:5-6 And he brought him forth abroad, and said, Look now toward heaven, and tell the stars, if thou be able to number them: and he said unto him, So shall thy seed be. *⁶And he believed in the LORD; and he counted it to him for righteousness.*

King Solomon, when asked of God what he would want for himself, had this to say about his father, King David:

> 1 Kings 3:6 And Solomon said, Thou hast shewed unto thy servant David my father great mercy, *according as he walked before thee in truth, and in*

## The Great Clothing Exchange

*righteousness, and in uprightness of heart with thee*; and thou hast kept for him this great kindness, that thou hast given him a son to sit on his throne, as it is this day.

King David wrote numerous psalms in the Book of Psalms, many including discussions about righteousness. A few of them are:

Psalm 4:1  To the chief Musician on Neginoth, A Psalm of David. Hear me when I call, *O God of my righteousness*: thou hast enlarged me when I was in distress; have mercy upon me, and hear my prayer.

Psalm 23:3  He restoreth my soul: he leadeth me in the paths of righteousness for his name's sake.

Psalm 24:3-6  Who shall ascend into the hill of the LORD? or who shall stand in his holy place? [4]He that hath clean hands, and a pure heart; who hath not lifted up his soul unto vanity, nor sworn deceitfully. *[5]He shall receive the blessing from the LORD, and righteousness from the God of his salvation.* [6]This is the generation of them that seek him, that seek thy face, O Jacob. Selah.

Psalm 103:17-18  But the mercy of the LORD is from everlasting to everlasting upon them that fear him, *and his righteousness unto children's children;* [18]*To such as keep his covenant, and to those that remember his commandments to do them.*

All italics in the verses above are mine due to the focus I wish for the reader to consider. Read those passages again as we move on to the prophet Isaiah:

Isaiah 45:24  Surely, shall one say, *in the LORD have I righteousness and strength*: even to him shall men come; and all that are incensed against him shall be ashamed.

# Dressed for Eternity

Isaiah 54:17 No weapon that is formed against thee shall prosper; and every tongue that shall rise against thee in judgment thou shalt condemn. *This is the heritage of the servants of the LORD, and their righteousness is of me, saith the LORD.*

By now it should be obvious that even in the times of the Old Testament under the Law, that God made it clear to various people that true righteousness was not something they could drum up on their own. It could only come from Him. There are far too many Scripture references to quote here displaying God's utter and complete disdain for those who attempted righteousness under their own strength. Some passages get quite sharp as God says such people will still die in their sins.

The reader might remember how in the discussion on the chains of the bridal headdress on page 109, that the Apostle Paul in Ephesians 6 wrote about the Breastplate of Righteousness, urging the believer to put this on.

Being a Pharisaical student of the Torah, and by extension the prophets as well under the leadership of the best teachers Judaism had to offer, Paul no doubt was making a direct reference to another passage in Isaiah:

Isaiah 59:17 For he put on righteousness as a breastplate, and an helmet of salvation upon his head; and he put on the garments of vengeance for clothing, and was clad with zeal as a cloke.

This passage is in the middle of a discourse where Isaiah prophesies God coming to Israel's rescue. Notice how Isaiah says that God Himself is dressed. It would stand to reason then, that if God Himself wears righteousness as a breastplate, then we who are called His sons and daughters should wear it too.

**Where do we get the Robe of Righteousness?**

As we move from references in the Old Testament to references in the New, let me begin with a quote from the book of Hebrews.

## The Great Clothing Exchange

Pay careful attention to this:

> Hebrews 7:1-4  For this Melchisedec, king of Salem, priest of the most high God, who met Abraham returning from the slaughter of the kings, and blessed him;  ²To whom also Abraham gave a tenth part of all; first being by interpretation *King of righteousness, and after that also King of Salem, which is, King of peace;*  ³Without father, without mother, without descent, having neither beginning of days, nor end of life; *but made like unto the Son of God;* abideth a priest continually.  ⁴Now consider how great this man was, unto whom even the patriarch Abraham gave the tenth of the spoils.

Truly of whom is this passage speaking? Let us carry on in this chapter:

> Hebrews 7:11-21  If therefore perfection were by the Levitical priesthood, (for under it the people received the law,) what further need was there that another priest should rise after the order of Melchisedec, and not be called after the order of Aaron?  ¹²For the priesthood being changed, there is made of necessity a change also of the law.  ¹³For he of whom these things are spoken pertaineth to another tribe, of which no man gave attendance at the altar.  ¹⁴For it is evident that our Lord sprang out of Juda; of which tribe Moses spake nothing concerning priesthood.  ¹⁵And it is yet far more evident: for that after the similitude of Melchisedec there ariseth another priest,  ¹⁶Who is made, not after the law of a carnal commandment, but after the power of an endless life.  ¹⁷For he testifieth, Thou art a priest for ever after the order of Melchisedec.  ¹⁸For there is verily a disannulling of the commandment going before for the weakness and unprofitableness thereof.  ¹⁹For the law made nothing perfect, but the bringing in of a better hope did; by the which we draw nigh unto God.  ²⁰And inasmuch as not without an oath he was made priest:  ²¹(For those priests were made without an oath; but this with an oath by him that said unto him, The Lord sware and will not repent, Thou art a priest for ever after the order of Melchisedec:)

We see in these passages, a life with no beginning and no end, without father or mother. Being as no human has ever been described this way, guess who built Jerusalem? We see God speaking again during the time of the Kings:

**Dressed for Eternity**

1 Kings 11:36   And unto his son will I give one tribe, that David my servant may have a light alway before me in Jerusalem, the city which I have chosen me to put my name there.

. . . And indeed God did put His name there!

Jerusalem is built on and around several hills.  One of God's names is "Shaddai". El Shaddai means God Almighty.  The letter Shin in the Hebrew alphabet contains three arms.  When I first found this back in the early 2000's, it was a sketch only, so I went looking for a topographical map of Jerusalem, and then darkened the valleys.  This is what resulted on the next page: (see darkened green areas)

# The Great Clothing Exchange

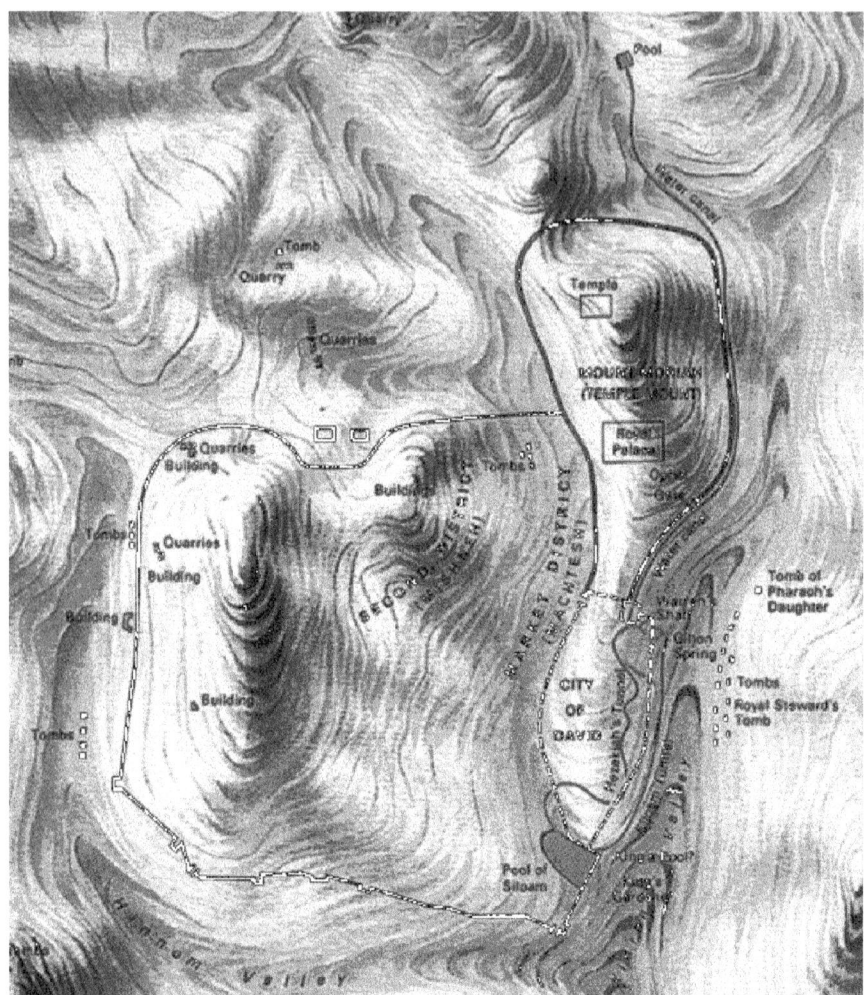

Now if you were to hold up three fingers as in counting three to a friend, and hold two fingers closer to the right, you'd end up with a similar appearance to the darkened green areas of this image. A blog author wrote about this again in 2010, and not only does she point out the above imagery on her blog, but she points out the side profile of the human heart, and how the letter Shin can be seen there as well. (a link to her discussion is in the appendix)

How does all this tie into our discussion about righteousness? The very first King of Righteousness; the builder of this eternal city; the Priest-King without mother or father and with no beginning and no end; while known to mankind at the time as Melchisedec, is none other than Jesus Christ Himself – King of

Kings, and Lord of Lords, our Heavenly High Priest and Bridegroom to the Church! Only the King of Righteousness can impart righteousness to those who would accept His gift of Salvation. Only God commanded that tithes be brought into the storehouse.

> Malachi 3:8  Will a man rob God? Yet ye have robbed me. But ye say, Wherein have we robbed thee? In tithes and offerings.

> Malachi 3:10  Bring ye all the tithes into the storehouse, that there may be meat in mine house, and prove me now herewith, saith the LORD of hosts, if I will not open you the windows of heaven, and pour you out a blessing, that there shall not be room enough to receive it.

Peter continues the dialogue as follows:

> 1 Peter 2:24-25  Who his own self bare our sins in his own body on the tree, *that we, being dead to sins, should live unto righteousness: by whose stripes ye were healed.* ²⁵For ye were as sheep going astray; but are now returned unto the Shepherd and Bishop of your souls.

Notice my italics again. Whose stripes are being spoken of here? The prophet Isaiah spoke of this person in Isaiah 53. Jesus told His disciples this would happen at the Last Supper, and indeed when the time came for His ultimate sacrifice for the sins of mankind, the whips came out just as prophesied so long ago.

Indeed it is Christ that imparts this Robe of Righteousness to all who believe, to all who call upon His name. There is nothing we can do to earn it, as Paul's dissertation in Romans will point out, but there is much we can do to look after it.

**Maintenance and Care of the Robe of Righteousness:**

This Robe of Righteousness requires care and attention to keep it looking its best. James puts it this way:

## The Great Clothing Exchange

James 1:27 Pure religion and undefiled before God and the Father is this, To visit the fatherless and widows in their affliction, and to keep himself unspotted from the world.

Paul says

1 Corinthians 10:11-15 Now all these things happened unto them for ensamples: and they are written for our admonition, upon whom the ends of the world are come. [12]Wherefore let him that thinketh he standeth take heed lest he fall. [13]There hath no temptation taken you but such as is common to man: but God is faithful, who will not suffer you to be tempted above that ye are able; but will with the temptation also make a way to escape, that ye may be able to bear it. [14]Wherefore, my dearly beloved, flee from idolatry. [15]I speak as to wise men; judge ye what I say.

Galatians 6:1-4 Brethren, if a man be overtaken in a fault, ye which are spiritual, restore such an one in the spirit of meekness; considering thyself, lest thou also be tempted. [2]Bear ye one another's burdens, and so fulfil the law of Christ. [3]For if a man think himself to be something, when he is nothing, he deceiveth himself. [4]But let every man prove his own work, and then shall he have rejoicing in himself alone, and not in another.

King David wrote in Psalm 119:

Psalm 119:9 BETH. Wherewithal shall a young man cleanse his way? by taking heed thereto according to thy word.

The word righteous simply means "right living". Right living according to God's Word is living life in a manner pleasing to Him. Christ said:

John 14:15 If ye love me, keep my commandments.

# Dressed for Eternity

It's one thing to be given the Robe of Righteousness, but it is another to maintain it through how we choose to live our everyday lives. God's Word tells us to take care that we do not fall back into sin. We are told to be ambassadors to the world, but we are told not to entangle ourselves with the world again.

> Galatians 5:1  Stand fast therefore in the liberty wherewith Christ hath made us free, and be not entangled again with the yoke of bondage.

I would encourage the reader to take a moment to read the entire second chapter of Peter 2. Eventually Peter brings us to this particular thought:

> 2 Peter 2:20  For if after they have escaped the pollutions of the world through the knowledge of the Lord and Saviour Jesus Christ, they are again entangled therein, and overcome, the latter end is worse with them than the beginning.

The discussion in 2 Peter chapter 2 actually discusses the problem of false teachers entering the Church and leading people astray. In this train of thought then, it is not merely the world and its sinful ways that we must resist the temptation to be like, but we must also make sure to know God's Word inside and out so that we are not led astray by false teachers as well.

Proverbs, that very practical book all about learning to live a righteous life, has this to say:

> Proverbs 4:18-27  But the path of the just is as the shining light, that shineth more and more unto the perfect day. $^{19}$The way of the wicked is as darkness: they know not at what they stumble. $^{20}$My son, attend to my words; incline thine ear unto my sayings. $^{21}$Let them not depart from thine eyes; keep them in the midst of thine heart. $^{22}$For they are life unto those that find them, and health to all their flesh. $^{23}$Keep thy heart with all diligence; for out of it are the issues of life. $^{24}$Put away from thee a froward mouth, and perverse lips put far from thee. $^{25}$Let thine eyes look right on, and let thine eyelids look straight before thee. $^{26}$Ponder the path of thy feet, and let all thy ways be established. $^{27}$Turn not to the right hand nor to the left: remove thy foot from evil.

## The Great Clothing Exchange

Almost the entire book of Romans and the General Electric Power Company (Galatians, Ephesians, Philippians, and Colossians) echo these same sentiments. For as King David observed in Psalm 119, the more we spend time in God's Word, the less likely we are to engage the sinful nature and walk the ways of the world.

Paul says in Galatians that if we walk in the Spirit, we will not fulfill the lusts of the flesh.

From time to time this robe needs washing, and again the Apostle Paul comes to the rescue with the best laundry soap this side of Heaven:

> Romans 12:1-2  I beseech you therefore, brethren, by the mercies of God, that ye present your bodies a living sacrifice, holy, acceptable unto God, which is your reasonable service.  ²And be not conformed to this world: but be ye transformed by the renewing of your mind, that ye may prove what is that good, and acceptable, and perfect, will of God.

We are to live out, or work out as Paul puts it, the salvation God has given us.

> Philippians 2:12-16  Wherefore, my beloved, as ye have always obeyed, not as in my presence only, but now much more in my absence, work out your own salvation with fear and trembling.  ¹³For it is God which worketh in you both to will and to do of his good pleasure.  ¹⁴Do all things without murmurings and disputings:  ¹⁵That ye may be blameless and harmless, the sons of God, without rebuke, in the midst of a crooked and perverse nation, among whom ye shine as lights in the world;  ¹⁶Holding forth the word of life; that I may rejoice in the day of Christ, that I have not run in vain, neither laboured in vain.

There are two notes in this passage that such a discussion on righteousness would be completely remiss not to bring up.

The first is that this working out, this putting into practise, is done with a level of understanding that failure to do so could have disastrous effects on our lives in eternity.  As we are told in Ephesians (Ephesians 2:8-9  For by grace are ye saved through faith; and that not of yourselves: it is the gift of God: ⁹Not of works, lest any man should boast.), we can't earn our salvation. We do not work to earn it. We work to put it into practise in our daily lives as we come into contact with those of the world.

The second is that this working out is not to be of our own effort, but God working through us. Notice I didn't say for us, I said through us. We must submit to God's efforts in our lives to make us into the Bride He longs for us to be. But if we are gallivanting around worldly haunts and getting spots of sin dotting our precious garments, we become as those in 2 Peter Chapter 2 who were led away.

Notice how the remainder of that passage echoes the passage shared from Proverbs. God doesn't change and nor do His expectations of how His people are to behave. Even King David understood that the only way He'd meet these expectations was to a) spend time in God's Word and b) keep a clean slate before Him.

So we see that maintenance of our Robes of Righteousness require alertness, choices, spending time in God's Word, and through submission to the Holy Spirit, working out what we read in God's Word as both the outworking of the Salvation God has given us, and the display of our love for Him.

## Beauty for Ashes

> Isaiah 61:1-3  The Spirit of the Lord GOD is upon me; because the LORD hath anointed me to preach good tidings unto the meek; he hath sent me to bind up the brokenhearted, to proclaim liberty to the captives, and the opening of the prison to them that are bound;  ²To proclaim the acceptable year of the LORD, and the day of vengeance of our God; to comfort all that mourn;  ³To appoint unto them that mourn in Zion, *to give unto them beauty for ashes*, the oil of joy for mourning, the garment of praise for the spirit of heaviness; that they might be called trees of righteousness, the planting of the LORD, that he might be glorified.

Earlier in Isaiah 61, we come to the passage that Christ read in the Synagogue on the day He officially began His ministry.  Christ stopped reading in verse 2, but the passage carries on.  Our next few discussions will focus on verse 3 above.  In some cases, we will return to a similar format to the first two sections of this book so that we get a deeper, practical understanding of what is being shared here.

Let us begin with our focus on the italicized phrase above, "Beauty for ashes".

## From Scripture:

Ashes are mentioned in Scripture only 43 times.  Some are mentioned in judgements of cities such as:

> 2 Peter 2:6  And turning the cities of Sodom and Gomorrha into ashes condemned them with an overthrow, making them an ensample unto those that after should live ungodly;

## The Great Clothing Exchange

But the vast majority mentions ashes as a display of either great contrition, great sadness, or great mourning. Tamar mourned the loss of her virginity. Esther's uncle mourned the decree by Haman and all the Jews of Persia followed suit:

> Esther 4:3   And in every province, whithersoever the king's commandment and his decree came, there was great mourning among the Jews, and fasting, and weeping, and wailing; and many lay in sackcloth and ashes.

In one of David's psalms, he expresses his emotions this way:

> Psalm 102:9  For I have eaten ashes like bread, and mingled my drink with weeping,

The prophet Daniel, after reading the book of Jeremiah, found himself in deep contrition:

> Daniel 9:3-5  And I set my face unto the Lord God, to seek by prayer and supplications, with fasting, and sackcloth, and ashes:  ⁴And I prayed unto the LORD my God, and made my confession, and said, O Lord, the great and dreadful God, keeping the covenant and mercy to them that love him, and to them that keep his commandments;  ⁵We have sinned, and have committed iniquity, and have done wickedly, and have rebelled, even by departing from thy precepts and from thy judgments:

## Sackcloth pairing:

The reference in Isaiah could be said by some to be a shortened version of the phrase "sackcloth and ashes", but invariably, anywhere in Scripture where sackcloth is donned, ashes are very close by.

The wearing of sackcloth also denoted sorrow, contrition or mourning. Easton's Bible Dictionary says this:
Sackcloth
  Cloth made of black goats' hair, coarse, rough, and thick, used for sacks,

## Dressed for Eternity

and also worn by mourners (Gen_37:34; Gen_42:25; 2Sa_3:31; Est_4:1, Est_4:2; Psa_30:11, etc.), and as a sign of repentance (Mat_11:21). It was put upon animals by the people of Nineveh (Jon_3:8).

**What is Sackcloth?**

Apparently an entire industry built up around this concept of wearing a piece of irritating cloth close to the skin as a form of penitence, sorrow or mourning, and the cloth was actually given a name after the city in Turkey where this industry is said to have originated. An article of clothing made of coarse hair or other irritations is said to be a Cilice, after Cilicia in Asia Minor under Roman rule. (see link in appendix)

According to some sources, this garment's rough, coarse, and generally itchy nature wasn't enough to prove the wearer's intent, and some manufacturers would insert bits of wire or twigs to make it even more uncomfortable. Monks were known to wear it often, and it became a tradition in the Catholic church right up to present day, supposedly being in use by devout Catholics to a wider degree than the common man would believe.

So by the time Isaiah mentions ashes in chapter 61, the connotation is clearly that of mourning, of sadness and possibly even that of self-defacing according to such usage occasionally engaged in earlier in Biblical times.

**Sackcloth and Ashes Replaced:**

But God says He will replace the ashes with beauty. What kind of beauty is He talking about?! If we consider ashes to be at one end of the spectrum, with all its weeping, sorrow, sadness, contrition and mourning, then beauty is at the other end of the spectrum. God gives us glimpses as to what this beauty is:

> 1 Peter 3:3-4 Whose adorning let it not be that outward adorning of plaiting the hair, and of wearing of gold, or of putting on of apparel; *⁴But let it be the hidden man of the heart, in that which is not corruptible*, even the ornament of a meek and quiet spirit, which is in the sight of God of great price.

## The Great Clothing Exchange

Proverbs 1:8-9 *My son, hear the instruction of thy father, and forsake not the law of thy mother:* ⁹For they shall be an ornament of grace unto thy head, and chains about thy neck.

Proverbs 3:3-4 *Let not mercy and truth forsake thee:* bind them about thy neck; write them upon the table of thine heart: ⁴So shalt thou find favour and good understanding in the sight of God and man.

Proverbs 3:21-24 My son, let not them depart from thine eyes: *keep sound wisdom and discretion:* ²²*So shall they be life unto thy soul, and grace to thy neck.* ²³Then shalt thou walk in thy way safely, and thy foot shall not stumble. ²⁴When thou liest down, thou shalt not be afraid: yea, thou shalt lie down, and thy sleep shall be sweet.

Proverbs 4:7-9 *Wisdom is the principal thing; therefore get wisdom: and with all thy getting get understanding.* ⁸Exalt her, and she shall promote thee: she shall bring thee to honour, when thou dost embrace her. ⁹She shall give to thine head an ornament of grace: a crown of glory shall she deliver to thee.

Proverbs 6:20-22 *My son, keep thy father's commandment, and forsake not the law of thy mother:* ²¹*Bind them continually upon thine heart, and tie them about thy neck.* ²²When thou goest, it shall lead thee; when thou sleepest, it shall keep thee; and when thou awakest, it shall talk with thee.

Proverbs 25:11-12 A word fitly spoken is like apples of gold in pictures of silver. ¹²*As an earring of gold, and an ornament of fine gold, so is a wise reprover upon an obedient ear.*
1 Chronicles 16:29 Give unto the LORD the glory due unto his name: bring an offering, and come before him: *worship the LORD in the beauty of holiness.*

Psalm 90:14-17 O satisfy us early with thy mercy; that we may rejoice and be glad all our days. ¹⁵Make us glad according to the days wherein thou hast afflicted us, and the years wherein we have seen evil. ¹⁶Let thy work appear unto thy servants, and thy glory unto their children. ¹⁷*And let the* *beauty of the LORD our God be upon us*: and establish thou the work of our hands upon us; yea, the work of our hands establish thou it.

Proverbs 31:30  Favour is deceitful, and beauty is vain: *but a woman that feareth the LORD, she shall be praised.*

Hosea 14:5-7  I will be as the dew unto Israel: he shall grow as the lily, and cast forth his roots as Lebanon.  ⁶His branches shall spread, and his beauty shall be as the olive tree, and his smell as Lebanon.  ⁷They that dwell under his shadow shall return; they shall revive as the corn, and grow as the vine: the scent thereof shall be as the wine of Lebanon.

Notice again the italicized words.  Those are mine for emphasis.

From these verses, and there very well could be more, we see the following thoughts God has regarding what beauty is to Him.

- A meek and quiet spirit is an ornament adorning the inner man, an ornament of great worth to God.  There are 31 references to meekness being a trait among God's people.  The vast majority of these references come with realities those who are meek will partake of:

    - The meek shall eat and be satisfied (Psalm 22:26)
    - The meek shall be guided in judgement (Psalm 25:9)
    - The meek shall be taught God's ways (Psalm 25:9)
    - The meek shall inherit the earth (Psalm 76:9, Matthew 5:5)
    - The meek shall delight in the abundance of peace (Psalm 37:11)
    - The meek shall be lifted up (Psalm 147:6)
    - The meek shall be beautified with salvation (Psalm 149:4)
    - The meek shall increase their joy in the Lord (Isaiah 29:19)

Meekness is described as great power under great control.  Jesus was meek, but unlike the world's definition of meekness, He was anything but weak!  A few more points about meekness:

## The Great Clothing Exchange

- ○ It is a fruit of the Spirit (Galatians 5:23)
- ○ It is proof of being a child of God (Colossians 3:12, James 1:21, James 3:13)
- ○ It is paired with gentleness, humility, wisdom and quietness of spirit (Ephesians 4:2, Colossians 3:12, Titus 3:2, 1 Peter 3:4)

There is so much more that could be discussed here regarding this ornament of the inner man known as a meek and quiet spirit, particularly in the last sub-point given above. Suffice to say that this is a trait that is not natural to much of the human race! In order to don this particular ornament of beauty, one needs to humble his/herself before God, submit to the Holy Spirit, and allow this fruit of the Spirit to be lived out through them.

- Listening to parental instruction is considered an ornament of grace to one's head and chains around their neck. Scripture has much to say on this one as well. Obedience and respect for one's parents is mentioned as a command very early in the Scriptures:
  - ○ Exodus 20:12 Honour thy father and thy mother: that thy days may be long upon the land which the LORD thy God giveth thee.

This is the first commandment with a promise attached to it, which shows just how important this is to God.

- ○ Leviticus 19:3 Ye shall fear every man his mother, and his father, and keep my sabbaths: I am the LORD your God.

This reference begins immediately after God telling the Hebrew people to be holy as He is holy. We will discuss more about holiness in a bit here, but it is interesting that God begins His explanatory list with this command to respect and honour one's parents.

But how is respect for one's parents an ornament of grace? Grace has various definitions, only one of which is the commonly espoused concept of granting others what they do not deserve. If we left it at this, then saying that obedience and respect for one's parents as an ornament of grace would be claiming parents do not deserve it but children are to give it anyway. While this is true in some cases where parents have fallen short in their responsibilities before God to their children, this is not the case for all parents.

Another definition of grace is "to honour or favour". In this definition, obedience and respect of one's parents causes God to honour and favour that person with long life.

- Sound wisdom and discretion, as opposed to worldly wisdom, are considered grace to one's neck, a crown of glory. Both the longest and shortest paragraph that could be written about wisdom and discretion is to read the entire book of Proverbs! The contrasts between worldly and sound wisdom occur on practically every page several times and then some. Once again we see God choosing to honour the person who adheres to and acts on sound wisdom. God goes so far as to refer to it as a crown of glory.

The concept of wisdom being of a glorious nature is reflected in comments God makes in Proverbs about the hoary head:

Proverbs 16:31 The hoary head is a crown of glory, if it be found in the way of righteousness.

Various places in Scripture pair glory with wise decision-making. This requires use of the grey-matter God has given each and every one of us. We have to think to process what is right from wrong, best from worst, pleasing and displeasing, honouring and dishonouring, and then act on that knowledge appropriately, which leads us to the next item in this partial list of what God thinks is beautiful.

- A wise reprover to a listening, obedient ear is an earring of gold. This is already discussed in the discussion on earrings on page 119. But two people are required for this particular ornament to appear.
    - The first person is the wise reprover. Both Jesus and Paul explain how to approach someone caught in sin to restore them.

## The Great Clothing Exchange

Galatians 6:1-2 Brethren, if a man be overtaken in a fault, ye which are spiritual, restore such an one in the spirit of meekness; considering thyself, lest thou also be tempted. ²Bear ye one another's burdens, and so fulfil the law of Christ.

Matthew 18:15-17 Moreover if thy brother shall trespass against thee, go and tell him his fault between thee and him alone: if he shall hear thee, thou hast gained thy brother. ¹⁶But if he will not hear thee, then take with thee one or two more, that in the mouth of two or three witnesses every word may be established. ¹⁷And if he shall neglect to hear them, tell it unto the church: but if he neglect to hear the church, let him be unto thee as an heathen man and a publican.

- o The second person is the obedient ear. It's all well and good for the wise person who sees a problem to come and carefully point it out to the person in the hopes they will be restored to right-living before God again. But if that person is not willing to listen and obey, the reproof is as if it fell on the ears of a fool according to Proverbs.

Proverbs 9:8 Reprove not a scorner, lest he hate thee: rebuke a wise man, and he will love thee.

This is why both he that reproves wisely and he that listens and obeys such reproof is an earring of gold.

- Holiness is considered beautiful to God. Now here is a subject that has filled entire volumes over the centuries as people have sought to understand what it means to be holy before God. The basic definition of "holy" is simply, "set apart". God is set apart from sin and longs for His people to be set apart from sin also. In varying ways God has said:

1 Peter 1:15-16 But as he which hath called you is holy, so be ye holy in all manner of conversation; 16 Because it is written, Be ye holy; for I am holy.

Sin is a black, sickening blot to God.

> Habakkuk 1:12-13  Art thou not from everlasting, O LORD my God, mine Holy One? we shall not die. O LORD, thou hast ordained them for judgment; and, O mighty God, thou hast established them for correction. [13]Thou art of purer eyes than to behold evil, and canst not look on iniquity: wherefore lookest thou upon them that deal treacherously, and holdest thy tongue when the wicked devoureth the man that is more righteous than he?

Now we know the answer to this question is due to God's wrath being far more patient than ours, but that the judgement of the wicked will indeed come. It is because God cannot look upon sin that we are only able to stand before Him dressed in Christ's Robe of Righteousness.  But as pointed out already, that robe can become stained, spotted and torn by choices we make to deliberately entertain sin.  See the earlier discussion on the Robe of Righteousness on page 147.

Holiness has been misconstrued as a list of do's and don'ts by the modern church.  In reality, God spells out two ways of being holy.  There is the list of commands under the Old Testament law, and then there are the two commands given by Christ in Matthew.

> Matthew 22:36-40  Master, which is the great commandment in the law? [37]Jesus said unto him, Thou shalt love the Lord thy God with all thy heart, and with all thy soul, and with all thy mind.  [38]This is the first and great commandment.  [39]And the second is like unto it, Thou shalt love thy neighbour as thyself.  [40]On these two commandments hang all the law and the prophets.

When we wholeheartedly engage in these two commandments, all the holiness commandments of the Old Testament are merely common sense.  But when we choose to attempt holiness apart from an intimate, loving relationship with God, then any commandment is a chore, holiness or otherwise.

## The Great Clothing Exchange

Holiness pleases God more than anything else, because it is a complete separation from the ways of sin that have doomed unregenerate man to an eternity in hell.

- God's own beauty is in His holiness and in His glory. The Scriptures tell us that the beauty we see in God is precisely because of His separation from the world. There is something attractive about something clean and pure, and God is all that and more.

- Beauty is likened to the olive tree. For this author, this will be the third time in a single week where God has brought the olive tree to mind. The first was in research for oil in the discussion on food fit for the Bride of Christ on page 141. The second was at mid-week study when God pointed out to me that the tree in Psalm 1 is patterned after the olive tree in its nature. Now here we are in this list of how God defines beauty, and we see the olive tree again.

The olive tree grows where no other tree will grow. It seems to prefer the wild, dry, rocky places and yet somehow stays green all year round. For a deciduous, that's quite a feat! Its fruit, the olive, has been furnishing the Hebrew people with oil ever since they entered the land of Canaan after fleeing Egypt, and is both an import and an export in modern-day Israel. See the discussion on oil on page 141 for more information, and see the links in the appendix to learn more about this amazing tree.

- God feels a woman more concerned with reverence for God than outward appearance is to be praised.

Lastly, for the sake of this discussion, we come to how God views the beauty of a woman. The woman who concerns herself more with the ways and reverence of God than how others view her outward appearance, is a woman God honours.

> Proverbs 31:30 Favour is deceitful, and beauty is vain: but a woman that feareth the LORD, she shall be praised.

## Dressed for Eternity

In today's modern society, men seem to put as much effort into outward appearances as women do. So it behooves the church, made up of both men and women, to recognize that God is more enamoured with their mind and heart, than with their outward attempts at impressing people. We will discuss more about this point at the end of the book in a section devoted solely to modesty.

## Oil of Joy

> Isaiah 61:1-3  The Spirit of the Lord GOD is upon me; because the LORD hath anointed me to preach good tidings unto the meek; he hath sent me to bind up the brokenhearted, to proclaim liberty to the captives, and the opening of the prison to them that are bound; ²To proclaim the acceptable year of the LORD, and the day of vengeance of our God; to comfort all that mourn; ³To appoint unto them that mourn in Zion, to give unto them beauty for ashes, *the oil of joy for mourning*, the garment of praise for the spirit of heaviness; that they might be called trees of righteousness, the planting of the LORD, that he might be glorified.

Second in this list of replaced adornment, is the Oil of Joy for mourning. See my italics above.

## The Holy Spirit's reference in anointing:

The Holy Spirit has been described in the New Testament, as the oil of anointing. We see this first mentioned when Jesus was baptized in the Jordan.

> Matthew 3:13-17  Then cometh Jesus from Galilee to Jordan unto John, to be baptized of him. ¹⁴But John forbade him, saying, I have need to be baptized of thee, and comest thou to me?  ¹⁵And Jesus answering said unto him, Suffer it to be so now: for thus it becometh us to fulfil all righteousness. Then he suffered him. ¹⁶And Jesus, when he was baptized, went up straightway out of the water: and, lo, the heavens were opened unto him, a*nd he saw the Spirit of God descending like a dove, and lighting upon him*.  ¹⁷And lo a voice from heaven, saying, This is my beloved Son, in whom I am well pleased.

> Acts 10:37-38  That word, I say, ye know, which was published throughout all Judaea, and began from Galilee, after the baptism which John preached;  ³⁸How *God anointed Jesus of Nazareth with the Holy Ghost* and with power: who went about doing good, and healing all that were oppressed of the devil; for God was with him.

## The Great Clothing Exchange

Later we see Christ quoting from the very passage in Isaiah:

> Luke 4:18-21 *The Spirit of the Lord is upon me*, because *he hath anointed me to preach the gospel to the poor;* he hath sent me to heal the brokenhearted, to preach deliverance to the captives, and recovering of sight to the blind, to set at liberty them that are bruised, [19]To preach the acceptable year of the Lord. [20]And he closed the book, and he gave it again to the minister, and sat down. And the eyes of all them that were in the synagogue were fastened on him. [21]And he began to say unto them, This day is this scripture fulfilled in your ears.

## The Anointing Oil of the Tabernacle:

This concept of the Holy Spirit as an anointing oil began back in the desert when God told Moses to make special oil for the anointing of the priests and Tabernacle implements:

> Exodus 30:22-25 Moreover the LORD spake unto Moses, saying, [23]Take thou also unto thee principal spices, of pure myrrh five hundred shekels, and of sweet cinnamon half so much, even two hundred and fifty shekels, and of sweet calamus two hundred and fifty shekels, [24]And of cassia five hundred shekels, after the shekel of the sanctuary, and of oil olive an hin: [25]And thou shalt make it an oil of holy ointment, an ointment compound after the art of the apothecary: it shall be an holy anointing oil.

The quoted passage above gives us a brief but detailed look at the anointing oil that was used in Tabernacle priestly service. As anointing oil is mentioned in Isaiah 61 as one of God's replacements in adornment for the Bride of Christ, we will spend some time now discussing its make up, its usage, and what that means for the Bride of Christ.

The first thing to note about the above passage, are the ingredients. The very first list of anointing oil ingredients included the following:

Myrrh, cinnamon, calamus, cassia, and olive oil.

### Dressed for Eternity

As in previous pieces of research, the spices that God requested of Moses for the purpose of making this anointing oil had to come from somewhere. That somewhere was Egypt.

## Make-up and Characteristics

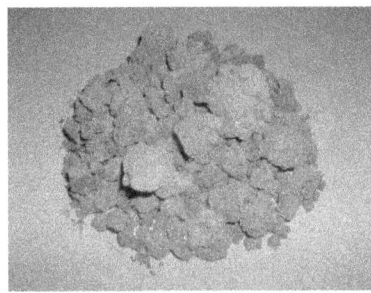

**Myrrh** not only has a sweet smell and bitter taste, but it has medicinal properties as well. According to sources cited by Wikipedia, Myrrh has made it into various medical practises down through the years. Research has revealed that Myrrh has assisted with glucose intolerance, acted as an analgesic for pain, been known in Egypt to treat oral parasitic ailments, lower bad cholesterol, increase good cholesterol, and inhibit some forms of cancer growth. It is no wonder this spice has made it into not only Middle Eastern pharmaceutical practises, but Far Eastern and Western medical practises as well.

**Cinnamon** has a long and ancient history both in harvesting and usage as well as in confusion with another ingredient in our list, Cassia. True Cinnamon, as the variant from the tree Cinnamomum Verum is known, is what was referred to as the correct Cinnamon in the recipe God gave to Moses. Cinnamon was being imported by Egypt according to known records, as far back as 2000 BC, long before Jacob took his family to Egypt under Joseph's watchful gaze. It is highly likely that Egypt's traders imported it from India. According to ancient historical records, Cinnamon was a pricey spice, fetching a pretty denari in Rome at the time of Pliny.

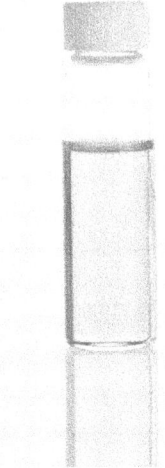

The medicinal uses of cinnamon are ancient and long, but not unfounded. Research has verified many of the health-related claims of

### The Great Clothing Exchange

the spice and proposed that many others are possible. One common usage today is to mix one 1/4 teaspoon of cinnamon with 1 tablespoon of unpasteurized honey to produce a compound that when swallowed, aids in curing the common cold. Other research has found some variants of cinnamon to help with HIV-1, herpes, diabetes, some colon issues, and more.

**Calamus** comes from a reed or rush-like plant and has apparently gone by a wide variety of names, including myrtle grass or sweet cinnamon. It is said that calamus has been known to satisfactorily replace cinnamon in baking. Unlike cinnamon, it is said to have a sweet as opposed to sharp scent. According to a papyrus note that was found, Calamus was imported into Egypt as early as the 1300's BC. Considering the proposed dates of the Exodus, if this dating is accurate, then Egypt may have only begun trading in calamus just years before the Hebrew nation up and fled.

According to this same papyrus, it wasn't listed as having too many medicinal uses, but was apparently included in a mix of spices in a wrap aimed at aiding stomach ailments. It was more widely used in far eastern medicines than middle eastern. To that end, this spice addition to the anointing oil may have purely been for its scent.

**Cassia,** as already noted, has occasionally been confused with cinnamon, largely because it comes from the cinnamon family of plants. According to sources quoted on Wikipedia, this is the "version" of cinnamon sold in North America, (this author had to check her package of "organic cinnamon". It was Cassia) while the "true cinnamon" discussed earlier is sold in the Middle East and beyond. The cassia spoken of in our text comes from the Cinnamomum Iners plant typically grown in the Arabian area and Ethiopia. Again, this lends itself to trade with the Egyptian people. Not much is known about its medicinal benefits other than that it is similar to cinnamon in that regard.

**Dressed for Eternity**

Research keeps pointing to cassia coming out of the Far East and possibly as close as India. So the only way Egyptians would have had access was via traders.

**Olive oil** has already been given a decent description over on page 141. So I welcome the reader to flip there to learn more about olive oil.

**Recipe for Anointing Oil**

What is interesting about the recipe, is that the measurements used were according to the weight of a coin that has been found by archaeologists. This has allowed for a modern translation of the recipe as follows:

To quote Wikipedia (see source in appendix):

- Pure Myrrh ( מר דרור  mar deror) 500 shekels (about 6 kg)
- Sweet Cinnamon ( קינמון בשם  kinnemon besem) 250 shekels (about 3 kg)
- Sweet Calamus ( קְנֵה שָׂ -ם  kaneh bosm) 250 shekels (about 3 kg)
- Cassia ( קדה  kiddah) 500 shekels (about 6 kg)
- Olive oil ( שמן זית  shemen sayith) one hin (about 5 quarts according to Adam Clarke; about 4 liters according to Shiurei Torah, 7 liters according to the Chazon Ish)

See the link in the appendix for further links ascribing the details above.

This transcribing from the shekel weight to modern kilograms allows for the modern recreation of this oil today.

The combination of these spices would have created a very sweet/spicy scent as it was suspended in the olive oil, very much like that of a perfume oil when all was said and done.

# The Great Clothing Exchange

## What does this mean for the Bride of Christ?

The anointing oil represents the Holy Spirit's desire to bring healing, joy, and power to the life of the believer and to present the Bride as a sweet smelling savour before the Lord.

## Myrrh

Myrrh represents the bitterness of the suffering we are called to endure just as Christ suffered.

> Ephesians 5:1-2  Be ye therefore followers of God, as dear children; [2]And walk in love, as Christ also hath loved us, and hath given himself for us an offering and a sacrifice to God for a sweetsmelling savour.

Christ taught that anyone who is not willing to count the cost of their faith, isn't worthy of following Him:

> Matthew 10:37-39  He that loveth father or mother more than me is not worthy of me: and he that loveth son or daughter more than me is not worthy of me. [38]And he that taketh not his cross, and followeth after me, is not worthy of me. [39]He that findeth his life shall lose it: and he that loseth his life for my sake shall find it.

> Matthew 16:24-26  Then said Jesus unto his disciples, If any man will come after me, let him deny himself, and take up his cross, and follow me. [25]For whosoever will save his life shall lose it: and whosoever will lose his life for my sake shall find it. [26]For what is a man profited, if he shall gain the whole world, and lose his own soul? or what shall a man give in exchange for his soul?

> Luke 21:12-19  But before all these, they shall lay their hands on you, and persecute you, delivering you up to the synagogues, and into prisons, being brought before kings and rulers for my name's sake. [13]And it shall turn to you for a testimony. [14]Settle it therefore in your hearts, not to

meditate before what ye shall answer: [15]For I will give you a mouth and wisdom, which all your adversaries shall not be able to gainsay nor resist. [16]And ye shall be betrayed both by parents, and brethren, and kinsfolks, and friends; and some of you shall they cause to be put to death. [17]And ye shall be hated of all men for my name's sake. [18]But there shall not an hair of your head perish. [19]In your patience possess ye your souls.

But for all these sufferings, those that endure to the end will be honoured:

Mark 13:13 And ye shall be hated of all men for my name's sake: but he that shall endure unto the end, the same shall be saved.

So we see that Myrrh teaches us to endure through the suffering thrust on us by the world for our choice to be obedient to the things of God. The Bride of Christ then, must endure, must not falter under attack, and must stand strong until her Heavenly Bridegroom returns.

## Cinnamon

Cinnamon has often been considered the spice of joy, which also happens to be the second Fruit of the Spirit.

Galatians 5:22 But the fruit of the Spirit is love, joy, peace, longsuffering, gentleness, goodness, faith,

It is said that the flowers of this tree have a foul smell, and it's also been said that cinnamon improves flavour of bitter foods. Christ asks us to find joy in the suffering we must endure while walking this earth, knowing that we share in His suffering and will one day receive a crown of righteousness.

The fact the oil mentioned in Isaiah is referred to as the "oil of joy" is a direct reference to this fruit of the Spirit. Without the Holy Spirit's efforts in our lives, we will not find true Joy.

# The Great Clothing Exchange

## Calamus

Calamus apparently smells nice not only as a spice, but as the plant in which it grows. It has apparently been used in various perfumes due to its rich and pleasing scent. The Christian is encouraged by the Apostle Paul:

> 2 Corinthians 2:14-16  Now thanks be unto God, which always causeth us to triumph in Christ, and maketh manifest the savour of his knowledge by us in every place. [15]For we are unto God a sweet savour of Christ, in them that are saved, and in them that perish: [16]To the one we are the savour of death unto death; and to the other the savour of life unto life. And who is sufficient for these things?

Put another way, Christ says in Matthew:

> Matthew 5:13-16  Ye are the salt of the earth: but if the salt have lost his savour, wherewith shall it be salted? it is thenceforth good for nothing, but to be cast out, and to be trodden under foot of men. [14]Ye are the light of the world. A city that is set on an hill cannot be hid. [15]Neither do men light a candle, and put it under a bushel, but on a candlestick; and it giveth light unto all that are in the house. [16]Let your light so shine before men, that they may see your good works, and glorify your Father which is in heaven.

The book of Proverbs adds another take to this:

> Proverbs 11:27  He that diligently seeketh good procureth favour: but he that seeketh mischief, it shall come unto him.

> Proverbs 22:1  A good name is rather to be chosen than great riches, and loving favour rather than silver and gold.

> Proverbs 28:23  He that rebuketh a man afterwards shall find more favour than he that flattereth with the tongue.

> Luke 2:52  And Jesus increased in wisdom and stature, and in favour with God and man.

I mention these various verses to allow Scripture to explain itself here. If we are to be a sweet smelling savour to the world around us, we need to reflect the ways of God in how we conduct ourselves in daily matters. Scripture says that:

> Proverbs 16:7  When a man's ways please the LORD, he maketh even his enemies to be at peace with him.

So our goal as the Bride of Christ is to be such a reflection of our Heavenly Bridegroom as to draw the world to Him in a manner that is pleasing to God. When we please God first, those that matter to us will also be pleased.

We won't please everyone. Salt not only seasons food, but cleanses, and if in a wound, that cleansing can sting to high heck! Light not only illuminates darkness, but it also exposes those who would rather stay in the darkness, so they get upset. But we aren't to allow those who get upset to put our lights under bowls and deaden the impact we are to have in the world.

## Cassia

Cassia's flowers are purple, which as we know, is the colour of royalty. It grows in high altitudes, making the Far East a perfect breeding ground, but also speaks to the victory we are to have in Christ over sin and worldly ways. This spice has been used in incense, which in Scripture references to our prayer life, and in garments in at least one passage in Song of Solomon.

> Psalm 141:1-3  A Psalm of David. LORD, I cry unto thee: make haste unto me; give ear unto my voice, when I cry unto thee. ²Let my prayer be set forth before thee as incense; and the lifting up of my hands as the evening sacrifice. ³Set a watch, O LORD, before my mouth; keep the door of my lips.

> Revelation 8:3-4  And another angel came and stood at the altar, having a golden censer; and there was given unto him much incense, that he should

## The Great Clothing Exchange

offer it with the prayers of all saints upon the golden altar which was before the throne. [4]And the smoke of the incense, which came with the prayers of the saints, ascended up before God out of the angel's hand.

We first see incense mentioned in preparations for the Tabernacle in Exodus:

Exodus 30:1  And thou shalt make an altar to burn incense upon: of shittim wood shalt thou make it.

Exodus 40:27  And he burnt sweet incense thereon; as the LORD commanded Moses.

We won't go into the recipe for the incense as that is beyond the scope of the immediate discussion. However, it consisted of similar spices to those used in the anointing oil.

The concept that our prayers are as incense before God should encourage us to enter into that place of conversation with Him more often than we do. God loves to listen to His children, loves to engage in two-way communication, loves to hear our praises and our expressions of love, worship and devotion.

The purple of this spice, as already observed, speaks to royalty. So it isn't the voice of any commoner that God looks forward to hearing from, but the Bride of Christ herself, the Church!

Altogether, we see that the Bride of Christ, when filled with the Holy Spirit, will find strength from Joy as a fruit of the Spirit living through her, enabling her to endure the sufferings of this present time so that she may spread the sweet aroma of Salvation to the world around her, granting victory to heaven as each soul comes to Christ.

## Garments of Praise

> Isaiah 61:3 To appoint unto them that mourn in Zion, to give unto them beauty for ashes, the oil of joy for mourning, *the garment of praise for the spirit of heaviness*; that they might be called trees of righteousness, the planting of the LORD, that he might be glorified.

> Isaiah 61:6 But ye shall be named the Priests of the LORD: men shall call you the Ministers of our God: ye shall eat the riches of the Gentiles, and in their glory shall ye boast yourselves.

We are now looking at the third item in this list, as noted by my italics above. First God gives His Bride beauty in place of sadness and mourning. Then He gives us His Holy Spirit, the Oil of Joy, also to replace our mourning. This third replacement is described as "Garments of Praise". The KJV uses the term "spirit of heaviness" here, while other translations have used the term mourning, although heaviness of spirit is not necessarily indicative of mourning specifically, but of the heaviness that can come from a weighted down over one's shame, mistakes, etc.

Of course the question must be begged, what are these garments, and why are they specifically called garments "of praise"?

First off, we must understand that God says in His Word that He inhabits the praises of His people.

> Psalm 22:1-5 To the chief Musician upon Aijeleth Shahar, A Psalm of David. My God, my God, why hast thou forsaken me? why art thou so far from helping me, and from the words of my roaring? ²O my God, I cry in the daytime, but thou hearest not; and in the night season, and am not silent. *³But thou art holy, O thou that inhabitest the praises of Israel.* ⁴Our fathers trusted in thee: they trusted, and thou didst deliver them. ⁵They cried unto thee, and were delivered: they trusted in thee, and were not confounded.

## The Great Clothing Exchange

Verse three is italicized on the previous page for emphasis. Notice that it is couched between two sets of attitudes toward God. First, there is the crying out for help, the "roaring" as David puts it, the incessant calling out and crying for help. Following verse three however, there is trust, there is a crying out from within that trust and God responds. The difference between the two is found in verse three.

Verse three gives us the key to verses four and five quite strongly. Even today, the tendency is to make demands of God from a place of fear, urgency, even tears and anger and wondering why He seems so far off. But when we come to God in a spirit of humility and lift up and praise His name, God shows up and is far more likely to act. His choice to act is freed by our trust, and trust is strengthened as we praise and extol Him for Who He is and all He's done for us. To praise a child is to tell them how well they did something. To praise God is to thank Him and show Him our gratitude for all He's done in, through and for us.

No one likes to be treated like an ungrateful servant being ordered around by a demanding boss, least of all the Creator of the Universe. But if we are respectful, if we are appreciative, if we are humble before Him, He responds to that as any loving Father and benevolent King would respond. But remember, God sees the heart where mankind often cannot. God knows when we are "buttering Him up" and when we don't really mean the words coming out of our mouths.

> Isaiah 29:13 Wherefore the Lord said, Forasmuch as this people draw near me with their mouth, and with their lips do honour me, but have removed their heart far from me, and their fear toward me is taught by the precept of men:

> Mark 7:6-9 He answered and said unto them, Well hath Esaias prophesied of you hypocrites, as it is written, This people honoureth me with their lips, but their heart is far from me. ⁷Howbeit in vain do they worship me, teaching for doctrines the commandments of men. ⁸For laying aside the commandment of God, ye hold the tradition of men, as the washing of pots and cups: and many other such like things ye do.

> ⁹And he said unto them, Full well ye reject the commandment of God, that ye may keep your own tradition.

> Hebrews 10:22 Let us draw near with a true heart in full assurance of faith, having our hearts sprinkled from an evil conscience, and our bodies washed with pure water.

This preparation mentioned in Hebrews from the perspective of the eternal state of the human heart, received its physical outworking way back in the preparations for worship in the Tabernacle. We have established that God does not like lip service, does not like being ordered around, but does appreciate a heart of praise. The preparations of the heart took on physical form in the Old Testament as a type of what God expects in the inner man. We return now to the book of Exodus:

**Levitical Priestly Clothing:**

> Exodus 28:40-43 And for Aaron's sons thou shalt make coats, and thou shalt make for them girdles, and bonnets shalt thou make for them, for glory and for beauty. ⁴¹And thou shalt put them upon Aaron thy brother, and his sons with him; and shalt anoint them, and consecrate them, and sanctify them, that they may minister unto me in the priest's office. ⁴²And thou shalt make them linen breeches to cover their nakedness; from the loins even unto the thighs they shall reach: ⁴³And they shall be upon Aaron, and upon his sons, when they come in unto the tabernacle of the congregation, or when they come near unto the altar to minister in the holy place; that they bear not iniquity, and die: it shall be a statute for ever unto him and his seed after him.

## The Great Clothing Exchange

We see that those who would serve in the Tabernacle were to wear certain clothing. From the High Priest to the average Levite, the following four pieces were to make up the basics of the priestly garments:

- Coats
- Girdles
- Bonnets
- Breeches

In this passage on the previous page, only the breeches are specified to be in linen. A lengthy passage we will look at in a moment, mentions that the entire list above was made out of fine linen. No wool was to be worn by the priests, and there were stipulations that they should not wear anything that would make them sweat.

Fine linen, as we learned on page 91, was a much more labour-intensive cloth to make, and therefore typically worn only by the rich, the bride, the priest, or royalty. We learned that fine linen represents righteousness given to the Bride of Christ by God Himself, being provided through Christ's atonement on the Cross of Calvary.

## Breeches

We are covered on the outside by a coat or robe of righteousness. But the breeches, being classified as an undergarment, tell us that righteousness is to be a thing of the hidden places as well, not merely for what others might see on the outside, but what only God can see on the inside.

> 1 Samuel 16:7 But the LORD said unto Samuel, Look not on his countenance, or on the height of his stature; because I have refused him: for the LORD seeth not as man seeth; for man looketh on the outward appearance, but the LORD looketh on the heart.

> 1 Kings 8:39 Then hear thou in heaven thy dwelling place, and forgive, and do, and give to every man according to his ways, whose heart thou knowest; (for thou, even thou only, knowest the hearts of all the children of men;)

> Jeremiah 17:10 I the LORD search the heart, I try the reins, even to give every man according to his ways, and according to the fruit of his doings.

> Luke 6:45 A good man out of the good treasure of his heart bringeth forth that which is good; and an evil man out of the evil treasure of his heart bringeth forth that which is evil: for of the abundance of the heart his mouth speaketh.

## Bonnet

The fine linen bonnet reminds us that Christ is our covering, just as we learned in our discussion on ornaments on page 99 when we discussed the Roman soldier's helmet. One of the definitions of "bonnet" is that of a hill, or high place, or a lifting up.

> Psalm 3:3-4 But thou, O LORD, art a shield for me; my glory, and the lifter up of mine head. ⁴I cried unto the LORD with my voice, and he heard me out of his holy hill. Selah.

> Psalm 121:1-2 A Song of degrees. I will lift up mine eyes unto the hills, from whence cometh my help. ²My help cometh from the LORD, which made heaven and earth.

Many teachers and many songwriters have assumed that the hills to which David lifts his eyes in Psalm 121, are not the Hill of the Lord where the Temple stood, but the hills upon which altars to false gods stood instead. They say he is asking a question here, instead of making a statement.

However, what if he's speaking of the hills of Jerusalem? What if it is not a question he is asking at all, but a statement instead. In Psalm 3, David says God heard him out of where? God's holy hill! In Psalm 121, David lifts his eyes to the Maker of ALL the hills! God is greater than the groves under which false gods were worshipped. Remember we learned a few pages back that God stamped His initial into the Jerusalem hills.

## The Great Clothing Exchange

Psalm 15:1-2  A Psalm of David. LORD, who shall abide in thy tabernacle? who shall dwell in thy holy hill?  ²He that walketh uprightly, and worketh righteousness, and speaketh the truth in his heart.

Psalm 24:3-6  Who shall ascend into the hill of the LORD? or who shall stand in his holy place?  ⁴He that hath clean hands, and a pure heart; who hath not lifted up his soul unto vanity, nor sworn deceitfully.  ⁵He shall receive the blessing from the LORD, and righteousness from the God of his salvation.  ⁶This is the generation of them that seek him, that seek thy face, O Jacob. Selah.

Psalm 99:9  Exalt the LORD our God, and worship at his holy hill; for the LORD our God is holy.

But notice who may worship there?  Can an unclean heart worship in God's Holy Hill?  Can a man with dirty hands stand in His holy place?

Sadly, eventually the people of Israel thought they could, and God had to bring judgement down on the Levite tribe.  This passage in Ezekiel is long, but it must be read to get the whole picture of what is being discussed here:

Ezekiel 44:10-23  And the Levites that are gone away far from me, when Israel went astray, which went astray away from me after their idols; they shall even bear their iniquity.  ¹¹Yet they shall be ministers in my sanctuary, having charge at the gates of the house, and ministering to the house: they shall slay the burnt offering and the sacrifice for the people, and they shall stand before them to minister unto them.

¹²Because they ministered unto them before their idols, and caused the house of Israel to fall into iniquity; therefore have I lifted up mine hand against them, saith the Lord GOD, and they shall bear their iniquity.  ¹³And they shall not come near unto me, to do the office of a priest unto me, nor to come near to any of my holy things, in the most holy place: but they shall bear their shame, and their abominations which they have committed.  ¹⁴But I will make them keepers of the charge of the house, for all the service thereof, and for all that shall be done therein.

¹⁵But the priests the Levites, the sons of Zadok, that kept the charge of my sanctuary when the children of Israel went astray from me, they shall come near to me to minister unto me, and they shall stand before me to offer unto me the fat and the blood, saith the Lord GOD:  ¹⁶They shall enter into my sanctuary, and they shall come near to my table, to minister unto me, and they shall keep my charge.

¹⁷And it shall come to pass, that when they enter in at the gates of the inner court, they shall be clothed with linen garments; and no wool shall come upon them, whiles they minister in the gates of the inner court, and within.  ¹⁸They shall have linen bonnets upon their heads, and shall have linen breeches upon their loins; they shall not gird themselves with any thing that causeth sweat.  ¹⁹And when they go forth into the utter court, even into the utter court to the people, they shall put off their garments wherein they ministered, and lay them in the holy chambers, and they shall put on other garments; and they shall not sanctify the people with their garments.  ²⁰Neither shall they shave their heads, nor suffer their locks to grow long; they shall only poll their heads.  ²¹Neither shall any priest drink wine, when they enter into the inner court.  ²²Neither shall they take for their wives a widow, nor her that is put away: but they shall take maidens of the seed of the house of Israel, or a widow that had a priest before.  ²³And they shall teach my people the difference between the holy and profane, and cause them to discern between the unclean and the clean.

Truly, God's Holy Hill had been profaned.  Amazingly enough, God did not banish the Levitical priests from His courts.  He only banished them from His presence.  They were demoted to the outer courts where the sacrifices took place, serving the people.  But the true service of serving God would now be done by the priests among the sons of Zadok of the Levite tribe.

Again, God specifies the clothing they were to wear; this time, unlike the passage in Exodus, stating the entire outfit was to be in fine linen.

# The Great Clothing Exchange

## Girdle

Once again, continuing with the original list here, we see the girdle, which we learned on page 92, is the Belt of Truth in Ephesians 6.

So in a very similar manner to Bridal Attire already discussed, the priestly garments speak of Christ being the lifter of our head, our righteousness, our covering and protector, and that God cares about the inner man as well as the outer man.

## Changing our Garments

We learn that we cannot come to God as the rebellious Levites tried to do, with the blood of sin and spiritual adultery on our hands. We must wash ourselves and be made clean before we can enter into God's courts with praise. But we can't do that ourselves. Allow me another Old Testament example before we move on:

> Zechariah 3:1-8  And he shewed me Joshua the high priest standing before the angel of the LORD, and Satan standing at his right hand to resist him. ²And the LORD said unto Satan, The LORD rebuke thee, O Satan; even the LORD that hath chosen Jerusalem rebuke thee: is not this a brand plucked out of the fire? ³Now Joshua was clothed with filthy garments, and stood before the angel. ⁴And he answered and spake unto those that stood before him, saying, Take away the filthy garments from him. And unto him he said, Behold, I have caused thine iniquity to pass from thee, and I will clothe thee with change of raiment. ⁵And I said, Let them set a fair mitre upon his head. So they set a fair mitre upon his head, and clothed him with garments. And the angel of the LORD stood by. ⁶And the angel of the LORD protested unto Joshua, saying, ⁷Thus saith the LORD of hosts; If thou wilt walk in my ways, and if thou wilt keep my charge, then thou shalt also judge my house, and shalt also keep my courts, and I will give thee places to walk among these that stand by.

> ⁸Hear now, O Joshua the high priest, thou, and thy fellows that sit before thee: for they are men wondered at: for, behold, I will bring forth my servant the BRANCH.

A few chapters after Isaiah 61:3, we come to Isaiah 64. I encourage the reader to read the verses surrounding this one at your leisure:

> Isaiah 64:6 But we are all as an unclean thing, and all our righteousnesses are as filthy rags; and we all do fade as a leaf; and our iniquities, like the wind, have taken us away.

So if our spiritual clothing is so filthy, how are we to make them clean again? This is where God steps in. Remember it was Christ who read the first few verses of Isaiah 61 at the official beginning of His earthly ministry. It is only through the accepting of Jesus' gift of Salvation that we can be washed, that our sin can be taken from us, that the old man can be put off and the new man put on.

**The new man:**

> Ephesians 2:11-19 Wherefore remember, that ye being in time past Gentiles in the flesh, who are called Uncircumcision by that which is called the Circumcision in the flesh made by hands; ¹²That at that time ye were without Christ, being aliens from the commonwealth of Israel, and strangers from the covenants of promise, having no hope, and without God in the world: ¹³But now in Christ Jesus ye who sometimes were far off are made nigh by the blood of Christ. ¹⁴For he is our peace, who hath made both one, and hath broken down the middle wall of partition between us; ¹⁵Having abolished in his flesh the enmity, even the law of commandments contained in ordinances; for to make in himself of twain one new man, so making peace; ¹⁶And that he might reconcile both unto God in one body by the cross, having slain the enmity thereby: ¹⁷And came and preached peace to you which were afar off, and to them that were nigh. ¹⁸For through him we both have access by one Spirit unto the Father. ¹⁹Now therefore ye are no more strangers and foreigners, but fellow citizens with the saints, and of the household of God;

## The Great Clothing Exchange

Ephesians 4:21-24  If so be that ye have heard him, and have been taught by him, as the truth is in Jesus: [22]That ye put off concerning the former conversation the old man, which is corrupt according to the deceitful lusts; [23]And be renewed in the spirit of your mind; [24]And that ye put on the new man, which after God is created in righteousness and true holiness.

Colossians 3:8-17  But now ye also put off all these; anger, wrath, malice, blasphemy, filthy communication out of your mouth. [9]Lie not one to another, seeing that ye have put off the old man with his deeds; [10]And have put on the new man, which is renewed in knowledge after the image of him that created him: [11]Where there is neither Greek nor Jew, circumcision nor uncircumcision, Barbarian, Scythian, bond nor free: but Christ is all, and in all. [12]Put on therefore, as the elect of God, holy and beloved, bowels of mercies, kindness, humbleness of mind, meekness, longsuffering; [13]Forbearing one another, and forgiving one another, if any man have a quarrel against any: even as Christ forgave you, so also do ye. [14]And above all these things put on charity, which is the bond of perfectness. [15]And let the peace of God rule in your hearts, to the which also ye are called in one body; and be ye thankful. [16]Let the word of Christ dwell in you richly in all wisdom; teaching and admonishing one another in psalms and hymns and spiritual songs, singing with grace in your hearts to the Lord. [17]And whatsoever ye do in word or deed, do all in the name of the Lord Jesus, giving thanks to God and the Father by him.

The old man, the sinful nature, separates man from God. Mankind cannot even hope to come into God's presence with praise and gratitude if he or she is still clothed in the self-serving, rebellious nature of sin. The old man must be taken off and the new man put on.

Christ made the way for this to be permanently possible. What the Old Testament priest had to do with physical clothing sewn to specific instructions out of special material, Christ now made a reality in the spirit realm. The new man in Christ is made possible at the point of salvation, but after that, choices need to be made. Just because we now wear Christ's Robe of Righteousness does not mean we are able to go and play in the ways of the world again. Doing so will soil our garments and if we aren't careful, will remove our place in the Bride of Christ and relegate us to the guests at the Marriage Supper of the Lamb. We may not lose our salvation as such, but we have not regularly washed in the Word, have not regularly abstained from the ways of sin, have not allowed the Holy Spirit to live through us whereby we'd lose our interest in the things of sin.

Ezekiel 36:25-27  Then will I sprinkle clean water upon you, and ye shall be clean: from all your filthiness, and from all your idols, will I cleanse you. $^{26}$A new heart also will I give you, and a new spirit will I put within you: and I will take away the stony heart out of your flesh, and I will give you an heart of flesh. $^{27}$And I will put my spirit within you, and cause you to walk in my statutes, and ye shall keep my judgments, and do them.

Romans 8:1-6  There is therefore now no condemnation to them which are in Christ Jesus, who walk not after the flesh, but after the Spirit. $^{2}$For the law of the Spirit of life in Christ Jesus hath made me free from the law of sin and death. $^{3}$For what the law could not do, in that it was weak through the flesh, God sending his own Son in the likeness of sinful flesh, and for sin, condemned sin in the flesh: $^{4}$That the righteousness of the law might be fulfilled in us, who walk not after the flesh, but after the Spirit. $^{5}$For they that are after the flesh do mind the things of the flesh; but they that are after the Spirit the things of the Spirit. $^{6}$For to be carnally minded is death; but to be spiritually minded is life and peace.

Galatians 5:13-18  For, brethren, ye have been called unto liberty; only use not liberty for an occasion to the flesh, but by love serve one another. $^{14}$For all the law is fulfilled in one word, even in this; Thou shalt love thy neighbour as thyself. $^{15}$But if ye bite and devour one another, take heed that ye be not consumed one of another. $^{16}$This I say then, Walk in the Spirit, and ye shall not fulfil the lust of the flesh. $^{17}$For the flesh lusteth against the Spirit, and the Spirit against the flesh: and these are contrary the one to the other: so that ye cannot do the things that ye would. $^{18}$But if ye be led of the Spirit, ye are not under the law.

## The Great Clothing Exchange

Galatians 5:22-25   But the fruit of the Spirit is love, joy, peace, longsuffering, gentleness, goodness, faith, [23]Meekness, temperance: against such there is no law. [24]And they that are Christ's have crucified the flesh with the affections and lusts. [25]If we live in the Spirit, let us also walk in the Spirit.

## Looking forward

1 Peter 2:4-10   To whom coming, as unto a living stone, disallowed indeed of men, but chosen of God, and precious, [5]Ye also, as lively stones, are built up a spiritual house, an holy priesthood, to offer up spiritual sacrifices, acceptable to God by Jesus Christ.   [6]Wherefore also it is contained in the scripture, Behold, I lay in Sion a chief corner stone, elect, precious: and he that believeth on him shall not be confounded.   [7]Unto you therefore which believe he is precious: but unto them which be disobedient, the stone which the builders disallowed, the same is made the head of the corner,   [8]And a stone of stumbling, and a rock of offence, even to them which stumble at the word, being disobedient: whereunto also they were appointed.   [9]But ye are a chosen generation, a royal priesthood, an holy nation, a peculiar people; that ye should shew forth the praises of him who hath called you out of darkness into his marvellous light:   [10]Which in time past were not a people, but are now the people of God: which had not obtained mercy, but now have obtained mercy.

Isn't it interesting how similar the garments of praise are to the Bridal attire spoken of in Ezekiel?   The Bride of Christ is not just any royal princess and heir, but she is also a priest unto her God.   Her bridegroom is a High Priest after the order of Melchisedec, and He has decked her out in finery not only fitting that of a bride, but that of a priest as well.   She is clothed in holiness, in righteousness, in royalty, and displays such status to the entire world.   She worships in the courts of Almighty God and spreads the Gospel of Peace to all who will hear.   She influences the culture in which she lives, she rescues the perishing and keeps her wedding garments pure and white for the day when the Trumpet will sound!

## "Without Spot or Wrinkle"

> Ephesians 5:23-32   For the husband is the head of the wife, even as Christ is the head of the church: and he is the saviour of the body. ²⁴Therefore as the church is subject unto Christ, so let the wives be to their own husbands in every thing. ²⁵Husbands, love your wives, **_even as Christ also loved the church, and gave himself for it;_** **_²⁶That he might sanctify and cleanse it with the washing of water by the word,_** **_²⁷That he might present it to himself a glorious church, not having spot, or wrinkle, or any such thing; but that it should be holy and without blemish._** ²⁸So ought men to love their wives as their own bodies. He that loveth his wife loveth himself.  ²⁹For no man ever yet hated his own flesh; but nourisheth and cherisheth it, even as the Lord the church: ³⁰For we are members of his body, of his flesh, and of his bones. ³¹For this cause shall a man leave his father and mother, and shall be joined unto his wife, and they two shall be one flesh.  ³²This is a great mystery: but I speak concerning Christ and the church.

We've spent the last several sections learning how God adorns His Bride. In this next section we are going to learn about the concepts in the above bolded and italicized text. Those embellishments are mine for emphasis.

As almost every human being knows and understands, failure to properly look after an article of clothing or a piece of jewelry will result in that item eventually breaking down and becoming unusable. It is this author's desire to make the concepts in verses 26 and 27 as real and as applicable as possible to the reader.

We will examine the concepts of sanctification and cleansing with the washing of water by the Word; what spots, wrinkles and blemishes are, and talk a bit about holiness. After that, we will take a closer look at the parable of the 10 virgins. Some of these concepts have already been touched on in other discussions to this point. But we are going to look at them more directly here.

We will also learn how to care for our Bridal attire so that we are ready when Christ returns for us.

Are you ready to learn how to do the spiritual laundry? Are you ready to learn how to shine your spiritual jewelry? Here we go...

## Sanctification

Let us begin with a bit of a word study. While there are those who consider use of such words as "sanctification" to be some sort of "Christianese" that should not be used by the person trying to reach the common man, the word does appear in Scripture, and it appeared to those who otherwise technically should not have easily understood what it meant. This must mean it has a fairly simple definition to suggest its use to the common people back in the days Scripture was written.

The Strong's Hebrew Dictionary says this:

קדשׁ

qâdash

kaw-dash'

A primitive root; to be (causatively make, pronounce or observe as) clean (ceremonially or morally): - appoint, bid, consecrate, dedicate, defile, hallow, (be, keep) holy (-er, place), keep, prepare, proclaim, purify, sanctify (-ied one, self), X wholly.

The Strong's Greek Dictionary says this:

αγἁ ζω

hagiazō

hag-ee-ad'-zo

From G40; to make holy, that is, (ceremonially) purify or consecrate; (mentally) to venerate: - hallow, be holy, sanctify.

As we can see above, in either the Greek or the Hebrew, this word is loaded with meaning.

Visiting google.ca, we see the common modern translation:

Verb

Set apart as or declare holy; consecrate.

Make legitimate or binding by religious sanction.

## Spots and Wrinkles

Synonyms
hallow - consecrate - dedicate – bless

The first mention we see in Scripture of the act of sanctification is at the very first official celebration of Passover:

> Exodus 13:1-2  And the LORD spake unto Moses, saying, ²Sanctify unto me all the firstborn, whatsoever openeth the womb among the children of Israel, both of man and of beast: it is mine.

As an act of gratitude and remembrance, every family was to sanctify their first born child. As the definitions above state, this meant that every first born child was now set apart for any purpose to which God might call them, at any time and for any reason.

This act of sanctification for God's usage and purposes would continue through to the establishment of Tabernacle worship. The sanctification of the Tabernacle and priests for service is also the first place where we see the anointing oil in use. It is interesting to observe that not much further along in the sanctification of the Tabernacle that God says in Leviticus:

> Leviticus 20:7  Sanctify yourselves therefore, and be ye holy: for I am the LORD your God.

This time, the call to sanctification is not to the firstborn, nor is it to the Levitical priests. This time, the entire congregation of the people is being told to sanctify themselves and be holy as God is holy.

It is impossible to talk about sanctification without talking about holiness. The reason for this is that sanctification is the process of becoming holy. It is the process of being set apart from the world and from sin and set apart toward a holy God.

Looking at the various verses where this word is used brought up an unusual verse in Isaiah:

> Isaiah 8:11-18  For the LORD spake thus to me with a strong hand, and instructed me that I should not walk in the way of this people, saying, *¹²*Say ye not, A confederacy, to all them to whom this people shall say, A confederacy; neither fear ye their fear, nor be afraid. *¹³Sanctify the LORD of hosts himself; and let him be your fear, and let him be your dread. ¹⁴And he shall be for a sanctuary; but for a stone of stumbling and for a rock of offence to both the houses of Israel, for a gin and for a snare to the inhabitants of Jerusalem. ¹⁵And many among them shall stumble, and fall, and be broken, and be snared, and be taken.* ¹⁶Bind up the testimony, seal the law among my disciples.  ¹⁷And I will wait upon the LORD, that hideth his face from the house of Jacob, and I will look for him.  ¹⁸Behold, I and the children whom the LORD hath given me are for signs and for wonders in Israel from the LORD of hosts, which dwelleth in mount Zion.

Now sadly, to this day many in Israel stumble over the Lord of hosts.  We know from later in the New Testament, that Christ is this stone of stumbling and Rock of offence.

> Matthew 21:43-44  Therefore say I unto you, The kingdom of God shall be taken from you, and given to a nation bringing forth the fruits thereof. ⁴⁴And whosoever shall fall on this stone shall be broken: but on whomsoever it shall fall, it will grind him to powder.

However, the focus here is on a phrase in verse 13 of Isaiah 8: "Sanctify the LORD of hosts himself; and let him be your fear, and let him be your dread." Wow. . . What is God saying here?

God wants to be set apart as holy within our own thoughts and within our own hearts.  When so many things grapple for our attention, our time, and our resources, God wants to be the consecrated One in our lives, the One who gets first priority.  God wants to be the One who is revered, held in high esteem, honoured and loved above all else.  We see this same thought from the Apostle Peter when he writes:

> 1 Peter 3:15-16  But sanctify the Lord God in your hearts: and be ready always to give an answer to every man that asketh you a reason of the

## Spots and Wrinkles

> hope that is in you with meekness and fear: <sup>16</sup>Having a good conscience; that, whereas they speak evil of you, as of evildoers, they may be ashamed that falsely accuse your good conversation in Christ.

The first time we see this word used in the New Testament, we come across Christ praying in the Garden:

> John 17:15-19 I pray not that thou shouldest take them out of the world, but that thou shouldest keep them from the evil. <sup>16</sup>They are not of the world, even as I am not of the world. *<sup>17</sup>Sanctify them through thy truth: thy word is truth.* <sup>18</sup>As thou hast sent me into the world, even so have I also sent them into the world. *<sup>19</sup>And for their sakes I sanctify myself, that they also might be sanctified through the truth.*

Here we see God in the flesh, Jesus Christ, setting Himself apart from the things of the world so that His disciples may be sanctified also. Here also, we see the first direct reference to sanctification through the Word of God. King David did not use the word sanctification, but he gave the exact same concept when he wrote in Psalm 119:

> Psalm 119:9 BETH. Wherewithal shall a young man cleanse his way? by taking heed thereto according to thy word.

Because God's Word is truth and because Christ has prayed that God would sanctify His people through His Truth, we have the Apostle Paul writing:

> Romans 12:1-2 I beseech you therefore, brethren, by the mercies of God, that ye present your bodies a living sacrifice, holy, acceptable unto God, which is your reasonable service. <sup>2</sup>And be not conformed to this world: but be ye transformed by the renewing of your mind, that ye may prove what is that good, and acceptable, and perfect, will of God.

The process of sanctification, that act of being set apart from the world and being made holy toward God, produces a transformation in how we think, how we speak, how we act, and where we go. Indeed, as we spend time in God's Word, the way God thinks and acts begins to influence the way we think and

## Dressed for Eternity

act and we begin to change. It is said that a person takes on the characteristics of the five people they hang around the most. It is also said that a couple who has been married for a long time will not only begin to laugh and speak alike, but they almost begin to look alike too.

So it should be with the Bride of Christ and the Heavenly Bridegroom. Does she spend so much time with the Holy Spirit that she begins to act and talk like Jesus Christ? Does she spend so much time either in or pondering the Word of God that she begins to mimic how God does things simply by sheer association?

**Cleansing**

This ongoing act of sanctification by necessity involves the act of cleansing.

This concept of cleansing first appears in lengthy commands to Moses in making first preparations to use the Tabernacle implements ahead of official implementation of the entire Mosaic Law. This cleansing was done via the blood of the animal sacrificed on the altar. In fact, that very altar had to go through its own purification ritual.

> Exodus 29:36-37 And thou shalt offer every day a bullock for a sin offering for atonement: and thou shalt cleanse the altar, when thou hast made an atonement for it, and thou shalt anoint it, to sanctify it. [37]Seven days thou shalt make an atonement for the altar, and sanctify it; and it shall be an altar most holy: whatsoever toucheth the altar shall be holy.

In the verses prior to this, Aaron and his sons were to go through seven days of consecration, which just happens to be one of the definitions of sanctification.

Cleansing was prescribed for a wide range of hygienic, relational, and social laws as well as those of redemption from sin. Many of these hygienic laws have influenced modern-day hygiene not only in the home and public places, but in hospitals as well. For many nations around the globe, Jews settling in foreign lands would be the first they'd hear of properly draining meat, handling

## Spots and Wrinkles

menstruation, dealing with mold and mildew, and more. Notice how all these examples involve the act of cleaning away the harmful to make the person or object clean and ready for use again?

King David understood this concept of washing to be clean very well! His greatest recorded example is found in Psalm 51:

> Psalm 51:2 Wash me throughly from mine iniquity, and cleanse me from my sin.
>
> Psalm 51:6-7 Behold, thou desirest truth in the inward parts: and in the hidden part thou shalt make me to know wisdom. ⁷Purge me with hyssop, and I shall be clean: wash me, and I shall be whiter than snow.
>
> Psalm 51:10-12 Create in me a clean heart, O God; and renew a right spirit within me. ¹¹Cast me not away from thy presence; and take not thy holy spirit from me. ¹²Restore unto me the joy of thy salvation; and uphold me with thy free spirit.

Notice David is not praying to the High Priest, nor is he praying to himself. He is calling on God to do the cleansing of his heart. This is inward, not outward as so many references in the law pertained. But King David understood the types in the carrying out of the Law, and knew that true cleansing only came from God Himself.

Notice also, that David understands that such cleansing from God comes through God's truth, that it is through the Holy Spirit he gains wisdom. Truly King David understood many things about a healthy relationship with God that most people of his day completely missed.

From David we come to his son, King Solomon, writing the book of Proverbs.

> Proverbs 20:30 The blueness of a wound cleanseth away evil: so do stripes the inward parts of the belly.

This actually becomes another reference to blood cleansing away sin. When a bruise is blue, that means there has been some level of bleeding in the affected muscle. The vessels are torn and the bruise turns blue and purple and red before it eventually turns brown and yellow and green. Dirty blood is typically purple when seen on the surface, outside the body. So we are shown once again, this time in an example of discipline, that blood by its very nature, cleanses as well as transmits nutrients.

As a side note on our journey through this topic, the discipline spoken of here explains in just a few words, the benefit of correction as it pertains to change of heart and mind in a person. Sometimes God's children need discipline before we will leave our sinful ways behind. When we do wrong, we need to be brought back on track.

> Hebrews 12:4-11 Ye have not yet resisted unto blood, striving against sin. ⁵And ye have forgotten the exhortation which speaketh unto you as unto children, My son, despise not thou the chastening of the Lord, nor faint when thou art rebuked of him: ⁶For whom the Lord loveth he chasteneth, and scourgeth every son whom he receiveth. ⁷If ye endure chastening, God dealeth with you as with sons; for what son is he whom the father chasteneth not? ⁸But if ye be without chastisement, whereof all are partakers, then are ye bastards, and not sons. ⁹Furthermore we have had fathers of our flesh which corrected us, and we gave them reverence: shall we not much rather be in subjection unto the Father of spirits, and live? ¹⁰For they verily for a few days chastened us after their own pleasure; *but he for our profit, that we might be partakers of his holiness.* ¹¹Now no chastening for the present seemeth to be joyous, but grievous: nevertheless afterward it yieldeth the peaceable fruit of righteousness unto them which are exercised thereby.

However, as much as this was intended as a side note, this chastening spoken of by King Solomon and the writer of Hebrews both have the same result. A cleansing takes place and we are brought that much closer to the holiness of God.

## Spots and Wrinkles

After the book of Proverbs, cleansing takes on the form we are used to seeing in the New Testament, that of the cleansing of one's heart unto holiness before God. The cleansing via the blood of animals continues, but God begins to communicate more regarding the heart of man.

But for all the times where God will do the cleansing of sin, the Bride of Christ is expected to take part in this cleansing as pointed out in Romans 12:1 and 2 already. Paul mentions again:

> 2 Corinthians 7:1 Having therefore these promises, dearly beloved, let us cleanse ourselves from all filthiness of the flesh and spirit, perfecting holiness in the fear of God.

The immediately preceding verses referred to above are these:

> 2 Corinthians 6:14-18 Be ye not unequally yoked together with unbelievers: for what fellowship hath righteousness with unrighteousness? and what communion hath light with darkness? ¹⁵And what concord hath Christ with Belial? or what part hath he that believeth with an infidel? ¹⁶And what agreement hath the temple of God with idols? *for ye are the temple of the living God; as God hath said, I will dwell in them, and walk in them; and I will be their God, and they shall be my people.* ¹⁷*Wherefore come out from among them, and be ye separate, saith the Lord, and touch not the unclean thing; and I will receive you,* ¹⁸And will be a Father unto you, and ye shall be my sons and daughters, saith the Lord Almighty.

Many debates have arisen as to what these verses mean. Some call these verses into direct contradiction to Jesus sitting with sinners to have a meal with them. What is being spoken of here is not the social aspect whereby relationships are formed to bring people out of their sin and into the Light, but rather the agreement with sinful ways, thoughts, and lifestyles instead. We are called to reach out, but not to fall into sin ourselves in the process. When we agree with sinful things, we eventually either engage in them, or support them; neither of which is becoming to the child of God aiming at living a holy life pleasing to Him.

We are to come out from among those that would defile us; we are to avoid engaging in activities that would soil our Robe of Righteousness. This is a difficult message for those of the more liberal persuasion in Christianity. But there clearly is a difference between a relationship that pulls a sinner out of their sin, and a relationship that joins the sinner in their sin and even approves of it.

Therefore, as Paul continues in chapter 7, we are to take steps to push sin away and keep it away. This behaviour shows God that we mean business, that we love Him more than the sin that could tempt us, and that we are willing to be set apart for His glory.

Now in order for all this talk of sanctification and cleansing to truly make sense for the Bride of Christ, we need to spend a little time discussing the spots and wrinkles Christ wants to cleanse her from with the washing of the Word.

# Dressed for Eternity

**Spots and Wrinkles**

The Bride of Christ looks positively stunning in her royal regalia, all decked out in fine white linen, silk, embroidery, badger skin shoes, and amazing jewelry. Science-fiction games like to mention something called "armour-weave", where metal is woven into the clothing for protection of the wearer. That this would be science-fiction and not history is amazing, considering the Egyptians perfected the art of weaving gold strands into their clothing and passed this ability on to the Hebrew people.

The Bride of Christ's wedding attire also happens to be her battle attire, and she is fully protected because of the glory of God and His Righteousness surrounding her and being displayed through her in all that she does.

But sometimes stints on the battlefield can cause this soldier-Bride to get a little dirty at times. Unfortunately, down through history and to this very day, there are soldiers in the army of God who have not only gotten a little dirty in the course of their duties, but sadly, enjoyed the experience so much that they allowed the mud and dirt to stay on their clothing and on their person. Some have even died in this sorry state of affairs. How does this happen? What can be done about such a situation to either prevent or deal with it?

There are two known answers to the first question in Scripture. One is wandering eyes, as God was so often getting upset with Israel for as she repeatedly went whoring after other gods.

> Hosea 9:1 Rejoice not, O Israel, for joy, as other people: for thou hast gone a whoring from thy God, thou hast loved a reward upon every cornfloor.

Wandering eyes are seen in the prodigal son when he thought life away from home would be better and found out otherwise as he sat in a muddy pig pen trying to eat their corn husks.

## Spots and Wrinkles

> Luke 15:15-16  And he went and joined himself to a citizen of that country; and he sent him into his fields to feed swine. ¹⁶And he would fain have filled his belly with the husks that the swine did eat: and no man gave unto him.

Many of God's children have been led astray by the supposedly more exciting, shiny, and enticing things of the world once they were exposed to them.

> James 1:13-15  Let no man say when he is tempted, I am tempted of God: for God cannot be tempted with evil, neither tempteth he any man: ¹⁴But every man is tempted, when he is drawn away of his own lust, and enticed. ¹⁵Then when lust hath conceived, it bringeth forth sin: and sin, when it is finished, bringeth forth death.

The other is found in the dangers of relational evangelism. Let's look at these verses below:

> Galatians 6:1  Brethren, if a man be overtaken in a fault, ye which are spiritual, restore such an one in the spirit of meekness; considering thyself, lest thou also be tempted.

> Galatians 5:1  Stand fast therefore in the liberty wherewith Christ hath made us free, and be not entangled again with the yoke of bondage.

> 1 Corinthians 10:12  Wherefore let him that thinketh he standeth take heed lest he fall.

This is happening with regards to Christians, the Church, and alternative lifestyle issues.  There are not merely individual Christians falling into sin because of this issue, but entire churches choosing to disobey God's Word on the matter for the sake of making those caught in sin feel good about themselves and feel accepted.  But it isn't the only example of the warnings being offered above.  Christians have been caught into alcoholism, prostitution, and others for similar reasons.  The human nature has difficulty separating the sin from the sinner, and thus these warnings are given.

## Dressed for Eternity

Let us take a few minutes and look deeper into what these spots and wrinkles are. Keep in mind the lists given here are not exhaustive by any means. There may be other things that you as the reader may wish to add to these lists.

## Spots

Spots in Scripture are first mentioned in the Old Testament when Jacob is cheating Labon out of his flocks by first making a deal and then taking steps to deliberately alter the appearance of the flocks in his favour.

> Genesis 30:31-32  And he said, What shall I give thee? And Jacob said, Thou shalt not give me any thing: if thou wilt do this thing for me, I will again feed and keep thy flock: ³²I will pass through all thy flock to day, removing from thence all the speckled and spotted cattle, and all the brown cattle among the sheep, and the spotted and speckled among the goats: and of such shall be my hire.

The next time we see spots mentioned is in relation to health issues throughout the book of Leviticus. Any spot that appeared on the skin for any reason and did not go away immediately, was to be brought before the priest who would assess the situation, and quarantine the person if need be.

One of the worst spots a person could get at that time was that of Leprosy. Leprosy was a symptom of poor hygiene, and was present internally long before it broke out onto the skin.  Once it surfaced on the skin, it was considered incurable and the person would be sent outside the camp, or later on, outside the city.

Sin has been likened to leprosy because just like leprosy, sin can seem innocuous, inconspicuous even.  It might be misconstrued as a minor inconvenience, a twinge of discomfort that is easily brushed off.  But just like leprosy, it grows until it consumes the person, body, soul and spirit.

The first time in Scripture that spots are mentioned in a negative context for animals is in Numbers:

## Spots and Wrinkles

> Numbers 19:2-3  This is the ordinance of the law which the LORD hath commanded, saying, Speak unto the children of Israel, that they bring thee a red heifer without spot, wherein is no blemish, and upon which never came yoke: ³And ye shall give her unto Eleazar the priest, that he may bring her forth without the camp, and one shall slay her before his face:

Now the fact that this female red heifer was to be the sin offering should not escape notice. Her colouring was to be perfectly uniform; any deviation from that colour was considered a spot and marked her as unclean and therefore unfit to be the sin sacrifice.

The next number of times we see spots mentioned in a negative light, it is in direct reference to sin and rebellion against God in both the Old and New Testament.

Peter and Jude take the concept of the spot and apply it to false teachers.

> 2 Peter 2:12-14  But these, as natural brute beasts, made to be taken and destroyed, speak evil of the things that they understand not; and shall utterly perish in their own corruption;  ¹³And shall receive the reward of unrighteousness, as they that count it pleasure to riot in the day time. Spots they are and blemishes, sporting themselves with their own deceivings while they feast with you;  ¹⁴Having eyes full of adultery, and that cannot cease from sin; beguiling unstable souls: an heart they have exercised with covetous practices; cursed children:

> Jude 1:10-12  But these speak evil of those things which they know not: but what they know naturally, as brute beasts, in those things they corrupt themselves.  ¹¹Woe unto them! for they have gone in the way of Cain, and ran greedily after the error of Balaam for reward, and perished in the gainsaying of Core.  ¹²These are spots in your feasts of charity, when they feast with you, feeding themselves without fear: clouds they are without water, carried about of winds; trees whose fruit withereth, without fruit, twice dead, plucked up by the roots;

Read each book's respective chapter in its entirety to get the full message found in these verses quoted above.

When we consider that in the Old Testament, a spot of colour different from the overall colour of the animal made it unfit for use in the sacrificial system, this should say something about doctrinal teaching within the church. If a teaching enters the church that is a different gospel than the one of the Scriptures, it is truthfully said to be "off colour" and should be avoided. We already say that an "off colour" remark is generally unacceptable, not necessary, in poor humour, etc. We get that from the Scriptures.

The Bride of Christ needs to be certain she is not engaging in off-colour teaching and doctrine, because engaging in such things becomes a spot on her garment just as bleach removes colour from its target.

**Wrinkles**

If false teachers are spots, then the false teachings they spread are the wrinkles. Wrinkles occur naturally in two different circumstances:

1) Wrinkles occur in clothing if they have been bunched up and tossed in a corner. They occur naturally in clothing that goes through the dryer coming out wrinkled and needing ironing.

2) Wrinkles can occur on skin along with folds if a person is over-weight. They also occur as a person ages, when the elasticity and firmness of their skin fades and sinks. The skin develops wrinkles as it folds in on itself in this process.

If we apply these naturally-occurring situations to life for the Bride of Christ, we see a couple areas that can be prone to wrinkles. The first is that of adding to Scripture, and the second is removing things from the Scriptures:

Deuteronomy 4:2 "Ye shall not add unto the word which I command you, neither shall ye diminish ought from it, that ye may keep the commandments of the LORD your God which I command you."

Revelation 22:18-19 For I testify unto every man that heareth the words of the prophecy of this book, If any man shall add unto these things, God shall add unto him the plagues that are written in this book: [19]And if any man shall take away from the words of the book of this prophecy, God shall take away his part out of the book of life, and out of the holy city, and from the things which are written in this book.

There have always been people throughout history who have added to the Word of God. Christ got after the Pharisees for how they handled the Law. They had added so many of their own rules and regulations that the concept of maintaining the Law for one's self was deemed darn near impossible to all but the trained clergy.

## Spots and Wrinkles

> Mark 7:6-9  He answered and said unto them, Well hath Esaias prophesied of you hypocrites, as it is written, This people honoureth me with their lips, but their heart is far from me. ⁷Howbeit in vain do they worship me, teaching for doctrines the commandments of men. ⁸For laying aside the commandment of God, ye hold the tradition of men, as the washing of pots and cups: and many other such like things ye do. ⁹And he said unto them, Full well ye reject the commandment of God, that ye may keep your own tradition.

Adding to Scripture as the Pharisees did, would be saying that we know better than God. We are saying that He gave us the skeleton but left us to flesh it out. This flies in the face of Scripture when it says:

> 2 Timothy 3:16-17  All scripture is given by inspiration of God, and is profitable for doctrine, for reproof, for correction, for instruction in righteousness:  ¹⁷That the man of God may be perfect, throughly furnished unto all good works.

We see examples of this kind of behaviour within some denominations to this day, as they add to the commands of Scripture to fit with their liturgical ideas. This concept was rampant during the Dark Ages and earned the Medieval time period that title for that very reason.

The Bride of Christ needs to be wary of people who come claiming a new doctrine, a new Gospel, etc. Such "new ideas" become rolls of fat on her body and wrinkles in her robes.

As mentioned above, the second thing that contributes to wrinkles in the Bride of Christ is the taking away of Scripture. We see this most obviously in conversations where people say they will accept one portion of the Bible, but not others. They are, in effect, rejecting the whole counsel of God by doing this.

> Jeremiah 42:20-21  For ye dissembled in your hearts, when ye sent me unto the LORD your God, saying, Pray for us unto the LORD our God; and according unto all that the LORD our God shall say, so declare unto

us, and we will do it. ²¹And now I have this day declared it to you; but ye have not obeyed the voice of the LORD your God, nor any thing for the which he hath sent me unto you.

This passage above is followed by drastic discipline for choosing not to obey the whole counsel of God. The discipline handed out here seems pale compared to the eternal punishment mentioned in Revelation 22.

Let us look at a couple incidents in the prophet Samuel's day, where disobedience and adding to the commands of God cost a King his crown:

1 Samuel 13:11-14 And Samuel said, What hast thou done? And Saul said, Because I saw that the people were scattered from me, and that thou camest not within the days appointed, and that the Philistines gathered themselves together at Michmash; ¹²Therefore said I, The Philistines will come down now upon me to Gilgal, and I have not made supplication unto the LORD: I forced myself therefore, and offered a burnt offering. ¹³And Samuel said to Saul, Thou hast done foolishly: *thou hast not kept the commandment of the LORD thy God, which he commanded thee*: for now would the LORD have established thy kingdom upon Israel for ever. ¹⁴But now thy kingdom shall not continue: the LORD hath sought him a man after his own heart, and the LORD hath commanded him to be captain over his people, *because thou hast not kept that which the LORD commanded thee.*

1 Samuel 15:13-26 And Samuel came to Saul: and Saul said unto him, Blessed be thou of the LORD: I have performed the commandment of the LORD. ¹⁴And Samuel said, What meaneth then this bleating of the sheep in mine ears, and the lowing of the oxen which I hear? ¹⁵And Saul said, They have brought them from the Amalekites: for the people spared the best of the sheep and of the oxen, to sacrifice unto the LORD thy God; and the rest we have utterly destroyed. ¹⁶Then Samuel said unto Saul, Stay, and I will tell thee what the LORD hath said to me this night. And he said unto him, Say on. ¹⁷And Samuel said, When thou wast little in thine own sight, wast thou not made the head of the tribes of Israel, and the LORD anointed thee king over Israel? ¹⁸And the LORD sent thee on a journey, and said, Go and utterly destroy the sinners the

## Spots and Wrinkles

Amalekites, and fight against them until they be consumed. *[19]Wherefore then didst thou not obey the voice of the LORD, but didst fly upon the spoil, and didst evil in the sight of the LORD?* [20]And Saul said unto Samuel, Yea, I have obeyed the voice of the LORD, and have gone the way which the LORD sent me, and have brought Agag the king of Amalek, and have utterly destroyed the Amalekites. [21]But the people took of the spoil, sheep and oxen, the chief of the things which should have been utterly destroyed, to sacrifice unto the LORD thy God in Gilgal. *[22]And Samuel said, Hath the LORD as great delight in burnt offerings and sacrifices, as in obeying the voice of the LORD? Behold, to obey is better than sacrifice, and to hearken than the fat of rams.* [23]For rebellion is as the sin of witchcraft, and stubbornness is as iniquity and idolatry. Because thou hast rejected the word of the LORD, he hath also rejected thee from being king. [24]And Saul said unto Samuel, I have sinned: for I have transgressed the commandment of the LORD, and thy words: because I feared the people, and obeyed their voice. [25]Now therefore, I pray thee, pardon my sin, and turn again with me, that I may worship the LORD. [26]And Samuel said unto Saul, I will not return with thee: for thou hast rejected the word of the LORD, and the LORD hath rejected thee from being king over Israel.

When we disregard one command of the Lord and add to another command He has given, we produce wrinkles in the Bride of Christ. Both behaviours are in full disobedience to the commands of Scripture. But how many people say they will live by one command and not another?

Now for sake of clarification, those commands given in the Old Testament that had to do with redemption, perfection, and the sacrifices for sin, have all been completed and fulfilled in the death and resurrection of Christ Himself. For example, the concept of the Sabbath has gone from being a literal day on the calendar to a place of rest in the heart.

Exodus 31:12-18  And the LORD spake unto Moses, saying, [13]Speak thou also unto the children of Israel, saying, Verily my sabbaths ye shall keep: for it is a sign between me and you throughout your generations; that ye may know that I am the LORD that doth sanctify you. [14]Ye shall keep the sabbath therefore; for it is holy unto you: every one that defileth it shall surely be put to death: for whosoever doeth any work therein, that soul shall be cut off from among his people. [15]Six days may work be done; but in the seventh is the sabbath of rest, holy to the LORD: whosoever doeth any work in the sabbath day, he shall surely be put to death. [16]Wherefore the children of Israel shall keep the sabbath, to observe the sabbath throughout their generations, for a perpetual covenant. [17]It is a sign between me and the children of Israel for ever: for in six days the LORD made heaven and earth, and on the seventh day he rested, and was refreshed. [18]And he gave unto Moses, when he had made an end of communing with him upon mount Sinai, two tables of testimony, tables of stone, written with the finger of God.

Colossians 2:6-10 As ye have therefore received Christ Jesus the Lord, so walk ye in him: [7]Rooted and built up in him, and stablished in the faith, as ye have been taught, abounding therein with thanksgiving. [8]Beware lest any man spoil you through philosophy and vain deceit, after the tradition of men, after the rudiments of the world, and not after Christ. [9]For in him dwelleth all the fulness of the Godhead bodily. 10 And ye are complete in him, which is the head of all principality and power:

Colossians 2:14-23 Blotting out the handwriting of ordinances that was against us, which was contrary to us, and took it out of the way, nailing it to his cross; [15]And having spoiled principalities and powers, he made a shew of them openly, triumphing over them in it. [16]Let no man therefore judge you in meat, or in drink, or in respect of an holyday, or of the new moon, or of the sabbath days: [17]Which are a shadow of things to come; but the body is of Christ. [18]Let no man beguile you of your reward in a voluntary humility and worshipping of angels, intruding into those things which he hath not seen, vainly puffed up by his fleshly mind, [19]And not holding the Head, from which all the body by joints and bands having nourishment ministered, and knit together, increaseth with the increase of God. [20]Wherefore if ye be dead with Christ from the rudiments of the world, why, as though living in the world, are ye subject to ordinances, [21](Touch not; taste not; handle not; [22]Which all are to perish with the using;) after the commandments and doctrines of men?

## Spots and Wrinkles

²³Which things have indeed a shew of wisdom in will worship, and humility, and neglecting of the body; not in any honour to the satisfying of the flesh.

Hebrews 4:3-11 For we which have believed do enter into rest, as he said, As I have sworn in my wrath, if they shall enter into my rest: although the works were finished from the foundation of the world. ⁴For he spake in a certain place of the seventh day on this wise, And God did rest the seventh day from all his works. ⁵And in this place again, If they shall enter into my rest. ⁶Seeing therefore it remaineth that some must enter therein, and they to whom it was first preached entered not in because of unbelief: ⁷Again, he limiteth a certain day, saying in David, To day, after so long a time; as it is said, To day if ye will hear his voice, harden not your hearts. ⁸For if Jesus had given them rest, then would he not afterward have spoken of another day. ⁹There remaineth therefore a rest to the people of God. ¹⁰For he that is entered into his rest, he also hath ceased from his own works, as God did from his. ¹¹Let us labour therefore to enter into that rest, lest any man fall after the same example of unbelief.

This issue of keeping the sabbath has become a hot button in recent years, and is an example of adding to a completed doctrine. Paul urges caution on listening to people who will say that certain things have NOT been fulfilled by Christ and therefore must still be engaged in. The sabbath rest has gone from a day to an eternal position in Christ. To return to maintaining it as a day would be to bring one's self back under the rest of the sacrificial Law, completely undoing the Gospel of Grace.

Even worse than trying to return those born into Grace back under the Law, are those who would turn the concept of Grace into an excuse for sin. Modern day teachers merely refer to this as "Liberal Christianity":

Jude 1:3-4 Beloved, when I gave all diligence to write unto you of the common salvation, it was needful for me to write unto you, and exhort you that ye should earnestly contend for the faith which was once delivered unto the saints.

> ⁴For there are certain men crept in unawares, who were before of old ordained to this condemnation, *ungodly men, turning the grace of our God into lasciviousness, and denying the only Lord God, and our Lord Jesus Christ.*

> Romans 6:12-16 Let not sin therefore reign in your mortal body, that ye should obey it in the lusts thereof. ¹³Neither yield ye your members as instruments of unrighteousness unto sin: but yield yourselves unto God, as those that are alive from the dead, and your members as instruments of righteousness unto God. ¹⁴For sin shall not have dominion over you: for ye are not under the law, but under grace. *¹⁵What then? shall we sin, because we are not under the law, but under grace? God forbid.* ¹⁶Know ye not, that to whom ye yield yourselves servants to obey, his servants ye are to whom ye obey; whether of sin unto death, or of obedience unto righteousness?

Using Grace as a license to sin is more of a spot than a wrinkle, but it is listed here. However, the latter part of the quote from Jude above states why it is listed here instead. When we deny the grace of God, we are taking out the foundation of our faith. That firmness and elasticity found in our skin disappears and we are left looking like a wrinkled skeleton of the Bride we were intended to be.

The Grace of God is indeed elastic in its very definition: granting to someone what they don't deserve. But that elasticity is completely stretched out of shape in today's modern mantra of tolerance. God's grace was not designed to wrap around sin. It was designed to liberate mankind from sin instead. Grace is not a license to sin, but a passport to living a holy life before God.

> Romans 6:1-2 What shall we say then? Shall we continue in sin, that grace may abound? ²God forbid. How shall we, that are dead to sin, live any longer therein?

Let me finish this discussion with a few more words from Paul on spots and wrinkles in the Church:

**Spots and Wrinkles**

2 Corinthians 11:2-4  For I am jealous over you with godly jealousy: for I have espoused you to one husband, that I may present you as a chaste virgin to Christ. ³But I fear, lest by any means, as the serpent beguiled Eve through his subtilty, so your minds should be corrupted from the simplicity that is in Christ. ⁴For if he that cometh preacheth another Jesus, whom we have not preached, or if ye receive another spirit, which ye have not received, or another gospel, which ye have not accepted, ye might well bear with him.

2 Corinthians 11:10-15  As the truth of Christ is in me, no man shall stop me of this boasting in the regions of Achaia. ¹¹Wherefore? because I love you not? God knoweth. ¹²But what I do, that I will do, that I may cut off occasion from them which desire occasion; that wherein they glory, they may be found even as we. ¹³For such are false apostles, deceitful workers, transforming themselves into the apostles of Christ. ¹⁴And no marvel; for Satan himself is transformed into an angel of light. ¹⁵Therefore it is no great thing if his ministers also be transformed as the ministers of righteousness; whose end shall be according to their works.

Now that we've identified some of the kinds of spots and wrinkles faced by the Bride of Christ, we will now turn our attention to looking after her health and her bridal attire.

# Dressed for Eternity

**Learning how to do spiritual laundry**

As we saw in the last two discussions, spots and wrinkles don't merely affect the Bride's outfit, but her own health as well. Anything that is allowed to come into contact with sin gets soiled, and when it enters the body, the body gets sick. It was said earlier that in order for the concepts of sanctification and cleansing to make sense, we needed to understand a bit about what those spots and wrinkles are that Christ wants to remove via the washing of the Word.

So how exactly does the Bride of Christ keep herself clean and her bridal attire clean and pressed?

**Prevention:**

Step number one in maintaining optimal health and clean clothes, is to avoid coming into contact with sin in the first place. God tried to teach this concept through the Levitical law by saying in various ways for various situations by various people, that if a person came into contact with something God had deemed unclean, that they were to purify themselves a certain number of days in a certain manner. Failure to do so extended the prescribed number of days in which they would be classified as unclean themselves. The idea here was as much about prevention as it was purification, because if a person understood that a certain thing would make them unclean, it stood to reason that they would avoid it whenever possible.

In a similar manner under the Law of Grace, we are told to steer clear of things God has stated as being sin. An interesting discourse on this subject is given in the book of Acts. Rather than quote the entire chapter here, let me urge the reader to open their Bible to Acts 15, and take a seat in the back of one of the very first church council meetings. Pay attention to the following verses:

## Spots and Wrinkles

Acts 15:19-20 Wherefore my sentence is, that we trouble not them, which from among the Gentiles are turned to God: [20]But that we write unto them, that they abstain from pollutions of idols, and from fornication, and from things strangled, and from blood.

Acts 15:28-29 For it seemed good to the Holy Ghost, and to us, to lay upon you no greater burden than these necessary things; [29]*That ye abstain from meats offered to idols, and from blood, and from things strangled, and from fornication: from which if ye keep yourselves, ye shall do well.* Fare ye well.

1 Thessalonians 4:1-8 Furthermore then we beseech you, brethren, and exhort you by the Lord Jesus, that as ye have received of us how ye ought to walk and to please God, so ye would abound more and more. [2]For ye know what commandments we gave you by the Lord Jesus. [3]*For this is the will of God, even your sanctification, that ye should abstain from fornication:* [4]*That every one of you should know how to possess his vessel in sanctification and honour;* [5]Not in the lust of concupiscence, even as the Gentiles which know not God: [6]That no man go beyond and defraud his brother in any matter: because that the Lord is the avenger of all such, as we also have forewarned you and testified. [7]For God hath not called us unto uncleanness, but unto holiness. [8]He therefore that despiseth, despiseth not man, but God, who hath also given unto us his holy Spirit.

1 Thessalonians 5 is another great chapter on this subject; the following verses being the focus for today's discussion:

1 Thessalonians 5:19-24 Quench not the Spirit. [20]Despise not prophesyings. [21]*Prove all things; hold fast that which is good.* [22]*Abstain from all appearance of evil.* [23]*And the very God of peace sanctify you wholly; and I pray God your whole spirit and soul and body be preserved blameless unto the coming of our Lord Jesus Christ.* [24]Faithful is he that calleth you, who also will do it.

The passages on this page are not an exhaustive list of Scriptures on the matter of prevention, but they help to lay out a few thoughts and guidelines.

# Dressed for Eternity

Prevention begins by choosing not to engage in those things that Scripture says are wrong. Galatians 5 carries such a list prior to discussing the Fruit of the Spirit. Similar lists are scattered throughout the New Testament. Some of the items on the list are mentioned in these passages above. When we know what the Scriptures say about sin, we are able to make conscious choices regarding wilful participation. Galatians 5 also tells us the best way to go about avoiding the decisions that cause us to fall into sin:

> Galatians 5:16-18 This I say then, Walk in the Spirit, and ye shall not fulfil the lust of the flesh. [17]For the flesh lusteth against the Spirit, and the Spirit against the flesh: and these are contrary the one to the other: so that ye cannot do the things that ye would. [18]But if ye be led of the Spirit, ye are not under the law.

> Galatians 5:24-25 And they that are Christ's have crucified the flesh with the affections and lusts. [25]If we live in the Spirit, let us also walk in the Spirit.

**Diet:**

As with anything in life, part of prevention is not merely the mental choice to avoid certain kinds of engagement. It also requires lifestyle choices. As Paul says above, choosing to walk in the Spirit is a lifestyle choice. Feeding on God's Word is also a lifestyle choice.

> 1 Peter 2:1-3 Wherefore laying aside all malice, and all guile, and hypocrisies, and envies, and all evil speakings, [2]As newborn babes, desire the sincere milk of the word, that ye may grow thereby: [3]If so be ye have tasted that the Lord is gracious.

It all begins with the nurturing of milk, doesn't it? A human baby needs Mom's milk in order to inherit her immunity, as well as to gain the strength to grow. But eventually, baby must be weaned onto food it can feed itself. Unfortunately, not everyone is willing to be weaned or we wouldn't have this admonition in the book of Hebrews:

## Spots and Wrinkles

> Hebrews 5:12-14  For when for the time ye ought to be teachers, ye have need that one teach you again which be the first principles of the oracles of God; and are become such as have need of milk, and not of strong meat. ¹³For every one that useth milk is unskilful in the word of righteousness: for he is a babe. ¹⁴But strong meat belongeth to them that are of full age, even those who by reason of use have their senses exercised to discern both good and evil.

Ouch! A healthy diet of God's Word doesn't merely accept the surface lessons available to all newborns in the faith, but dives deeper into God's Word, uncovering the nuggets hidden there. As the child of God grows and matures, they learn how to discern between good and evil because of the food God has given them.

2 Timothy 3, the entire chapter, not only contains lists of kinds of sin to avoid and the kinds of people who engage in them, but it ends with this well-known exhortation:

> 2 Timothy 3:14-17  But continue thou in the things which thou hast learned and hast been assured of, knowing of whom thou hast learned them; ¹⁵And that from a child thou hast known the holy scriptures, which are able to make thee wise unto salvation through faith which is in Christ Jesus. ¹⁶All scripture is given by inspiration of God, and is profitable for doctrine, for reproof, for correction, for instruction in righteousness: ¹⁷That the man of God may be perfect, throughly furnished unto all good works.

Studying God's Word has many health benefits for the Bride of Christ.

1) First, she learns the doctrines of God as set down by God Himself
2) Second, any time she trips and falls, God's Word is there to reprove and correct her so that
3) Third, she receives instruction to guide her into living a life righteous and pleasing before God.

# Dressed for Eternity

Such a diet equips her to engage in the works that God ordained in advance for her to do.

> Ephesians 2:7-10 That in the ages to come he might shew the exceeding riches of his grace in his kindness toward us through Christ Jesus. [8]For by grace are ye saved through faith; and that not of yourselves: it is the gift of God: [9]Not of works, lest any man should boast. [10]For we are his workmanship, created in Christ Jesus unto good works, which God hath before ordained that we should walk in them.

Now notice above that the works prepared for the Bride do not include her Salvation. There is nothing we can do to earn our way into heaven and anyone telling you otherwise is a spot teaching a wrinkle.

This same concept of prevention works for her clothing too, because invariably, what the Bride of Christ comes into contact with will not only make her sick, but will soil her clothes as well. We are told in James that:

> James 1:27 Pure religion and undefiled before God and the Father is this, To visit the fatherless and widows in their affliction, and to keep himself unspotted from the world.

So to avoid those spots whether on our clothes or on our skin, we must choose to live life in the Spirit, daily feeding on the Word of God.

**Bathing and Laundry**

> Romans 13:11-14 And that, knowing the time, that now is high time to awake out of sleep: for now is our salvation nearer than when we believed. [12]The night is far spent, the day is at hand: *let us therefore cast off the works of darkness, and let us put on the armour of light.* [13]*Let us walk honestly, as in the day; not in rioting and drunkenness, not in chambering and wantonness, not in strife and envying.* [14]*But put ye on the Lord Jesus Christ, and make not provision for the flesh, to fulfil the lusts thereof.*

## Spots and Wrinkles

Now what happens if you are doing your best to be in the Word every day, and you slip up? Being as we are all human beings, this will happen to the best of us at some point.

The passage on the previous page talks about choosing to put off the works of darkness and put on the armour of light. This is very much like the concept of taking off your dirty clothes to put on clean ones. The difference is that the clothing spoken of above is so dirty that it can't be washed and put back on. It must be completely done away with.

There is only one bathing ritual that must be engaged in to be cleansed of any sin you have become conscious of, and that is the shed blood of Jesus Christ:

> Mark 14:23-24 And he took the cup, and when he had given thanks, he gave it to them: and they all drank of it. [24]And he said unto them, This is my blood of the new testament, which is shed for many.

> Ephesians 1:6-7 To the praise of the glory of his grace, wherein he hath made us accepted in the beloved. [7]In whom we have redemption through his blood, the forgiveness of sins, according to the riches of his grace;

> Colossians 1:12-14 Giving thanks unto the Father, which hath made us meet to be partakers of the inheritance of the saints in light: [13]Who hath delivered us from the power of darkness, and hath translated us into the kingdom of his dear Son: [14]In whom we have redemption through his blood, even the forgiveness of sins:

> Hebrews 9:11-15 But Christ being come an high priest of good things to come, by a greater and more perfect tabernacle, not made with hands, that is to say, not of this building; [12]Neither by the blood of goats and calves, but by his own blood he entered in once into the holy place, having obtained eternal redemption for us. [13]For if the blood of bulls and of goats, and the ashes of an heifer sprinkling the unclean, sanctifieth to the purifying of the flesh: [14]How much more shall the blood of Christ, who through the eternal Spirit offered himself without spot to God, purge your conscience from dead works to serve the living God? [15]And for this

cause he is the mediator of the new testament, that by means of death, for the redemption of the transgressions that were under the first testament, they which are called might receive the promise of eternal inheritance.

1 John 1:5-9  This then is the message which we have heard of him, and declare unto you, that God is light, and in him is no darkness at all. ⁶If we say that we have fellowship with him, and walk in darkness, we lie, and do not the truth: ⁷But if we walk in the light, as he is in the light, we have fellowship one with another, and the blood of Jesus Christ his Son cleanseth us from all sin. ⁸If we say that we have no sin, we deceive ourselves, and the truth is not in us. ⁹If we confess our sins, he is faithful and just to forgive us our sins, and to cleanse us from all unrighteousness.

All these passages above echo the same concept; that it is only by the shed Blood of Jesus Christ that we can receive forgiveness for our sins, and have our hearts and minds washed and cleansed. So the bathing routine is this:

1) Turn away from the sin. Take off the dirty clothing.
2) Come to Christ in humility, asking forgiveness for that sin. Turn on the flow.
3) Receive Christ's forgiveness through His Blood shed at the Cross of Calvary. Stand under the crimson flow.

**Doing the laundry is a very similar process:**

Revelation 7:13-14  And one of the elders answered, saying unto me, What are these which are arrayed in white robes? and whence came they? ¹⁴And I said unto him, Sir, thou knowest. And he said to me, These are they which came out of great tribulation, and have washed their robes, and made them white in the blood of the Lamb.

When we soil our Robe of Righteousness, it must be washed. Scripture says that the only cleansing agent that will get out the stain of sin is the shed Blood of Jesus Christ.

## Spots and Wrinkles

Getting out the stains from our Robe of Righteousness then involves two more steps not listed above for bathing. These two concepts have already been shared at various times, but they will be recapped here.

1) Cleanse your mind through the reading of the Word.

Romans 12:1-2 I beseech you therefore, brethren, by the mercies of God, that ye present your bodies a living sacrifice, holy, acceptable unto God, which is your reasonable service. ²And be not conformed to this world: but be ye transformed by the renewing of your mind, that ye may prove what is that good, and acceptable, and perfect, will of God.

This might mean checking over the head piece to be sure there are no rips or tears, because it is in the mind where temptations to sin enter. As we learned about the helmet, our salvation in Christ is meant to protect our mind from the attacks of the enemy. The Blood of Jesus bought our salvation and is the flow under which we must go to reaffirm the strength of that helmet.

Failure to ensure that our Salvation is secure via true repentance and full acceptance of the Lordship of Christ in our lives, can cause a wide range of problems, troubles, and strange ideas to infect us and damage our spiritual clothing in the process.

2) Check the path we are on and if need be, switch to the path of the Holy Spirit.

Galatians 5:13-16 For, brethren, ye have been called unto liberty; only use not liberty for an occasion to the flesh, but by love serve one another. ¹⁴For all the law is fulfilled in one word, even in this; Thou shalt love thy neighbour as thyself. ¹⁵But if ye bite and devour one another, take heed that ye be not consumed one of another. ¹⁶This I say then, Walk in the Spirit, and ye shall not fulfil the lust of the flesh.

This requires checking our footwear. Are we still wearing those badgerskin shoes? The boots that carry the Gospel of Peace?

# Dressed for Eternity

If checking our footwear reveals that we've been going barefoot for awhile, it's time to bathe as mentioned earlier, then to submit to the Holy Spirit's efforts in our lives. The Fruit of the Spirit mentioned in Galatians 5 doesn't grow very well when the Bride of Christ is not allowing the Holy Spirit to have control.

Sometimes there are wrinkles that need to be ironed out of the clothing. The only way to get them out is through water and the Word. Now we must remember:

> Hebrews 4:12 For the word of God is quick, and powerful, and sharper than any twoedged sword, piercing even to the dividing asunder of soul and spirit, and of the joints and marrow, and is a discerner of the thoughts and intents of the heart.

Therefore:

> 1 Peter 4:12-13 Beloved, think it not strange concerning the fiery trial which is to try you, as though some strange thing happened unto you: $^{13}$But rejoice, inasmuch as ye are partakers of Christ's sufferings; that, when his glory shall be revealed, ye may be glad also with exceeding joy.

God doesn't send these trials against you, but uses them as a refiner uses fire. Remember our discussion on gold and silver smelting earlier in this book? (see pages 73 and 105)

> Malachi 3:3 And he shall sit as a refiner and purifier of silver: and he shall purify the sons of Levi, and purge them as gold and silver, that they may offer unto the LORD an offering in righteousness.

> Romans 8:28 And we know that all things work together for good to them that love God, to them who are the called according to his purpose.

The only known way to get the wrinkles out of the Bride's clothing is to iron them out. This takes heat and pressure, both of which don't feel very good to the human spirit.

## Spots and Wrinkles

A somewhat easier way is to sit under the steam of God's judgement.

> Psalm 7:8  The LORD shall judge the people: judge me, O LORD, according to my righteousness, and according to mine integrity that is in me.

> Psalm 26:1-3  A Psalm of David. Judge me, O LORD; for I have walked in mine integrity: I have trusted also in the LORD; therefore I shall not slide. ²Examine me, O LORD, and prove me; try my reins and my heart. ³For thy lovingkindness is before mine eyes: and I have walked in thy truth.

> Psalm 96:11-13  Let the heavens rejoice, and let the earth be glad; let the sea roar, and the fulness thereof. ¹²Let the field be joyful, and all that is therein: then shall all the trees of the wood rejoice ¹³Before the LORD: for he cometh, for he cometh to judge the earth: he shall judge the world with righteousness, and the people with his truth.

> Psalm 139:23-24  Search me, O God, and know my heart: try me, and know my thoughts: ²⁴And see if there be any wicked way in me, and lead me in the way everlasting.

> 1 Corinthians 11:27-32  Wherefore whosoever shall eat this bread, and drink this cup of the Lord, unworthily, shall be guilty of the body and blood of the Lord. ²⁸But let a man examine himself, and so let him eat of that bread, and drink of that cup. ²⁹For he that eateth and drinketh unworthily, eateth and drinketh damnation to himself, not discerning the Lord's body. ³⁰For this cause many are weak and sickly among you, and many sleep. ³¹For if we would judge ourselves, we should not be judged. 32 But when we are judged, we are chastened of the Lord, that we should not be condemned with the world.

When we willingly place ourselves under God's benevolent judgement, the act of cleansing away those things that should not be in our lives is a much easier task for God to take on. Remember, it is He who sanctifies us. Sanctification is the process of becoming holy, according to our earlier discussion.

# Dressed for Eternity

Sometimes spots, stains and wrinkles can be tough things to get out. Sometimes they have to be cut out! That's a really big ouch when that happens! But it's necessary if we truly want to live holy lives before God and be ready for when the Trumpet announces the coming of the Heavenly Bridegroom.

**Parable of the 10 Virgins**

Learning how to look after our bridal finery is so important, that Christ told a parable about it in the book of Matthew:

> Matthew 25:1-13 Then shall the kingdom of heaven be likened unto ten virgins, which took their lamps, and went forth to meet the bridegroom. ²And five of them were wise, and five were foolish. ³They that were foolish took their lamps, and took no oil with them: ⁴But the wise took oil in their vessels with their lamps. ⁵While the bridegroom tarried, they all slumbered and slept. ⁶And at midnight there was a cry made, Behold, the bridegroom cometh; go ye out to meet him. ⁷Then all those virgins arose, and trimmed their lamps. ⁸And the foolish said unto the wise, Give us of your oil; for our lamps are gone out. ⁹But the wise answered, saying, Not so; lest there be not enough for us and you: but go ye rather to them that sell, and buy for yourselves. ¹⁰And while they went to buy, the bridegroom came; and they that were ready went in with him to the marriage: and the door was shut. ¹¹Afterward came also the other virgins, saying, Lord, Lord, open to us. ¹²But he answered and said, Verily I say unto you, I know you not. ¹³Watch therefore, for ye know neither the day nor the hour wherein the Son of man cometh.

Before we carry on in this discussion, it is necessary to be reminded of the brief introduction given earlier on ancient Jewish wedding customs back on page 5. It bears repeating that the bride and her maidens did not know when exactly her groom would be coming for her. It was the custom back then for the groom to return to his father's home to build a room for himself and his bride, and only upon the approval of his father was he able to return to get her.

## Spots and Wrinkles

Other sources would note that part of this was due to the fact that the bride and groom would not leave this room for seven days, so it needed to be fully stocked with everything they would need for those days.

While the groom was preparing this room, the bride was to be busy preparing her wedding garments and making herself ready. This is what has been going on when we meet the 10 virgins in Matthew 25. Because the groom shows up in the middle of the night when everyone is sleeping, as was often the habit in ancient Israel at the time, the 10 virgins had fallen asleep. It was and still is common in orthodox Jewish circles to have the marriage banquet under the stars to remember Abraham's promise. So the trumpet blows and the call goes out, "Behold, the Bridegroom cometh!". Instantly, up jump the 10 virgins! But there's a problem, and one that would not be easily solved. You see, only five of the 10 virgins would actually be admitted to the marriage supper. The reason is found in our discussion on the Anointing Oil back on page 171.

> Ephesians 3:14-19 For this cause I bow my knees unto the Father of our Lord Jesus Christ, $^{15}$Of whom the whole family in heaven and earth is named, $^{16}$That he would grant you, according to the riches of his glory, to be strengthened with might by his Spirit in the inner man; $^{17}$That Christ may dwell in your hearts by faith; that ye, being rooted and grounded in love, $^{18}$May be able to comprehend with all saints what is the breadth, and length, and depth, and height; 19 And to know the love of Christ, which passeth knowledge, *that ye might be filled with all the fulness of God.*

> Ephesians 5:17-21 Wherefore be ye not unwise, but understanding what the will of the Lord is. $^{18}$And be not drunk with wine, wherein is excess; *but be filled with the Spirit;* $^{19}$Speaking to yourselves in psalms and hymns and spiritual songs, singing and making melody in your heart to the Lord; $^{20}$Giving thanks always for all things unto God and the Father in the name of our Lord Jesus Christ; $^{21}$Submitting yourselves one to another in the fear of God.

The Holy Spirit is not a thing that can be purchased. He is the third personality in the Trinity and takes up residence in us.

## Dressed for Eternity

> 1 Corinthians 6:17-20  But he that is joined unto the Lord is one spirit. [18]Flee fornication. Every sin that a man doeth is without the body; but he that committeth fornication sinneth against his own body. *[19]What? know ye not that your body is the temple of the Holy Ghost which is in you, which ye have of God, and ye are not your own?* [20]For ye are bought with a price: therefore glorify God in your body, and in your spirit, which are God's.

It wasn't enough for the five foolish virgins to get up and trim their lamps. Anyone can choose to cut out bad things in their lives in order to look fresh and new. But without the Holy Spirit in their lives to light their wicks, their lamps would not light.

It isn't enough to be filled just once with the Holy Spirit as many have erroneously thought. The Greek used in Ephesians 5 refers to "keep on being" filled. We need to continually submit and surrender ourselves to the Holy Spirit in order to remain ready for that great Trumpet blast.

The cost of not being ready is great. The five foolish tried to buy oil from the five wise virgins. The Holy Spirit will also not be bought or sold. Failure to keep in step with the Spirit results in missing out on the Marriage Supper of the Lamb.

This is not merely true in the parable, but is true for the body of Christ today, the Church. We need to continually humble ourselves before the Holy Spirit and ensure He has a clean and comfortable place to live.

> 1 Corinthians 6:16-20  What? know ye not that he which is joined to an harlot is one body? for two, saith he, shall be one flesh. [17]But he that is joined unto the Lord is one spirit. [18]Flee fornication. Every sin that a man doeth is without the body; but he that committeth fornication sinneth against his own body. [19]What? know ye not that your body is the temple of the Holy Ghost which is in you, which ye have of God, and ye are not your own? [20]For ye are bought with a price: therefore glorify God in your body, and in your spirit, which are God's.

## Modesty

Before we get into what modesty is according to the Word of God, let's pause for a moment and consider what modesty has become around the world.

It is important to consider modesty as a subject that goes beyond cultural inhibitions, laws, and acceptable practises in order for the subject to be useful to anyone of any culture. So to shape our discussion, we will look at various cultures and religions and what they consider to be modest and why.

After that, we will discuss what modesty is and isn't, what makes men and women lust after each other, issues of respect, and more. The end goal for this discussion is to arm the reader with a healthy understanding of what God says about modesty, presented in a way that can be applied to whatever culture that person lives in. Whenever the opportunity presents itself, examples of how coming into contact with the Word of God has affected cultural modesty will also be presented.

This is a huge topic, and a contentious one at that. There are those who are quite legalistic about their modesty and those who will stop at nothing to enforce immodesty as a personal right. Then of course there is the fact that modesty means different things to different people, religions and regions. The concept of modesty in various cultures has changed down through history as well. Even within the church across the globe, modesty has taken on various forms at various times in history, and ranged from almost anything-goes in some denominations to almost all skin covered in others to this day. This of course only seems to affect the outward appearance and how it is interpreted.

By the end of this section, it is the hope of this author that the reader will understand that modesty is not merely about appearance, historical time period, region, denomination, or people group, but that, as with everything else in the Kingdom of God, it begins in the mind and heart toward God first, and then toward others.

Due to the contentious nature of this section, the reader is not expected to agree with everything they read. Instead, they are encouraged to pray before they begin reading, that the Holy Spirit would quicken to them anything they should pay particular attention to, and then act on that knowledge appropriately. Let us begin.

# Dressed for Eternity

## Cultural Expressions of Modesty

Modesty looks and acts in various ways around the world.

### American Indians

Before the settler days of the US among the Navajo-Dine people: A woman who was not dressed in turquoise and silver jewelry, a traditional rug dress, and wrap moccasins was not fully dressed. A man without turquoise and silver jewelry, loin covering, leggings, and Navajo moccasins was not modest either. Both wore their hair in buns close to their head to keep their wisdom close. Many elder Navajo dress in modified versions of these outfits to this day.

### India

According to Wikipedia sources, modesty in India depends on where you are and what caste you belong to. It is interesting to note that the acceptance of male nudity is more common in poverty-stricken and/or rural areas. This seems to be in keeping with missionary observations that when a person's lot in life improves, their sense of modesty returns upon discovery that they have personal worth.

In the city, nudity is generally not tolerated. Men may go topless. Women must be properly dressed at all times.

### Islamic nations

Nations around the world with an Islamic government/culture typically require women to either be fully clothed, or fully-clothed and wearing either a head scarf or burka. Scholars who have delved into the Quran looking for information on why this is so, have not found much to go on. It appears that whether a woman is or is not required to partially or fully hide all face or body features is a sect/governmental requirement rather than one of the particular religion.

## Dubai

While technically an Islamic state, Dubai is probably one of the most lenient in their definition of modest appearance. The only time there is strict enforcement of Islamic modesty rules is when you visit a local temple. The rest of time, adequate covering in public simply asks that shoulders and knees be covered. How you appear at the pool or at a party looks very North American otherwise. Having said that, not even men are allowed to appear without a shirt in public.

## Jewish People

Orthodox Jews must follow a strict set of modesty guidelines with family, friends, strangers, crowds, and worship gatherings. Jewish people who do not follow the orthodox ways have a much more lenient view of modesty and tend to dress as the common folk of whichever country they are living in. Modern-day Israel as a result looks not much different than western society when it comes to dress. See the appendix for a link detailing orthodox Jewish modesty guidelines. This may be a handy reference for those who think some denomination of Christianity is too harsh; good for a perspective shift.

## Korea

In Korean culture, modesty is as much about behaviour as it is about appearance. Men will carry heavy loads for women as a matter of polite behaviour. Showing up at home or in public without a shirt is considered naked and therefore immodest. Women are to present themselves in a humble manner, not exaggerating accomplishments or showing off what they can do. They don't wear very short skirts in church and they don't accuse others or cheat.

Men are considered immodest if they start showing off in some way, or don't pay for the lady's dinner on a date. Women are considered immodest if in a group they are loud and boisterous, or show off their jewelry and finery.

## Japan

In Japanese culture, a man is considered modest if he is bright and cheerful, dressed appropriately for work or school, and hard working. A woman is considered modest if she is polite and helpful. Ordinary jeans and t-shirt is considered normal daily attire.

## Singapore

In Singapore, and perhaps most Asian culture, modesty is generally seen as conservative, meek, quiet, and blending in the crowd, as opposed to being brash, outspoken and loud.

In appearance, women are generally frowned upon if they show any cleavage at all. Skirts shorter than thigh-length are considered immodest. As in Dubai, modest dress takes on the context of where it occurs. Bare shoulders may be fine on the street for example, but not at the office. Bare mid-riffs are generally not acceptable. Dressing with any sort of intent to provoke the other gender sexually can happen regardless of how a woman is dressed. It is the intent she projects instead.

Men are frowned on for showing up in public without a shirt, and tight-fitting shirts are considered immodest as well. Swim shorts as opposed to tighter swim trunks are preferred at the beach or poolside. Even shorts or pants above the knee are considered both weird and immodest.

Modest behaviour in Singapore is similar to that of Korea and Japan. If you are loud, brash, boastful, showing off your wealth and accomplishments, etc., then you are considered immodest. A modest person in Singapore will not boast of their accomplishments, wealth, or stature. A lady who flaunts her wealth via her clothing and jewelry is considered immodest no matter how she dresses. A wealthy businessman is considered modest if he lives a simple lifestyle.

## What is Modesty?

There are a few problems with how modesty is being presented these days. The goals are noble, but the unintended messages are wreaking havoc.

Freedictionary.com brings together word definitions from various dictionaries that are available online. They list several interesting definitions of the word "modesty":

> Reserve or propriety in speech, dress, or behavior. / Lack of pretentiousness; simplicity. / (Clothing & Fashion) (modifier) designed to prevent inadvertent exposure of part of the body / regard for decency of behavior, speech, dress, etc. / lack of vanity.

First and foremost, modesty is an attitude of the heart and mind worked out in how one views both themselves and those around them. How a person behaves around others in various situations is a direct result of personal views and understandings of not only themselves, but how they will be perceived by others. In some ways, personal views and understandings of how others think and behave also play into this.

## Respect

At the top of this list of views, understandings, and behaviour, is the concept of respect.

Respect assumes two things: First, that the person showing respect has respect for themselves and will behave in a manner fitting of that respect. Second, that the person showing respect considers those they come into contact with as being worthy of that respect.

This issue of respect plays out in two arenas for the typical person growing up in a "western" nation. To varying degrees these same two arenas come into play in other regions of the world, and in some cases are more pronounced than they are in western nations.

# Modesty

**Arena number one:**

**Society's view of men and women.** Much of the world is patriarchal in nature. This doesn't have to be a bad thing, but thanks to the twisted nature of sin in our lives, it often very quickly leads to opinions and behaviours that are not conducive to healthy interaction between the genders.

Men are often seen one of two ways: Either they are seen as domineering and make the woman do their bidding to the point of beating her down and making her feel like dirt; or they are viewed as more than willing to let women use their powers of allurement and feel that if a woman dresses a certain way, then they are inviting trouble and will gladly give it. Neither of these views of men are healthy, and yet there are societies where such mindsets are considered normal and even encouraged. North American society for example, views men as uncontrolled sex demons who will pounce on a woman if she shows her cleavage or too much of her butt. Men are considered sexual consumers and women are the goods.

Women are often seen one of two ways as well: Either they are seen as submissive servants who do their masters' bidding no matter how demeaning and menial, or they are viewed as feminist Amazons flaunting their wares with a look-don't-touch glare and getting upset when what they advertise brings in unwanted business. In North America, women are objects used to sell cars, boats, motorbikes, clothes, perfumes, and more. A walk through any mall almost feels like a trip through a soft-porn magazine with the larger-than-life 90% naked advertising going on from store to store.

**Arena number two:**

**Personal views of one's self.** Unfortunately, most people have developed a personal view of themselves based on how others around them have treated them in some fashion. This is true the world over. Women growing up under oppressive leadership often grow up thinking they are worthless and will turn to various methods in an attempt to make themselves feel better and draw more favourable treatment. Men growing up under leadership that does not exhibit or teach self control often get a twisted idea of what manhood is, and take advantage of those around them to get a leg up the ladder in social circles. This can range from sexual prowess to financial wealth to political power of some level.

As you can see, none of the views and perceptions in either of these two arenas are conducive to building a culture of respect.

This need for respect is exacerbated by cultural attitudes as well. In a culture where family is lauded as the nuclear core of the community, men and women are more likely to respect each other than in a culture where individualism is lauded instead of community. Cultural norms that have put down or degraded women for eons are difficult to challenge and change. Cultural norms casting men as predators can be difficult to change as well.

The best place for change to occur with regards to respect, is in the individual's mind. There are some truths that need to be espoused before a person will adopt a new way of thinking about themselves and others.

1) God created mankind as man and woman. He didn't create an androgynous race that had to pick which gender it was. As much as there are people out there who feel God made a mistake when He gave them the gender they have, this is not due to God's design for them, but how family and society allowed them to grow up instead. God does not make mistakes.

2) Secondly, while God merely spoke everything else into being at the beginning of Creation, He chose to take extra care in making mankind:

Genesis 1:27-28 So God created man in his own image, in the image of God created he him; male and female created he them. ²⁸And God blessed them, and God said unto them, Be fruitful, and multiply, and replenish the earth, and subdue it: and have dominion over the fish of the sea, and over the fowl of the air, and over every living thing that moveth upon the earth.

**Modesty**

Chapter two of Genesis gives us more detail as to how God created mankind:

Genesis 2:7 And the LORD God formed man of the dust of the ground, and breathed into his nostrils the breath of life; and man became a living soul.

Genesis 2:18-24 And the LORD God said, It is not good that the man should be alone; I will make him an help meet for him. [19]And out of the ground the LORD God formed every beast of the field, and every fowl of the air; and brought them unto Adam to see what he would call them: and whatsoever Adam called every living creature, that was the name thereof. [20]And Adam gave names to all cattle, and to the fowl of the air, and to every beast of the field; but for Adam there was not found an help meet for him. [21]And the LORD God caused a deep sleep to fall upon Adam, and he slept: and he took one of his ribs, and closed up the flesh instead thereof; [22]And the rib, which the LORD God had taken from man, made he a woman, and brought her unto the man. [23]And Adam said, This is now bone of my bones, and flesh of my flesh: she shall be called Woman, because she was taken out of Man. [24]Therefore shall a man leave his father and his mother, and shall cleave unto his wife: and they shall be one flesh.

Then we come to a very popular passage of Scripture. This passage has become so popular that it's been turned into a cliche, and as with any cliche, the meaning has largely been overlooked, glanced over, or lost altogether on the hearer.

Psalm 139:13-16 For thou hast possessed my reins: thou hast covered me in my mother's womb. [14]I will praise thee; for I am fearfully and wonderfully made: marvellous are thy works; and that my soul knoweth right well. [15]My substance was not hid from thee, when I was made in secret, and curiously wrought in the lowest parts of the earth. [16]Thine eyes did see my substance, yet being unperfect; and in thy book all my members were written, which in continuance were fashioned, when as yet there was none of them.

## Dressed for Eternity

In order to develop a healthy respect for one's self and for others, we need to begin here. Every single person alive, including you dear reader, was designed by God Himself. There is a blueprint carefully planned out and not merely encased in your DNA, but on a shelf someplace in heaven, detailing every minute detail of who you are, what your body shape would be, what gender you would be, what time period you would live in, etc. You are created exactly the way God wanted you to be, minus the deformities the sin-nature has thrown into the mix.

Now before you shake your fist at God for some deformity you may have been born with, it is important to understand that we live in a sinful world. Deformities can occur because of parental habits while you were forming in the womb. Deformities and disease often occur because of sin's creation of genetic defects passed down through the family line. (and this may very well be exacerbated by genetically modifying our food sources going forward) As we know from Christ's response to the disciples before healing a blind man, not all deformities are caused because an ancestor in our family line sinned. Some are allowed in order to bring glory to God. God doesn't make mistakes, but He does teach that the actions of one person will be reflected down through the generations, whether that action was caused by a family member, or those outside the family.

He allows us to go through things or be born in certain ways that will shape our mission in His Kingdom. It is important to stop and consider that God wanted you short and stocky or tall and lanky for a reason. The job and purpose He intended for you required that build. God thought you would look cute in an oval face and veins on the back of your hand that look like a heart when you put your fists together. Have you ever looked at your thumb-print? Have those rings ever amazed you that no other thumb-print is exactly like yours?

When you realize the planning and effort God put into making you exactly the way you are, you come to realize that it is for His pleasure that you look the way you do. The colour of your eyes, the thickness of your hair, the colour of your skin, the shape of your body, God chose all that and He thought it was perfect for you.

**Modesty**

So the first truth is that God created you exactly how He wanted you to look and gave you the personality that you have, because He thought it suited you.

What is important to understand is that the views of mankind in general are not to be held to the same level as God's view of you. It's okay to respect their views to a point, but the ultimate source of pleasure should be from God.

The second truth is that God didn't just make you in a carefully planned out manner that pleased Him, He made those around you in the same thoughtful, caring, and careful way. It took nine months to make you and your friends exactly how He wanted you. When looking at your friends, and when looking at those of the opposite gender, it is important to remember that God took pleasure in making them as well.

These understandings are foundational to building a healthy level of respect for yourself and those around you.

**Respect requires pairing with humility.**

> Romans 12:3  For I say, through the grace given unto me, to every man that is among you, not to think of himself more highly than he ought to think; but to think soberly, according as God hath dealt to every man the measure of faith.

> Romans 12:9-10  Let love be without dissimulation. Abhor that which is evil; cleave to that which is good.  ¹⁰Be kindly affectioned one to another with brotherly love; in honour preferring one another;

> 1 Peter 2:17  Honour all men. Love the brotherhood. Fear God. Honour the king.

An older definition of respect is given in the verses that follow:

> Psalm 40:4  Blessed is that man that maketh the LORD his trust, and respecteth not the proud, nor such as turn aside to lies.

## Dressed for Eternity

James 2:1-9 My brethren, have not the faith of our Lord Jesus Christ, the Lord of glory, with respect of persons. ²For if there come unto your assembly a man with a gold ring, in goodly apparel, and there come in also a poor man in vile raiment; ³And ye have respect to him that weareth the gay clothing, and say unto him, Sit thou here in a good place; and say to the poor, Stand thou there, or sit here under my footstool: ⁴Are ye not then partial in yourselves, and are become judges of evil thoughts? ⁵Hearken, my beloved brethren, Hath not God chosen the poor of this world rich in faith, and heirs of the kingdom which he hath promised to them that love him? ⁶But ye have despised the poor. Do not rich men oppress you, and draw you before the judgment seats? ⁷Do not they blaspheme that worthy name by the which ye are called? ⁸If ye fulfil the royal law according to the scripture, Thou shalt love thy neighbour as thyself, ye do well: ⁹But if ye have respect to persons, ye commit sin, and are convinced of the law as transgressors.

In these two passages, we see respect being given where it shouldn't be. This is talking about treating people with different levels of respect or no respect at all. To show partiality, as verse four states above, is not what God meant when He said to treat each other fairly and with honour. However, society does this all the time.

In some cultures, women are given less respect than dogs. In other cultures, street people are given less respect than dogs. The fact remains that whether you are rich or poor, man or woman, you were created worthy of the respect God mentions in Ephesians 5:

Ephesians 5:19-21 Speaking to yourselves in psalms and hymns and spiritual songs, singing and making melody in your heart to the Lord; ²⁰Giving thanks always for all things unto God and the Father in the name of our Lord Jesus Christ; 21Submitting yourselves one to another in the fear of God.

True respect as we know the word in modern-day usage, requires humility. It requires putting others ahead of yourself and thinking of their needs before your own. Ephesians 5 goes on to talk about how husbands and wives should

## Modesty

treat each other, and while many patriarchal societies are quick to focus only on the woman's side of the equation, read this following passage and note the man's role:

> Ephesians 5:22-33 Wives, submit yourselves unto your own husbands, as unto the Lord. [23]For the husband is the head of the wife, even as Christ is the head of the church: and he is the saviour of the body. [24]Therefore as the church is subject unto Christ, so let the wives be to their own husbands in every thing. [25]Husbands, love your wives, even as Christ also loved the church, and gave himself for it; [26]That he might sanctify and cleanse it with the washing of water by the word, [27]That he might present it to himself a glorious church, not having spot, or wrinkle, or any such thing; but that it should be holy and without blemish. [28]So ought men to love their wives as their own bodies. He that loveth his wife loveth himself. [29]For no man ever yet hated his own flesh; but nourisheth and cherisheth it, even as the Lord the church: [30]For we are members of his body, of his flesh, and of his bones. [31]For this cause shall a man leave his father and mother, and shall be joined unto his wife, and they two shall be one flesh. [32]This is a great mystery: but I speak concerning Christ and the church. [33]Nevertheless let every one of you in particular so love his wife even as himself; and the wife see that she reverence her husband.

Wives: Submit to husband as to the Lord, not to a slave driver. Reverence in the KJV, or respect in modern language, her husband.

Husbands: Love his wife as his own body, and be willing to die for her as Christ did for the Church

Notice how neither of these directives are capable of lording it over the other.; submission and respect on one side, and love and sacrifice on the other. But you can't love someone you don't respect, nor will you die for someone you don't value. In both cases we see a clear example of putting the other first.

Now let's look at how God made men and women.

> 1 Peter 3:5-12  For after this manner in the old time the holy women also, who trusted in God, adorned themselves, being in subjection unto their own husbands: ⁶Even as Sara obeyed Abraham, calling him lord: whose daughters ye are, as long as ye do well, and are not afraid with any amazement. ⁷Likewise, ye husbands, dwell with them according to knowledge, giving honour unto the wife, as unto the weaker vessel, and as being heirs together of the grace of life; that your prayers be not hindered. ⁸Finally, be ye all of one mind, having compassion one of another, love as brethren, be pitiful, be courteous: ⁹Not rendering evil for evil, or railing for railing: but contrariwise blessing; knowing that ye are thereunto called, that ye should inherit a blessing. ¹⁰For he that will love life, and see good days, let him refrain his tongue from evil, and his lips that they speak no guile: ¹¹Let him eschew evil, and do good; let him seek peace, and ensue it. ¹²For the eyes of the Lord are over the righteous, and his ears are open unto their prayers: but the face of the Lord is against them that do evil.

Matthew Henry's Commentary has this to say about this passage:

> Christians ought to do their duty to one another, from a willing mind, and in obedience to the command of God. Wives should be subject to their husbands, not from dread and amazement, but from desire to do well, and please God. The husband's duty to the wife implies giving due respect unto her, and maintaining her authority, protecting her, and placing trust in her. They are heirs together of all the blessings of this life and that which is to come, and should live peaceably one with another. Prayer sweetens their converse. And it is not enough that they pray with the family, but husband and wife together by themselves, and with their children. Those who are acquainted with prayer, find such unspeakable sweetness in it, that they will not be hindered therein. That you may pray much, live holily; and that you may live holily, be much in prayer.

Notice where the ultimate focus lies in these admonished interactions. These directives are given for interpersonal respect, so that God Himself will be honoured. After all, He made us right? He expects us to respect His creation.

## Modesty

We choose to respect ourselves and each other because we are God's workmanship, each and every one of us.

## Men

Knowing this, we can look more closely at how He made each of us. Men, by nature, are more visual. This doesn't mean they are more base as some seem to say, it just means they have a higher appreciation for what they see than women do. This might amaze some of you, but it's true. This author's brother for example, can find the most amazing things hidden away in the back of stores and present gifts at Christmas that leave everyone in awe. Some guys I've known were better housekeepers than I'd ever be! Look at how most guys look after their cars and trucks and motorbikes! The chrome shines! The leather shines! The dash sparkles! The mags on the tires reflect their face perfectly, and the wax job is flawless! Why? Because they have a higher appreciation for beautiful things. Did you ever wonder why most gardeners are men? They have what it takes to ensure plants grow into beautiful works of art.

For all these amazing traits, they come with a curve-ball that sin threw into the mix the moment Adam ate of the fruit Eve handed him. This curve-ball is honestly no fault of the man, but is thoroughly at fault of the enemy of our souls, satan himself. Being as we are discussing respect, that name will not be capitalized in this book no matter how proper it is deemed to do so. He is not worthy of that level of respect in written literature.

Throughout Scripture we see satan throwing all manner of temptations at mankind hoping to trip them up and send them to hell. The biggest way to do this has always been with lust. Lust by the way, is not merely aimed at women. It is aimed at anything desirous to behold, period. It is a close cousin to envy. We see what has become termed "lust of the eyes" when satan beguiled Eve into eating of the fruit of the Tree of Good and Evil in Genesis chapter 2. As with any sin, the focus is self. The question is "what's in it for me?" "How can I obtain that?" "I want/need that and will get it at all costs!" This has led to some of the 10 Commandments:

# Dressed for Eternity

Exodus 20:13-17 Thou shalt not kill. 14 Thou shalt not commit adultery. [15]Thou shalt not steal. [16]Thou shalt not bear false witness against thy neighbour. [17]Thou shalt not covet thy neighbour's house, thou shalt not covet thy neighbour's wife, nor his manservant, nor his maidservant, nor his ox, nor his ass, nor any thing that is thy neighbour's.

Notice verse 17's focus does not stop at "thy neighbour's wife", but includes where the other couple lives, their employees, their animals and their possessions in general.

Therefore, lust is not merely a sexual issue as many have taught over the years. It is a case of man's uniquely intense ability to appreciate beauty, form and function, and having that ability negatively turned on its head by sin. The sin-nature is "me first", "I want", etc, and has little regard to the owner of the object or person being considered. We see too many examples of this every day to bother with quoting examples. Just look up your local news for an example in your area.

**Women**

Women have been given the ability to nurture, to care, and as a result, are more emotional creatures than men, 90% of the time. Women are culturally considered the weaker vessel due to the generally-prevalent somewhat lighter frame, and due to the hormonal make-up required to bear children, have lower stamina levels than men. Having said that, women generally have longer endurance levels in other areas. Women have been the ones to look after the children, cook the meals, manage household chores and grocery shopping. Before the days of the supermarket and general store, women managed the kitchen garden and sewed the clothing as well. The effort required to go into this level of management meant that crossing the lady of the house was typically the wrong thing to do and you feared her frying pan or rolling pin with good reason! Women were not physically weak thanks to what it took to keep house and home together. The woman of Proverbs 31 not only made clothes for her family, but she cooked for her servants before they were even up! She was a business woman and her husband praised her in the city gates.

**Modesty**

Here are the last few verses of that amazing chapter:

> Proverbs 31:20-31  She stretcheth out her hand to the poor; yea, she reacheth forth her hands to the needy. [21]She is not afraid of the snow for her household: for all her household are clothed with scarlet. [22]She maketh herself coverings of tapestry; her clothing is silk and purple. [23]Her husband is known in the gates, when he sitteth among the elders of the land. [24]She maketh fine linen, and selleth it; and delivereth girdles unto the merchant. [25]Strength and honour are her clothing; and she shall rejoice in time to come. [26]She openeth her mouth with wisdom; and in her tongue is the law of kindness. [27]She looketh well to the ways of her household, and eateth not the bread of idleness. [28]Her children arise up, and call her blessed; her husband also, and he praiseth her. [29]Many daughters have done virtuously, but thou excellest them all. [30]Favour is deceitful, and beauty is vain: but a woman that feareth the LORD, she shall be praised. [31]Give her of the fruit of her hands; and let her own works praise her in the gates.

Understanding the different ways God has created men and women to look at the world and live within it, gives a better foundation for respecting one another and looking out for each other. Understanding what sin has done to the way men and women relate is also necessary to gaining an understanding of the levels of respect required for healthy relationships to flourish.

**Vanity**

Various verses in Scripture speak to one of the definitions of modesty, "the lack of vanity". Before we look at those verses, what is vanity?

> Excessive pride in one's appearance or accomplishments; conceit / Lack of usefulness, worth, or effect; worthlessness / excessive pride in oneself or one's appearance; character or quality of being vain. / an instance of this quality or feeling. / something about which one is vain. / lack of real value; worthlessness. / something worthless, trivial, or pointless.

## Dressed for Eternity

This combination of the various definitions presented by thefreedictionary.com is very interesting. This combination presents us with the two basic roots upon which men and women struggle.

The first is that of being prideful in one's own appearance, abilities, character, etc. Generally when we are proud of something we have done, we want others to know about it and share in our feelings. When others don't feel our efforts were so great, we can get hurt feelings and sometimes even lash back. Vanity takes this enjoyment of one's appearance or accomplishments to unhealthy levels to the point where they are constantly fussing over themselves so that others will show them the level of appreciation they feel they deserve. One person was referred to as spending 3 hours of me-time in the bathroom in order to look just right. Guys will do this with their vehicles and gardens and house exteriors, spending inordinate amounts of time to get them looking not only their absolute best, but better than everyone else's around them.

The Pharisees behaved this way constantly, prompting Christ to respond:

> Matthew 23:2-12 Saying, The scribes and the Pharisees sit in Moses' seat: [3]All therefore whatsoever they bid you observe, that observe and do; but do not ye after their works: for they say, and do not. [4]For they bind heavy burdens and grievous to be borne, and lay them on men's shoulders; but they themselves will not move them with one of their fingers. [5]But all their works they do for to be seen of men: they make broad their phylacteries, and enlarge the borders of their garments, [6]And love the uppermost rooms at feasts, and the chief seats in the synagogues, [7]And greetings in the markets, and to be called of men, Rabbi, Rabbi. [8]But be not ye called Rabbi: for one is your Master, even Christ; and all ye are brethren. [9]And call no man your father upon the earth: for one is your Father, which is in heaven. [10]Neither be ye called masters: for one is your Master, even Christ. [11]But he that is greatest among you shall be your servant. [12]And whosoever shall exalt himself shall be abased; and he that shall humble himself shall be exalted.

Sadly this kind of vanity is still seen among some denominations of the church today.

## Modesty

The second part of vanity's definition often drives the first part, believe it or not. How many people today, either through family, media, friends, or the culture of the society in which they live, grow up feeling useless, worthless, and of no consequence? Generally, when an effort ends up being useless, we say it was done in vain. But how many people, women especially, dress up, change their hairstyle, and put on make-up in a vain attempt to get the attention they long for, while instead gaining the attention that only serves to make them further feel like dirt?

So what are those verses that talk about vanity?

> 1 Timothy 2:8-10 I will therefore that men pray every where, lifting up holy hands, without wrath and doubting. ⁹In like manner also, that women adorn themselves in modest apparel, with shamefacedness and sobriety; not with broided hair, or gold, or pearls, or costly array; ¹⁰But (which becometh women professing godliness) with good works.

> 1 Peter 3:1-5 Likewise, ye wives, be in subjection to your own husbands; that, if any obey not the word, they also may without the word be won by the conversation of the wives; ²While they behold your chaste conversation coupled with fear. ³Whose adorning let it not be that outward adorning of plaiting the hair, and of wearing of gold, or of putting on of apparel; ⁴But let it be the hidden man of the heart, in that which is not corruptible, even the ornament of a meek and quiet spirit, which is in the sight of God of great price. ⁵For after this manner in the old time the holy women also, who trusted in God, adorned themselves, being in subjection unto their own husbands:

Remember in previous discussions about the Bridal attire, that it was only the wealthy who could afford many of the decorations mentioned here. Therefore, showing up to church dressed this way could be seen as flaunting one's wealth, very much a form of vanity that can happen even today. There's nothing wrong with being able to afford expensive jewelry and outfits, but when it appears as if they are worn to show off the wealth of the wearer, the focus is no longer on God, but on themselves.

# Dressed for Eternity

## Modesty Failings in the Church

Compounding this problem has been the Church's negative fascination with the concept that discussing the sexual differences of men and women is bad; that sex itself is somehow dirty; and that to even think of being attractive in any way shape or form is asking to be raped.

God says in Hebrews:

> Hebrews 13:4-5 Marriage is honourable in all, and the bed undefiled: but whoremongers and adulterers God will judge. [5]Let your conversation be without covetousness; and be content with such things as ye have: for he hath said, I will never leave thee, nor forsake thee.

## Attacking Men

But what has caused the church to fall down in this discussion is something Christ said about men:

> Matthew 5:27-28 Ye have heard that it was said by them of old time, Thou shalt not commit adultery: [28]But I say unto you, That whosoever looketh on a woman to lust after her hath committed adultery with her already in his heart.

This echoes a passage in Proverbs:

> Proverbs 6:20-34 My son, keep thy father's commandment, and forsake not the law of thy mother: [21]Bind them continually upon thine heart, and tie them about thy neck. [22]When thou goest, it shall lead thee; when thou sleepest, it shall keep thee; and when thou awakest, it shall talk with thee. [23]For the commandment is a lamp; and the law is light; and reproofs of instruction are the way of life: [24]To keep thee from the evil woman, from the flattery of the tongue of a strange woman. [25]Lust not after her beauty in thine heart; neither let her take thee with her eyelids. [26]For by means of a whorish woman a man is brought to a piece of bread: and the adulteress

# Modesty

will hunt for the precious life. ²⁷Can a man take fire in his bosom, and his clothes not be burned? 28 Can one go upon hot coals, and his feet not be burned? ²⁹So he that goeth in to his neighbour's wife; whosoever toucheth her shall not be innocent. ³⁰Men do not despise a thief, if he steal to satisfy his soul when he is hungry; ³¹But if he be found, he shall restore sevenfold; he shall give all the substance of his house. ³²But whoso committeth adultery with a woman lacketh understanding: he that doeth it destroyeth his own soul. ³³A wound and dishonour shall he get; and his reproach shall not be wiped away. ³⁴For jealousy is the rage of a man: therefore he will not spare in the day of vengeance.

Now seeing as we are talking to men here, let's look at another verse:

Psalm 119:9-11 BETH. Wherewithal shall a young man cleanse his way? by taking heed thereto according to thy word. ¹⁰With my whole heart have I sought thee: O let me not wander from thy commandments. ¹¹Thy word have I hid in mine heart, that I might not sin against thee.

Notice that these passages do not leave men feeling that they have absolutely no way out.

1 Corinthians 10:12-13 Wherefore let him that thinketh he standeth take heed lest he fall. ¹³There hath no temptation taken you but such as is common to man: but God is faithful, who will not suffer you to be tempted above that ye are able; but will with the temptation also make a way to escape, that ye may be able to bear it.

The way of escape is found when a man spends time in God's Word. The godly man will be spending enough time getting to know God and His ways through His written Word such that when temptations come, and God said they would come, the godly man is able to keep himself pure before Him.

Remember, our lives are not meant solely for the approval and appreciation of others. Whether man or woman, our ultimate source of approval is God Himself. Seeking God's approval is not a substitute for Salvation however. There is no way to earn that. But God is pleased when we choose to take what

# Dressed for Eternity

He's taught us from the Scriptures and live them out in everyday life. Overcoming sexual temptation is one of those areas of everyday life that a man must face because sin has corrupted his God-given appreciation for all things beautiful.

This doesn't mean men are never to come into contact with women. It means that men should, whenever possible, encourage women in living godly lives themselves. This means showing them the kind of respect discussed earlier. Focus on the Family has published some excellent literature regarding how men can positively impact the lives of the women they come into contact with.

**Now about Women**

Women on the other hand are not to needlessly tempt men. Proverbs refers to women without discretion in this manner:

> Proverbs 11:22 As a jewel of gold in a swine's snout, so is a fair woman which is without discretion.

A wise woman then, will consider the strengths and weaknesses of the men in her life and conduct herself accordingly. Remember, she is the nurturer, therefore, rather than see it as a slam against her personal sense of style, she should welcome the opportunity to present her men to God in a manner He would be pleased with.

By nature of the very fact that God created women with a shape pleasing to men, there is a power women have over men that God talks about in the book of Proverbs. But notice the kind of woman that misuses her power:

> Proverbs 9:13-18 A foolish woman is clamorous: she is simple, and knoweth nothing. [14]For she sitteth at the door of her house, on a seat in the high places of the city, [15]To call passengers who go right on their ways: [16]Whoso is simple, let him turn in hither: and as for him that wanteth understanding, she saith to him, [17]Stolen waters are sweet, and bread eaten in secret is pleasant. [18]But he knoweth not that the dead are there; and that her guests are in the depths of hell.

# Modesty

Proverbs 14:1  Every wise woman buildeth her house: but the foolish plucketh it down with her hands.

How many women do you know who could be classified as airheads? Or perhaps they've called themselves that? How many of them also tend to engage in activities that make you raise an eyebrow, turn your head away in disgust, or get themselves into situations that ultimately compromise their Christian witness and/or virginity? When it comes to things of faith, respect, humility, and wise treatment of the other gender, there is no room for airheads on either side of the coin, male or female.

To those women who have been put down, degraded, told they were nothing, or told they were ugly, let me restate what was shared a few pages ago. God doesn't make junk! There is no need to jump on the vanity bandwagon, because you are already a jewel in God's crown. Let the vanity mirror go lonely. Forget the clothing styles that make you fall out of your top and peek through your skirts. The enemy would have you believe that if you advertise what you're not selling, you will be liked by the world.

Rock 'n roll and Pop stars are doing this constantly. As of the time of this writing, this author can think of at least three women who have been destroyed because they bought into the lie that to be popular, they had to all but bare it all. Unfortunately, dressing with exposure in mind tends to attract men who have no intention of exercising self control and who are more than willing to forcibly buy what you appear to be selling and run with it, leaving you feeling dirty and worthless. It is up to men to speak into the lives of their women that they are beautiful just as they are, they are loved just as they are, and they are worth protecting, worth providing for, and worth fighting for. Men will appreciate a woman's beauty regardless of what she is wearing. But a man has an easier time fending off the enemy's attacks when she's dressed appropriately, than when she flaunts herself instead.

Men and women have the right to wear anything they want. But they do not have the right to deliberately place temptations in the other's path. Scripture says:

1 Corinthians 10:23-24  All things are lawful for me, but all things are not expedient: all things are lawful for me, but all things edify not.  <sup>24</sup> Let no man seek his own, but every man another's wealth.

Or as the NIV puts it:

1 Corinthians 10:23 "I have the right to do anything," you say—but not everything is beneficial. "I have the right to do anything"—but not everything is constructive.
*Holy Bible, New International Version®, NIV® Copyright © 1973, 1978, 1984, 2011 by Biblica, Inc.® Used by permission. All rights reserved worldwide.*

Women would do well to consider how men are wired, and help them in their desire to exhibit self control instead of hinder them in the effort.

What this looks like differs from culture to culture, but the end result is the same: respect the different genders and honour them by how each gender presents themselves. The trick here is to get rid of the selfish, "I'll do whatever I want and don't tell me otherwise" attitude and adopt, "How may I help you walk pleasing before the Lord?"  This mind-set shift has no help from the media, or from many cultures around the globe. But it is necessary if men and women are to help each other toward a level of modesty in behaviour and dress that pleases God. Neither gender is off the hook here.

The Jewish people actually have an interesting take on this concept of modesty that I found while researching the Levitical garments earlier.

> Bear in mind that clothing is the outer gesture of our special stature in the world as human beings. No other creature has the need or the desire to fashion a covering for its naked and exposed body. No other creature can understand the profound concepts of modesty, humility or restraint that clothing fundamentally represents. These ideas are uniquely human, and are the product of the recognition of a Transcendent God in Whose constant presence we live. To don the garments of the Cohen Gadol (priestly garments) is to take on the mantle of living life as a sanctified person, whose every footstep bespeaks Godliness. (brackets mine)

# Modesty

http://www.messianic-torah-truth-seeker.org/Torah/Kohen/kohengadol.html

By now the reader should be able to see that the concept of modesty is so much more than a fixation on how a person looks and dresses. The world is very focused on this fixation, and the church has become that way too in many respects. The first thing we judge when a newcomer walks in the door, is how they are dressed.

At their core, every single person alive wants to be accepted for who they are, not for what they look like. To achieve this, we need a fundamental shift in where our focus lies, so that we can greet each other in a manner worthy of our shared status as members of God's family. When we realize that "it's not all about me", and that our bodies are actually being reserved as gifts for a spouse God is lining up (or has lined up) for us, then we won't go showing the contents of that gift to every man who walks along, and nor will every man seek to unwrap what is not yet his.

So many men and women are trapped in the fixation that if they don't address their body's flaws, if they fail to accentuate their assets, that the other gender won't even look at them, or worse, will take advantage of and use them. Yes, women can take advantage of men equally as well as the other way around. Most discussions about this however, tend to only focus on how women get treated, which is wrong. Body image means so much to men, that some of them will religiously show up at the gym just to have that hot look at the bar Friday night. While it's true women get a sense of security and safety from a man who can fight for her, that's just the issue. She wants a man who respects and loves her enough to fight for her and not fight to get every other woman out there too.

There are suggestions that can help men and women deal with the ravages of the sin-nature on their bodies. How we look should first of all please our Creator who delighted to give us the shape and appearance He did. When we please Him, it matters very little what others think and we can get off the outer-appearance treadmill and rest.

## Does all this talk of Modesty mean it's wrong to look nice?

Heck no! What it does mean is to put more focus on the inner man as discussed at length already. God has gifted mankind with creativity, one of which is with textiles such as those recorded in Genesis. The kinds of cloth, colours, embroidery, and decorations given throughout Scripture tell us that God appreciates the uses to which mankind has put his (as in mankind's) creativity.

The important thing to remember, is that there are common understandings of modesty that are not specific to any one culture. As more of the world warms up to western ways of doing things, western dress is travelling around the world too, and finding itself having to conform to, or having adverse effects on, the cultural modesty to which it has been introduced.

With the exception of a few cultures around the world, most cultures want men to at least be wearing trousers of some form, or a loin cloth or shorts at the minimum in public. They expect women to at least have their bust and loins covered as well, with many cultures going beyond that to outlaw bare midriffs, short hemlines and plunged necklines. People who get upset at these guidelines in Western nations forget what is considered modest elsewhere as well. These guidelines in other countries in no way hinder creativity in how one chooses the colours and adornment they put on, or even the shape and cut. Many cultures have incredible traditional clothing far more flashy than anything in western culture.

The concept of "looking good" is different in every culture, but there are some basics that can be of assistance when choosing styles of cut, pattern, or other forms of adornment that can be helpful.

## Body Shape:

Not only does God like variety in the creativity He gave us, but He likes variety in the body shapes He gives us as well. Some of us are tall, some of us are short. Some of us have long legs, others have short legs.

**Modesty**

Some of us have small hands, others have large hands. But due to the effect the sin-nature has had on life, sometimes the body God gave us can develop issues. Some of us might pack weight on where we shouldn't and find it difficult to get rid of. Some of us find one body part too big or too small. Now please understand that this author is not promoting dissatisfaction with how God created each of us. It is my desire rather, that every reader would grow to appreciate the form God gave them and seek to present that form in the best condition they are able, and in a modest fashion to the world around them in a manner pleasing to God first and foremost. But in a world where not everyone has arrived at that point, there are ways to dress and adorn one's self in a way they can feel good about.

Let's start at the top and work our way down, shall we?

**The Head:**

Different face shapes and hair types will denote what kind of hair style looks best. A person with a long forehead for example may look better with bangs of some kind. A person with a shorter forehead as part of a round face may look better without bangs, as that gives their eyebrows more room to shine. Where a person's crown is on their head will denote where their hair will most naturally lie and following the crown with any chosen hair style will help it behave better.

**The Neck:**

While the Mattel Barbie doll has an incredibly long neck, most of us don't have or want our necks to be quite that long. A short neck can be given the appearance of length with hair worn long, or long, light-weight earrings. A person who feels they have a really long neck should not wear low-cut tops, as collars can assist with the appearance of shortening the neck length.

One's choice of necklace can affect the visual appearance of a long or short neck as well.

**The Shoulders:**

A person with small shoulders will want to choose tops with padded or extended shoulders if they want to look broader. Conversely, a broad-shouldered person will want to avoid padded or extended shoulders on clothing unless they particularly like the football/hockey player look.

**The Bust:**

Not much to suggest here for men, other than the fact that tight-fitted shirts on a muscular frame may get eyeballs where you don't want them. Choose tops that fit, but that are modestly built.

For women, western culture has not been kind. While women of almost every other culture understand the need to only show their bust to their husband, western culture has somehow decided that the whole world should see your husband's prizes too. If you ever wanted a reason to rebel against society, this is a sure-fire area to do it in. There is such a thing as healthy rebellion. Did you know that? Choosing tops that will look good without advertising what you're not selling is doable, and allows for more creativity than trying to make sure you don't fall out of your neckline in public.

Women who have small shoulders and a small bust can choose patterns that contain horizontal striping or v-shaped striping with the v opening upward. Both of these patterns will give the visual illusion of more on top, if that's what you'd prefer.

Women who are naturally large on top will want that v going the other way, or wear vertical stripes to lessen the visual effect if for some reason they are not happy with being so large on top. Not all of us can afford surgery like Dolly Parton, to lessen how big we are, so use colours and patterns to your advantage.

## Modesty

### The Hands:

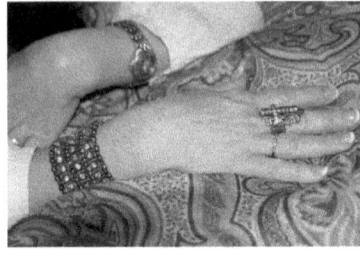

Every now and then, someone comes along who figures their hands are too big or too small. If a person thinks their hands are too big and their fingers too small, wear bracelets to direct the eye away from the palm of the hand. If someone figures their fingers are too long, wear rings on more than one finger. The larger the ring, the smaller the hand looks.

### The Waist and Hips:

This is another area that men and women seem to obsess over. If you are small in this area and want to look bigger, have the v shape going from mid-chest downward. However, if you have large hips and want them to look smaller, send the v shape the other way.

Short, stocky builds are slimmed by vertical stripes while tall, thin builds benefit from horizontal stripes. Both can make diagonal stripes work to their advantage if they are careful.

### The Legs:

Large hips on short legs benefit from skirts or pants that flair at the bottom. Long legs can wear the flair too, but it may make those legs merely look even longer. People with long legs can lessen the appearance, if they wish, by wearing tops that drape over their pants or skirts, stretching down to below the butt or reaching to the upper thigh.

## The Feet:

Some of us have really small feet, others have really big feet. First and foremost, make sure the shoe fits the foot properly. After that, the style, colour and pattern can make them look larger or smaller. Horizontal striping on a big foot just makes it look wider, for example, while length-wise striping can make it look longer.

## Conclusion on the Matter:

If you remember that your body is the Temple of the Holy Ghost; if you remember that the private areas of your body are meant as gifts for your lifelong mate; if you remember that how you look was designed by God and how you look after it pleases or saddens Him first, then how you present yourself to the world will reflect that.

Be creative, remember whose you are and who you are, and respect both yourself, God, and the other gender. The Bride of Christ thinks of others ahead of herself. She won't make a weaker brother or sister stumble, because she is humble and doesn't put her rights ahead of others. The Bride of Christ presents herself beautifully in a modest manner, knowing that true beauty comes as 1 Peter says:

> 1 Peter 3:4 But let it be the hidden man of the heart, in that which is not corruptible, even the ornament of a meek and quiet spirit, which is in the sight of God of great price.

# Dressed for Eternity

**Recap**

Let's a take a moment now and tie everything together. We've covered a lot of ground in this discussion and it may help a little if we just take some time to summarize what we've discovered about how God adorns His Bride in the Scriptures.

**Section One**

Section One of this book covered the New Jerusalem and the 12 Stones of Aaron's Breastplate. These were correlated quite heavily until we got to the pearly gates and golden streets, as those did not factor into Aaron's Breastplate. Along the way we learned about the meaning behind the names of each of the 12 Tribes of Israel, and the 12 Apostles. All these things came together to form the following observations:

In order for there to be forgiveness of sin, we must first look to the Sonship of Jesus Christ, without whom there would be no shed Blood for the remission of sins. Once cleansed of sin, the Bride of Christ is to lead a life of moral purity, shaking off the darts of temptation with the shield of faith and continually seeking God's wisdom. She is to live in the Light, and shine forth that Light, but to do so, she must stay connected to the Body of Christ, or risk her fire going out.

We learned that all good things come from God. The Bride of Christ is to be looking heavenward for the return of the Heavenly Bridegroom, and staying filled with the Holy Spirit so as to produce the Fruit of the Spirit until Christ comes. Remaining submitted to the fire of the Holy Spirit keeps our lives firmly rooted on the Rock of Salvation, Jesus Christ Himself.

We learned that the Body of Christ does not always agree in how things should be done, but that as the Body of Christ, we should remain committed to the Great Commission, to corporate gatherings of praise and worship, and living a holy life. Life for the Bride of Christ is banded with life and death, triumphs and defeats.

## Conclusion

However, she must never forget that victory has been won in Christ's death and resurrection. The Bride of Christ must never forget that she is royalty. As such, she should always be mindful of her speech, never grow complacent, and always seek out God's wisdom in her dealings with the world. The world, and sometimes the Church too, will cast aside its wounded. But the Bride of Christ can be grateful that God never casts her aside, but instead takes the lowly things of the world to confound the mighty. Each member of the Bride of Christ has been created with a purpose. All we have to do is answer His call.

We learned that in our weakness, God's strength is made perfect. This only happens via vulnerability to His hand and not trying to be strong and protect ourselves. We learned that a pure heart can only come via the shed Blood of Christ when He allowed His body to be sacrificed for our sins. The Bride of Christ must continually pass through the cleansing flow to stand pure and holy before Him. She is to reflect the glory of God, which often means passing through fires the way gold is purified, so that the reflection of Christ may be seen in her. The various colours of Christ's character will then play across the surface of her own character as the various colours of the Bride of Christ are seen by the world.

## Section Two

Section Two covered ancient Jewish Bridal attire as seen through the prophetic eyes of Ezekiel as God described Jerusalem. We were introduced to some amazing similarities between this attire and that of the Roman soldiers that attended Paul as he wrote to the Ephesians. These unlikely pairings gave us some interesting insights into how God adorns His Bride.

We learned that in the same way symbols were embroidered onto great standards carried by Roman soldiers parading into town, so we are marked by God's standard, the Holy Spirit. Just like those soldiers, each member of the Bride of Christ has a job to do, some less glamorous than others. Taking the Gospel to the streets is not always very glamorous at all, but it is needful.

# Dressed for Eternity

We learned that like linen, the Robe of Righteousness is designed to resist the dirt and stains caused by sin. However, we must be careful not to fall into sin and when we do, to make quick work of washing under the Blood again. We learned the dangers of trying to straddle both sin and Salvation together and how that could have disastrous effects on our eternal destiny. This destiny was bought with a price, and protects our hearts and minds via the shed Blood of Christ.

We learned about the refining process God takes us through when trials and tribulations come our way. This process is necessary for the Bride of Christ to accurately reflect the face of Christ to the world around her. Through the refining, the Bride of Christ is expected to use her mind and heart in ways that please God through the use of wise choices, discretion, tact, etc.

We learned about lost souls being the lost jewels in God's own crown. The forehead jewels of the Bride of Christ are her dowry, the Holy Spirit displayed to the world by living through her. The Holy Spirit is unable to live through her if she is merely hearing His Words. She must be a doer of the Word as well. In addition, doing the Word will produce purity of heart as she learns to be careful what influences she allows into her heart and mind.

We learned that God Himself is our crown, our diadem, which is totally fitting considering Who it is that provided us with the Helmet of Salvation. He is our Bread of Life as well, sustaining us through good times and bad. Dwelling on His word brings health to our spiritual walk and nourishes our spirit as we persevere through the trials and struggles that sometimes feel like deserts in our lives.

# Conclusion

## Section Three

In the third section we learned about the kinds of things God exchanges in our lives.

The over-arching theme in this section was the replacing of sadness, shame and mourning, with praise, joy, and righteousness. This exchange is not something the Bride of Christ is able to do on her own; rather, the Holy Spirit is necessary to enable the change in and through her.

We discovered parallels between the garments the Levitical priest wore, and the garments given to the Bride of Christ. The need to be dressed in the fine white linen of the Robe of Righteousness is necessary for those who stand before Jesus Christ, who is the Second person of the Trinity and Great High Priest.

We learned about the anointing oil, and the way in which it typifies the Holy Spirit and His work in our lives. Indeed, it is only through the Holy Spirit's work that we are able to become sweet-smelling savours not only to God, but to those who are perishing in the world around us.

## Section Four

In section four, we learned about some of the spots and wrinkles that can wreak havoc for the Bride of Christ. Some of these spots affect the Bride's body directly, others affect her Robe of Righteousness or tarnish her dowry. Some of the wrinkles can come from added folds of skin, or sunken areas of skin instead. We learned what can cause wrinkles in her clothes as well.

We also learned what is necessary to keep the body of Christ healthy, and how important the Word of God is to do spiritual laundry.

**Section Five**

Lastly, we covered the thorny issue of modesty for the Bride of Christ. We learned about the attitudes and mindsets necessary to take modesty from a drudgery to a blessing. We covered some of the abuses that go on in the ways governments, religions, and even denominations within Christianity have committed in trying to enforce ideas of modesty. We wrapped up this section with a quick introduction to ways in which a person may still take pride in their appearance without causing a brother or sister to stumble.

**Conclusion:**

We covered a lot of ground answering the question, "How does God adorn His Bride in the Scriptures?" It is this author's hope and desire that you, my reader, will have been able to glean something from this discussion that will aide you in living out your faith in Christ to a new level and degree of understanding. Understanding the ways in which we are clothed in heavenly realms can help us as we seek to live those things out in the world around us. Always keep in mind that it is submitting to the Holy Spirit's efforts as He teaches us, guides us, corrects us, and lives through us that the clothing discussed here becomes evident to those around us.

In the following pages you will find an appendix featuring links to many sources of research used in the writing of this book. These links are offered for further informational purposes and this author makes no claims that such links will remain in use years after this book is written.

# APPENDIX A

This is where you can find additional information on any topic for which a comment has been made to turn to this area of the book. Links offered here are for further information only, and due to the nature of the Internet, may or may not be available depending on website/server uptime or downtime, owners maintaining or changing their sites, etc. Therefore, this author is not liable in the event any link in this appendix is no longer permanently available, or temporarily goes down for any reason.

## INTRODUCTION

### The Bride of Christ and Israel:
http://www.spiritandtruth.org/teaching/Romans_9-11/09_Romans_11_16-24/webshow/09_Romans_11_16-24.pdf

### Wedding ceremonies
http://focusonjerusalem.com/jewishwedtrad2.html
http://www.themodernjewishwedding.com/jewish-wedding-traditions
http://answers.yahoo.com/question/index?qid=20071125172118AACTUSg
http://www.myjewishlearning.com/life/Life_Events/Weddings/Liturgy_Ritual_and_Custom/Mikveh.shtml
http://messianicfellowship.50webs.com/wedding.html

## SECTION ONE

### Introduction:
http://www.jjkent.com/articles/tribes-israel-symbolic-stones.htm
http://www.johnpratt.com/items/docs/lds/meridian/2005/12stones.html
http://www.jjkent.com/articles/foundation-stones-apostles.htm

### Mohs Scale of Hardness:
http://en.wikipedia.org/wiki/Mohs_hardness_scale

### Sardis
http://en.wikipedia.org/wiki/Ruby
http://en.wikipedia.org/wiki/Carnelian
http://en.wikisource.org/wiki/1911_Encyclopædia_Britannica/Sard

## Appendix A
### Topaz
http://en.wikipedia.org/wiki/Peridot
http://bibledictionaries.com/topaz.htm
http://gluedideas.com/content-collection/cyclopedia-of-biblical-literature/Pitdah.html

### Chrysoprase
http://en.wikipedia.org/wiki/Chrysoprase
http://en.wikipedia.org/wiki/Mohs_hardness_scale
http://gluedideas.com/Encyclopedia-Britannica-Volume-8-Part-1-Edward-Extract/Emerald.html
http://gluedideas.com/Encyclopedia-Britannica-Volume-5-Part-2-Cast-Iron-Cole/Chrysoprase.html

### Anthrax/Jacynth
http://en.wikipedia.org/wiki/Jacinth
http://www.gemselect.com/other-info/jacinth-gems.php
http://voices.yahoo.com/discovering-gemstone-called-jacinth-697499.html?cat=7
http://www.edelsteine.at/dictionary/granat/

### Sapphire
http://en.wikipedia.org/wiki/Sapphire
http://en.wikipedia.org/wiki/Chalcedony
http://en.wikipedia.org/wiki/Beryl#Aquamarine_and_maxixe

### Jasper
http://www.gemselect.com/gem-info/jasper/jasper-info.php
http://www.gemstone.org/index.php?option=com_content&view=article&id=125:sapphire&catid=1:gem-by-gem&Itemid=14

### Ligure
http://www.christianhospitality.org/resources/breastplate/birthstones.html
http://en.wiktionary.org/wiki/ligure
http://en.wikipedia.org/wiki/Sapphire
http://en.wikipedia.org/wiki/Lapis_lazuli

## Agate/Emerald
http://en.wikipedia.org/wiki/Agate
http://www.1911encyclopedia.org/Agate
http://en.wikipedia.org/wiki/Emerald
http://www.gemstone.org/index.php?option=com_content&view=article&id=84:sapphire&catid=1:gem-by-gem&Itemid=14

## Amethyst
http://www.galleries.com/Amethyst
http://en.wikipedia.org/wiki/Amethyst
http://www.israel-a-history-of.com/naphtali.html
http://www.gotquestions.org/Matthias-Judas-Paul.html

## Chrysoberyl
http://www.galleries.com/Chrysoberyl
http://en.wikipedia.org/wiki/Beryl
http://en.wikipedia.org/wiki/Chrysoberyl
http://www.minerals.net/gemstone/chrysoberyl_gemstone.aspx

## Beryl/Onyx/Diamond
http://en.wikipedia.org/wiki/Onyx
http://en.wikipedia.org/wiki/Beryl
http://www.christianhospitality.org/resources/breastplate/birthstones.html

## Onyx
http://www.gemselect.com/gem-info/jasper/jasper-info.php
http://en.wikipedia.org/wiki/Onyx

## Pearls
http://en.wikipedia.org/wiki/Pearl
http://www.mikimotoamerica.com/about-pearl-jewelry/how-to-buy-pearls/qualities-of-pearls/
http://www.purepearls.com/pearl-education/pearl-colors.html

## Gold
http://en.wikipedia.org/wiki/Gold

**Appendix A**

**SECTION TWO**

**Introduction**
http://www.ancient-hebrew.org/33_apparel.html

**'broidered work/Standards**
http://www.1902encyclopedia.com/E/EMB/embroidery.html
http://www.ancient-hebrew.org/33_apparel.html

**Badger's skin/boots**
http://www.zoocreation.com/biblespecies/badger.html
http://bibleencyclopedia.com/badger.htm
http://www.greenmeadows-stillwaters.com/types_the_ram_and_badgers_skins.htm
http://www.ancient-hebrew.org/33_apparel.html

**Fine linen/belt/sword**
http://en.wikipedia.org/wiki/Linen
http://www.reshafim.org.il/ad/egypt/timelines/topics/flax.htm
http://www.ancient-hebrew.org/33_apparel.html

**Silk**
http://en.wikipedia.org/wiki/Silk
http://ancienthistory.about.com/cs/china/g/silkroad.htm
http://www.silk-road.com/artl/egyptsilk.shtml
http://en.wikipedia.org/wiki/Silk_Route
http://www.israel-a-history-of.com/tabernacle-of-moses.html

**Ornaments/chains of gold/rows of jewels/helmet**
http://www.jewishvirtuallibrary.org/jsource/vjw/Yemen.html
http://en.wikipedia.org/wiki/Yemenite_Jews
http://www.ancient-hebrew.org/33_apparel.html
http://www.laydownlife.net/yedidah/AncientJewishWeddingCeremony.htm
http://messianicfellowship.50webs.com/wedding.html

**Dressed for Eternity**

**Bracelets**
http://antiquesilverjewelry.blogspot.ca/2012_04_01_archive.html
http://www.yemenite-art.com/Pages/Filigreejewelry.aspx
http://en.wikipedia.org/wiki/Silversmithery
http://en.wikipedia.org/wiki/Silver
http://www.therefinersfire.org/refiners_fire.htm
http://www.touregypt.net/featurestories/silver.htm
http://songdove.fa-ct.com/stuff/SmeltingAg.pdf

**Forehead jewel/shield**
http://biblehub.com/ezekiel/16-12.htm
http://pinterest.com/bcr8tive/jewelry-middle-east/
http://pinterest.com/mrvblkc/bridal-head-wear-forehead-jewelry/
http://en.wikipedia.org/wiki/Parable_of_the_Lost_Coin
http://library.timelesstruths.org/music/Jewels/
http://bibleillustration.blogspot.ca/2009/09/eastern-coin-head-dresses.html
http://www.bible-history.com/links.php?cat=39&sub=470

**Earrings**
http://phys.org/news/2012-05-unique-gold-earring-intriguing-ancient.html
http://www.arabiafelixjewels.com/tag/yemen-traditional-jewellery
http://www.britishmuseum.org/explore/highlights/highlight_objects/aes/g/gold_hoop-shaped_earring.aspx

**Crown**
http://en.wikipedia.org/wiki/Diadem
http://dictionary.reference.com/browse/diadem?s=t
http://www.perfect-wedding-day.com/bridal-tiaras-history-diadem.html

**Fine flour**
http://www.touregypt.net/featurestories/bread.htm
http://www.madehow.com/Volume-3/Flour.html
http://en.wikipedia.org/wiki/History_of_bread
http://en.wikipedia.org/wiki/Bread
http://www.cooksinfo.com/flour
http://en.wikipedia.org/wiki/Bread_of_Life_Discourse
http://www.thefreedictionary.com/staff+of+life

## Appendix A

### Honey
http://www.wired.com/wiredscience/2010/06/ancient-bees/
http://www.reshafim.org.il/ad/egypt/timelines/topics/beekeeping.htm
http://en.wikipedia.org/wiki/Honey
http://www.benefits-of-honey.com/honey-in-the-bible.html

### Oil
http://en.wikipedia.org/wiki/Seven_Species
http://www.mechon-mamre.org/p/pt/pt1302.htm#23
http://en.wikipedia.org/wiki/Ancient_Israelite_cuisine
http://www.gemsinisrael.com/e_article000008705.htm
http://www.goisrael.com/Tourism_Eng/Articles/Attractions/Pages/Olive%20Oil%20and%20Olive%20Presses.aspx

## SECTION THREE

### God's Name stamped on Jerusalem hills
http://promisedlandministries.wordpress.com/2010/03/14/shadows-of-the-messiah-where-gods-name-is-written/#comment-4266

### Sackcloth and Ashes
http://www.keyway.ca/htm2002/20020421.htm
http://dictionary.reference.com/browse/sackcloth
http://en.wikipedia.org/wiki/Sackcloth_and_ashes

### Anointing Oil
http://en.wikipedia.org/wiki/Myrrh
http://en.wikipedia.org/wiki/Cinnamon
http://en.wikipedia.org/wiki/Acorus_calamus
http://theepicentre.com/spice/cassia/
http://pastorpete.tripod.com/HAO.html
http://en.wikipedia.org/wiki/Holy_anointing_oil

# SECTION FIVE

## Modesty
http://en.wikipedia.org/wiki/Modesty
http://www.beautyredefined.net/modest-is-hottest-the-revealing-truth/
http://www.johnandellenduncan.com/jd_modesty.htm
http://www.christianityetc.org/modesty.php
http://guysonmodesty.com/tag/culture/
http://blog.cbeinternational.org/2013/04/on-modesty-and-male-privilege/
http://www.thefreedictionary.com/modesty

## Vanity
http://www.thefreedictionary.com/vanity

## Cultural Modesty
http://www.dimensionsofculture.com/2010/11/modesty-in-health-care-a-cross-cultural-perspective/
http://www.saupulse.com/2013/02/15/the-culture-of-modesty-2/
http://www.modestworld.com/laws.asp - Jewish orthodox teaching

## Suggested links:
http://www.charismanews.com/culture/40687-the-dos-and-don-ts-of-fashion-as-a-christian
http://guysonmodesty.com/tag/culture/
http://secretkeepergirl.com

## APPENDIX B

Notes on the Rapture and Tribulation as alluded to in "Aaron's Breastplate – Sapphire" on page 33.

What follows is a grouping together of various notes where Scripture is referenced with regards to the pre-trib view of the Rapture. Along with the Scriptures are the interpretation as given by Scripture,not just to me, but to most scholars of end-time eschatology. From my own personal study of Scripture, (and I don't read a lot of commentaries, I prefer to let Scripture speak for itself) we will be spared the wrath of God as it is poured out during the 7 year Tribulation period. Let us dive into what has been found:

What we see is a building up of things like war, famine, pestilence, economic recession, etc. When we see these things build in their intensity, we are told to look up, for our redemption draweth nigh. There are many verses in the Bible that support Revelations 3:10, especially if you look at those verses from the messianic Jewish perspective, as the Jewish fall feasts all speak of a pre-trib rapture, or natzhal(sp?) a catching away of the totally righteous, or tzaddikm before the Days of Awe, or the tribulation as we know it. Some of those verses fall into the law of double-fullfillment, and both were true for what happened then, as they will be in the near future.

What is the Rapture, and what is the Tribulation? Are they spoken of in Scripture? Do these terms actually exist? I can't find them in Scripture so how do I know someone didn't just make them up?

# Appendix B
## Tribulation:

Let me answer with a bit of a study. What is the Tribulation? The tribulation is referred to in the Old Testament as the Day of Wrath, or the Day of God's Wrath, or some variation of that theme. Below are verses and passages that outline what the Tribulation time period is about.

Isaiah 13, the whole chapter describes the Day of the Lord, in detail, and it sounds very similar to the book of Revelation.

Jeremiah 10:10

Ezekiel 7, again, describing the Wrath of the Lord, this time in reference to how men will act in that day.

Ezekiel 38:14-23 describes the wrath of God in relation to the battle of Armaggedon.

> Nahum 1:22 God is jealous, and the LORD revengeth; the LORD revengeth, and is furious; the LORD will take vengeance on his adversaries, and he reserveth wrath for his enemies.

Zephaniah 1, the whole chapter talks of the Day of the Lord,

Now we get to the New Testament.
Matthew 3:7 Christ asks the Pharisees if they are trying to escape the wrath to come.

> Romans 1:18 . . .the wrath of God is revealed from heaven against all ungodliness and unrighteousness of men, who hold the truth in unrighteousness;

> Ephesians 5:6 Let no man deceive you with vain words: for because of these things cometh the wrath of God upon the children of disobedience.

> Revelations 6:16,17 And said to the mountains and rocks, Fall on us, and hide us from the face of him that sitteth on the throne, and from the wrath of the Lamb: 17For the great day of his wrath is come; and who shall be able to stand?

# Dressed for Eternity

Let us examine what Christ said in Matthew

Matthew 24:4-30 And Jesus answered and said unto them, Take heed that no man deceive you. ⁵For many shall come in my name, saying, I am Christ; and shall deceive many. ⁶And ye shall hear of wars and rumours of wars: see that ye be not troubled: for all these things must come to pass, but the end is not yet. ⁷For nation shall rise against nation, and kingdom against kingdom: and there shall be famines, and pestilences, and earthquakes, in divers places. ⁸All these are the beginning of sorrows. ⁹Then shall they deliver you up to be afflicted, and shall kill you: and ye shall be hated of all nations for my name?s sake. ¹⁰And then shall many be offended, and shall betray one another, and shall hate one another. ¹¹And many false prophets shall rise, and shall deceive many. ¹²And because iniquity shall abound, the love of many shall wax cold. ¹³But he that shall endure unto the end, the same shall be saved. ¹⁴And this gospel of the kingdom shall be preached in all the world for a witness unto all nations; and then shall the end come.

(There is a clear indication here that he goes from speaking of what happens before the Tribulation to what happens during the Tribulation. In the section above, Christ is talking about the birth pangs leading up to the time of the end. We have seen these things begin to build and get closer and closer together and happen more often in strange places as time continues to march forward. What follows next is a description of the Tribulation period in a nutshell, from Christ's own mouth.)

¹⁵When ye therefore shall see the abomination of desolation, spoken of by Daniel the prophet, stand in the holy place, (whoso readeth, let him understand:) ¹⁶Then let them which be in Judaea flee into the mountains: ¹⁷Let him which is on the housetop not come down to take any thing out of his house: ¹⁸Neither let him which is in the field return back to take his clothes. ¹⁹And woe unto them that are with child, and to them that give suck in those days! ²⁰But pray ye that your flight be not in the winter, neither on the sabbath day: ²¹For then shall be great tribulation, such as was not since the beginning of the world to this time, no, nor ever shall be. ²²And except those days should be shortened, there should no flesh be saved: but for the elect?s sake those days shall be shortened. ²³Then if any man shall say unto you, Lo, here is Christ, or there; believe it not. ²⁴For there shall arise false Christs, and false prophets, and shall show great signs and wonders; insomuch that, if it

# Appendix B

were possible, they shall deceive the very elect. ²⁵Behold, I have told you before. ²⁶Wherefore if they shall say unto you, Behold, he is in the desert; go not forth: behold, he is in the secret chambers; believe it not. ²⁷For as the lightning cometh out of the east, and shineth even unto the west; so shall also the coming of the Son of man be. ²⁸For wheresoever the carcase is, there will the eagles be gathered together. ²⁹Immediately after the tribulation of those days shall the sun be darkened, and the moon shall not give her light, and the stars shall fall from heaven, and the powers of the heavens shall be shaken: ³⁰And then shall appear the sign of the Son of man in heaven: and then shall all the tribes of the earth mourn, and they shall see the Son of man coming in the clouds of heaven with power and great glory. ³¹And he shall send his angels with a great sound of a trumpet, and they shall gather together his elect from the four winds, from one end of heaven to the other.

So we see that although the actual terms "Rapture" and "Tribulation" are either not present at all as in the case of the term Rapture, or sparsely mentioned as in the case of the term Tribulation, that both are referred to much more often than most people realize. The catching away of the Church will happen before that great and terrible Day of the Lord.

**What is the Rapture?**

The word Rapture was a Latin translation of a Greek translation of the Jewish word for being caught away or hidden.

The term "Rapture" according to Holman's Bible Dictionary is:

RAPTURE The catching up of believers by Christ at the time of His return. The word came into use by way of the Latin rapio used to translate the Greek term of 1 Thessalonians 4:17, harpagesometha.

1 Thessalonians 4:16 For the Lord himself shall descend from heaven with a shout, with the voice of the archangel, and with the trump of God: and the dead in Christ shall rise first:

1Thessalonians 4:17 Then we which are alive and remain shall be caught up together with them in the clouds, to meet the Lord in the air: and so shall we ever be with the Lord.

A quick word-study then, follows:

harpazo   har-pad'-zo
From a derivative of aihreomai to seize (in various applications): - catch (away, up), pluck, pull, take (by force).

aihreomai   hahee-reh'-om-ahee
Probably akin to ah'ee-ro to take for oneself, that is, to prefer.

airo   ah'ee-ro
A primary verb; to lift; by implication to take up or away; figuratively to raise (the voice), keep in suspense (the mind); specifically to sail away (that is, weigh anchor); by Hebraism (compare naw-saw) to expiate sin: - away with, bear (up), carry, lift up, loose, make to doubt, put away, remove, take (away, up).

naw-saw', naw-saw'
A primitive root; to lift, in a great variety of applications, literally and figuratively, absolutely and relatively: - accept, advance, arise, (able to, [armour], suffer to) bear (-er, up), bring (forth), burn, carry (away), cast, contain, desire, ease, exact, exalt (self), extol, fetch, forgive, furnish, further, give, go on, help, high, hold up, honourable (+ man), lade, lay, lift (self) up, lofty, marry, magnify, X needs, obtain, pardon, raise (up), receive, regard, respect, set (up), spare, stir up, + swear, take (away, up), X utterly, wear, yield.

The Hebrew word pronounced naw-saw is used in various places of the Old Testament with the idea of the rapture being present. Here is a sampling of situations and thought patterns it is used in:

Psalm 24:5 Psalm 28:9 Psalm 32:1 Psalm 32:5 Isaiah 11:12 a catching up, forgiveness, gathering together

Isaiah 18:3 mentioned with trumpets, and this chapter goes on to discuss how the nation of Israel will once again worship, a nation that had been scattered.

Isaiah 33:24 uses this word also in the manner of forgiveness and again among verses that deal with how Israel will be treated in the last days.

Isaiah 46:4 deliverance is how this word is used here.

# Appendix B

Isaiah 51:6 used to tell the reader to look up and pay attention and describes what will happen and what will last. Isaiah 52:8 interesting verse speaking to watchmen, to those of us who are watching and waiting.

Isaiah 57:15 this time used in reference to where God is, and His position there.

Isaiah 63: 7-10 uses this word as well.

Ezekiel 3:12 and 14 the word is used when Ezekiel was taken up, and in verse 14, he didn't want to go where the Spirit wished to take him, but he went anyway.

Ezekiel 8:3 poor guy, here he's lifted away by a lock of his hair!

Ezekiel 11:1 This happened a lot to this prophet.

Next set of verses in:

John 14:1 Let not your heart be troubled: ye believe in God, believe also in me.

John 14:2 In my Father's house are many mansions: if it were not so, I would have told you. I go to prepare a place for you.

John 14:3 And if I go and prepare a place for you, I will come again, and receive you unto myself; that where I am, there ye may be also.

poreuomai   por-yoo'-om-ahee
Middle voice from a derivative of the same as peira; to traverse, that is, travel (literally or figuratively; especially to remove [figuratively die], live, etc.): - depart, go (away, forth, one's way, up), (make a, take a) journey, walk.

peira   pi'-rah
From the base of G4008 (through the idea of piercing); a test, that is, attempt, experience: - assaying, trial.

peran   per'-an
Apparently the accusative case of an obsolete derivation of peiro (to "peirce");

through (as adverb or preposition), that is, across: - beyond, farther (other) side, over.

These definitions on the previous page are given for the word "go" in John 14:2.

paralambano    par-al-am-ban'-o
From para and lambano to receive near, that is, associate with oneself (in any familiar or intimate act or relation); by analogy to assume an office; figuratively to learn: - receive, take (unto, with).

para    par-ah'
A primary preposition; properly near, that is, (with genitive case) from beside (literally or figuratively), (with dative case) at (or in) the vicinity of (objectively or subjectively), (with accusative case) to the proximity with (local [especially beyond or opposed to] or causal [on account of]). In compounds it retains the same variety of application: - above, against, among, at, before, by, contrary to, X friend, from, + give [such things as they], + that [she] had, X his, in, more than, nigh unto, (out) of, past, save, side . . . by, in the sight of, than, [there-]fore, with. In compounds it retains the same variety of application.

lambano    lam-ban'-o
A prolonged form of a primary verb, which is used only as an alternate in certain tenses; to take (in very many applications, literally and figuratively [probably objective or active, to get hold of; whereas dechomai is rather subjective or passive, to have offered to one; while aihreomai is more violent, to seize or remove]): - accept, + be amazed, assay, attain, bring, X when I call, catch, come on (X unto), + forget, have, hold, obtain, receive (X after), take (away, up).

aihreomai
hahee-reh'-om-ahee
Probably akin to ah'ee-ro to take for oneself, that is, to prefer. Some of the forms are borrowed from a cognate ( hellomai), which is otherwise obsolete: - choose. Some of the forms are borrowed from a cognate hellomai, hel-lom-ahee; which is otherwise obsolete.

dechomai    dekh'-om-ahee
Middle voice of a primary verb; to receive (in various applications, literally or figuratively): - accept, receive, take. Compare lambano.

# Appendix B

Just in those two sets of verses alone, we see that Christ is talking about catching away His Church, about taking us, what is rightfully His, and taking us to where He is about to go, His journey to that location beginning in a rather painful fashion, that word even referring to how it started, the piercing of His body)

The entire chapter of 1 Corinthians 15 is one to make me practically shout with Joy! But I'll just share a few verses here.

> 1 Corinthians 15:51-57 Behold, I shew you a mystery; We shall not all sleep, but we shall all be changed, $^{52}$In a moment, in the twinkling of an eye, at the last trump: for the trumpet shall sound, and the dead shall be raised incorruptible, and we shall be changed. $^{53}$For this corruptible must put on incorruption, and this mortal must put on immortality. $^{54}$So when this corruptible shall have put on incorruption, and this mortal shall have put on immortality, then shall be brought to pass the saying that is written, Death is swallowed up in victory. $^{55}$O death, where is thy sting? O grave, where is thy victory? $^{56}$The sting of death is sin; and the strength of sin is the law. $^{57}$But thanks be to God, which giveth us the victory through our Lord Jesus Christ.

koimao    koy-mah'-o
to put to sleep, that is, (passively or reflexively) to slumber; figuratively to decease: - (be a-, fall a-, fall on) sleep, be dead.

egeiro    eg-i'-ro
Probably akin to the base of agora (through the idea of collecting one's faculties); to waken (transitively or intransitively), that is, rouse (literally from sleep, from sitting or lying, from disease, from death; or figuratively from obscurity, inactivity, ruins, nonexistence): - awake, lift (up), raise (again, up), rear up, (a-) rise (again, up), stand, take up.

agora    ag-or-ah'
From "ageiro" (to gather; probably akin to egeiro); properly the town square (as a place of public resort); by implication a market or thoroughfare: - market (-place), street.

Ok first our loves ones are dead, then they get aroused from death and gathered together. Carrying on to the next concept of corruptible versus incorruptible:

# Dressed for Eternity

phthartos   fthar-tos'
From phtheiro decayed, that is, (by implication) perishable: - corruptible.

phtheiro   fthi'-ro
Probably strengthened from phthio̅ (to pine or waste): properly to shrivel or wither, that is, to spoil (by any process) or (genitive) to ruin (especially figuratively by moral influences, to deprave): - corrupt (self), defile, destroy.

aphtharsia   af-thar-see'-ah
From aphthartos incorruptibility; generally unending existence; (figuratively) genuineness: - immortality, incorruption, sincerity.

aphthartos   af'-thar-tos
From al'-fah(alpha) (as a negative particle) and a derivative of phtheiro̅ undecaying (in essence or continuance): - not (in-, un-) corruptible, immortal.

thnay-tos'
From thnay'-sko liable to die: - mortal (-ity).

thnay'-sko
A strengthened form of a simpler primary word ?a´?? thano̅ (which is used for it only in certain tenses); to die (literally or figuratively): - be dead, die.

athanasia   ath-an-as-ee'-ah
From a compound of al'-fah(alpha) (as a negative particle) and thanatos deathlessness: - immortality.

thanatos
than'-at-os
From thnay'-sko (properly an adjective used as a noun) death (literally or figuratively): - X deadly, (be . . .) death.

So we see in these verses that Christ intends to take our physical bodies and transform them from the temporal state in which we decay and die, to an eternal state where our bodies are glorified as Christ's was after He was resurrected. These verses clearly state that we will not ALL do this through death, but that those of us alive will also be changed and will rise to meet Christ in the air as stated in 1 Thessalonians 4:17.

**Appendix B**

The Rapture is referred to in Scripture as being caught away, taken up with Christ in the clouds, when the Holy Spirit is removed with the Church, etc.

**The debate:**

I studied a debate on the three views, pre- post- and mid trib rapture concepts and managed to find Scriptures that appeared to support all three views until I began to study the Jewish fall feasts in light of Christ as the Messiah. It became obvious that God has not intended nor will allow His Bride to go through the horrors that are about to befall the earth.

Personally, I find this to be a great comfort as I look around and see the unrest occurring both economically, climatically, socially, biologically, etc. To know that all that we see is merely a warning that our Lord is coming soon, is something I can grab hold of and look up in anticipation.

Romans 5:8,9
1 Thessalonians 1:10
1 Thessalonians 5:6-11

These verses tell me that in Christ, we will escape the wrath to come, therefore escaping the Tribulation period. As it is that time period where the wrath of God is poured out. Let me add yet more Scripture here. Again, these Scriptures talk not only of the coming wrath of God, but of deliverance for those who call out to Him for Salvation.

> Joel 2:28-32 And it shall come to pass afterward, that I will pour out my spirit upon all flesh; and your sons and your daughters shall prophesy, your old men shall dream dreams, your young men shall see visions: [29]And also upon the servants and upon the handmaids in those days will I pour out my spirit. [30]And I will show wonders in the heavens and in the earth, blood, and fire, and pillars of smoke. [31]The sun shall be turned into darkness, and the moon into blood, before the great and the terrible day of the LORD come. [32]And it shall come to pass, that whosoever shall call on the name of the LORD shall be delivered: for in mount Zion and in Jerusalem shall be deliverance, as the LORD hath said, and in the remnant whom the LORD shall call.